Praise for James Lileks'
Witty Humor Collection

FRESH LIES

"One might call Lileks . . . a *young* Dave Barry. . . . Lileks makes the grade."

—Neil A. Grauer, *Cleveland Plain Dealer*

"Those who have had the pleasure of reading the humor columns of James Lileks . . . will no doubt be on the lookout for more. Those who have not caught up yet with Lileks would be well advised to do so quickly."

—Roger Harris, *Newark Star-Ledger*

"[A] collection of comical syndicated columns along the lines of Lewis Grizzard's or, in particular, Dave Barry's. . . . Lileks turns out to be a heavyweight contender."

—*Kirkus Reviews*

"Entertaining. . . . Lileks . . . is a top-flight humorist who is at once imaginative, literate, and breezy."

—*Publishers Weekly*

"Wonderful. . . . If you need a chuckle—or, more accurately, a guffaw—buy it and enjoy."

—Rachel G. Thomas, *New Bedford Standard-Times*

"It's time we admit that the only sane reaction to life is a horse laugh and, by that standard, Lileks is a pretty sane guide to the (un)real world we grudgingly inhabit."

—John Louis Anderson, *St. Paul Pioneer Press*

Also by James Lileks

Notes of a Nervous Man

FRESH LIES

JAMES LILEKS

POCKET BOOKS

New York   London   Toronto   Sydney   Tokyo   Singapore

All of the columns in this work with the exception of "The Life and Times of Wile E. Coyote," "Office Life," and "Spokescreatures" were previously published.

POCKET BOOKS, a division of Simon & Schuster Inc.
1230 Avenue of the Americas, New York, NY 10020

Copyright © 1994 by James Lileks

All rights reserved, including the right to reproduce
this book of portions thereof in any form whatsoever.
For information address Washington Square Press,
1230 Avenue of the Americas, New York, NY 10020

ISBN: 0-671-73704-X

First Pocket Books trade paperback printing September 1995

10 9 8 7 6 5 4 3 2 1

POCKET and colophon are registered trademarks
of Simon & Schuster Inc.

Cover design by John Gall
Front cover photo © Sigrid Estrada

Printed in the U.S.A.

to the wisest, smartest, funniest, most astonishing person
the world has ever seen:
my boss

*(Actually, this book is for Sara, my wife, but
you don't get chances to suck up like this too often)*

Acknowledgments

Thanks to Bix Beiderbeck, who played trumpet while nearly all these pieces were composed; to Mr. Kim at the corner store, who gravely provided libations; to the howler monkees in the National Zoo up the road, who pretty much summed up my feelings about this joint; to Jane Chelius, who gives me money and dinner and good advice and, I think, worries about me; to my parents, who do the same and *definitely* worry about me. Thanks to Howard at the One Stop Store, the first person to make me feel welcome in D.C. (Aside from the panhandlers.) Particular salutes to the Bolus Warriors, the Valued Veterans, and my spiritual adviser, Etta Reid.

And, of course, thanks to everyone at Newhouse News Service.

With the exception of Jim Nesbitt.

Contents

Preface

~~~~~~

LET ME TELL YOU: THAT WAS THE LAST TIME I'LL EVER ACCEPT a job offer when I'm half in the bag.

I was at my boss's going-away party, held to send her off to her new job in Washington. I was having the sort of evening you have when life is good and someone else is driving, and was standing out on the porch watching the rain and considering how, by some miracle, my life had become precisely what I had wished it to be. I was newly married; I had a house of my own; I had a job held fast with the thick epoxy of a union contract; I wasn't all that bald, yet. I was a Minnesotan, yea, a Minnesotan, one of God's elect.

Then my boss strolled up, drew back, and took an axe to every strut that held me in place.

Would I like to come to D.C. and write a column?

Now?

I said yes, instantly. It was not the sort of thing to which you say no. Happiness is fleeting, but the chance to work in a city roundly reviled as a sinkhole of Byzantine influence and a blood-spattered slaughterhouse of random murder— well, you don't say nay to a chance like that. And so off I went. Sold the house for a dollar, bade my wife farewell—she had some time left in school—and set off for Washington.

It is easier to leave home than I thought. Take a deep

1

breath, close your eyes, pretend everything will all be frozen in place until you come back. One mistake: I trusted my possessions to White Trash Moving and Dumping, Inc. (Their Motto: 50 Years of Keeping the Difference Between the Two Straight, for the Most Part.) They pulled up to my house in a van the size of an ocean liner, and three guys with an average of four teeth each walked in and took away my life. Wrapped everything in white sheets of paper. Everything. A sandwich on the dining room table: wrapped and packed. Trash in the wastebasket: wrapped and packed. These guys probably went home at night, wrapped the newspaper, the dog, the cable remote, their supper, and were starting in on the children before they shook off their training. After two days everything was stowed in boxes with helpful labels like "Items: long and blue." I signed a piece of paper admitting that I had actually committed my goods to these cretins, and off they went. I followed a day later by train. I beat my possessions by three days; the movers got lost. Evidently they confused the map with something they had wrapped and were flummoxed when they unfolded it and there was nothing inside.

I spent my first year here without my wife—she stayed behind in Minnesota to finish law school—a period that saw me not just talking to myself but using pet names, and found me leaning up against the dryer during the spin cycle with a dreamy look on my face. For *hours.* During this interval I grew to know my new home, and detest it: helicopters circled my place like giant lawn mowers; car alarms sang songs to each other; the building next door was full of screams and wails unnervingly truncated and followed hours later by the sound of someone hosing down a tarpaulin outside (I could only assume they were dismembering people—which, in this city of instant-gratification shootings, shows an admirable sense of dedication to craft); cats copulated in the bushes with yowls of feral hatred; gunshots popped in the distance like champagne corks loosed by branch managers after a particularly good quarter. Oh, and then my neighborhood went up in riots in the spring of '91. Looting, burning, the usual. A curfew after two days. I was stuck at home with no food and called a pizza delivery service; they explained they couldn't deliver, because we were under martial law.

These things age a boy born on the planet North Dakota. In time I got the necessary calluses, learned to square my shoulders and endure; my wife arrived, and I began to settle into the comfortable parody of life I enjoy to this day. It's not bad, actually. We've discovered certain pleasures here, like buying bikes: we've had three stolen so far, and this affords us the opportunity of exploring all the various bike shops in the city. We like the international flavor of the city— the way the cable company has a level of technical proficiency and desire to serve that reminds one of the old Soviet telephone system; a bureaucracy that combines Italian efficiency with British warmth and a downright French sense of accommodation for the outsider; the presence of embassies from every nation, meaning that the city is a crossroads for foreign fungi. If the diplomats don't infect you, the service is cheerfully provided by the cab drivers.

The trek to D.C. is a journey made by a million other drones yearly—sharp-eyed pale things who come here to generate paper and policy most nicely into the billion-toothed machine. Some people, it seems, are born to service government, to stroke it and stroke it as if it were some inert queen bee secreting eggs and nectar. Others are put here to burrow into its lair from the outside, to bring sunlight into the dark chambers.

I am neither. In my tenure as a Washington-based columnist, I have so far managed to distinguish myself by my inability to penetrate Washington and by my disinterest in the Machiavellian plots and cabals that pass for a culture around here. I regard my life in Washington, D.C., as much like that of the Pope in Rome: in the world, but not of it.

There are, of course, several key differences.

THE POPE
- cool hat
- statements affect the inner lives of millions

- multilingual
- communes with the Great Almighty

MINOR SYNDICATED COLUMNIST IN D.C.
- pretentious fedora (see cover)
- statements briefly considered by dozens in Flint, Michigan
- wonders what the hell the Nigerian cab driver is saying to the dispatcher
- can't get the third assistant to the undersecretary to the Secretary of Hybrid Rutabaga Development to return his calls

But. *In the world, not of it.* This means that while I live here and work within spitting distance of the White House, my heart, soul, mind, and standards of reasonable real estate prices are back in the Midwest. I say this to assure you that this book is guaranteed to be free of any Washington insight or subject matter. Nothing comes from highly placed sources. Not a word from knowledgeable aides. I know it is fashionable to despise Washington, but I'm not trying to capitalize on that. I'm just being honest. When it comes down to the grand sweep of history, to the halting, zigzag path our nation is taking, I have no inside line. All I know is what I write in the papers.

—Washington, D.C.
June 7, 1993

P.S. Some of these pieces are lamer than others. You'll know them when you read them. I have spaced them throughout the book to give the worthwhile pieces some breathing room. If you hit what you believe are ten lame pieces in a row, however, it is possible that you don't find *any* of this amusing and have been given this book by someone who believes humor is universal. In this case you should put the book down and move along. Life's too short.

Office Life

ONCE UPON A TIME I STAYED UP LATE AS LONG AS I LIKED, spent the night in thick yeasty hours of sleep, woke late, and motor-scootered into the newspaper office just in time to have lunch, after which I would leave for home, where I would write all night. I had perfected the art of holding a job without actually being physically present. Today I have to go to bed early, wake after six thin hours of mealy sleep, walk three miles to work half asleep, and spend the day yoked to a desk. Every day I ask myself the same question, how did this happen? Did I sign something I should have read over more carefully? Should the stink of pitch in the air have told me something when I made this deal?

I should explain. The one thing I have strived to avoid all my life has been the nine-to-five job. Observation shows that it takes place mostly in offices, and offices are the lairs of the damned. Take the healthiest and happiest man in the world, put him in an office for five minutes, and he will have headaches, back pains, eyestrain, hemorrhoids, and shooting pains in his jaws from grinding his teeth. Offices do that. They're Hell with a floor plan.

My first office job was with a major seed manufacturer. I sat at a desk filling in numbers in forms, surrounded by chain-smoking women with tight perms and elaborate eyeglasses.

We all sat at big desks in an open room. I lasted two months and put down as my reason for leaving, "PREFER TO AVOID MURDERING EVERYONE AROUND ME WITH A BLUNT AXE." Consequently I have never understood those people who get fired and *then* go on a murderous rampage. Hey, they let you out; what more do you want?

My second job, as a compiler of television listings, lasted eight months. I should have fled in panic after the tour of the office, for it was a diorama of all the petty aesthetic miseries of office life: the tired plants gasping in the corner, the sink full of orphaned coffee mugs with their indelible rings, the beige and putty color scheme, the beige and putty people, the poster of a beige kitten desperately clinging to a tree branch with the words HANG IN THERE 'TIL FRIDAY! After which, what? Kitten drops to its death? Lands in the jaws of a dog? Ends up on a bar stool, complaining about another hard week on the branch?

I took the job anyway. I had a friend draw me a picture of the man from Edvard Munch's "The Scream" hanging from a branch. I bought a prestained coffee mug so I wouldn't stand out in the break room. I went through training sessions pretending to take great fascination in the work—which was filling in numbers in forms—and launched myself into thirty-two black pay-periods of skull-draining boredom. I learned several important lessons about office life.

1. There is always someone crazy who will not shut up. In this case it was a woman who laughed like a porpoise having an orgasm on laughing gas. You had to check on her occasionally to see if she'd swallowed her tongue. You were always disappointed.

2. Some people live to write huffy notes. These people clap their hands when the office gets a small fridge, because they know that in a month they can write huffy notes about cleaning out *Those Disgusting Sandwiches*. They believe that "not making coffee" or "not refilling the copier tray" should be capital crimes punishable by The International Convention of Anal-Retentive Office Despots. They love to end everything with THIS MEANS YOU! Sample huffy notes:

"A random survey of the back of people's drawers indicates that at least three (3) push pins (the valuable see-through variety) are loose in each drawer. Look in your drawer before raiding the supply closet, please. THIS MEANS YOU!" Or: "Some people are going through the revolving door downstairs at a rate of speed that is injurious to the lame and infirm. Check to see you don't propel the honored aged into the street at a high rate of speed! THIS MEANS YOU!" Or: "Ethnic tensions in the formerly Soviet Central Asian republics can only be soothed by the introduction of multiparty democracy, coupled with the rule of law. Order must be restored, or chaos will result. THIS MEANS YOU!"

3. The person in the office to whom you are the most attracted is already married. Or, worse yet, she isn't.

4. By some cruel fluke, everyone who truly knows how things should be done is subservient to management. Compounding the irony, *everyone who is clueless is in charge.* This odd, happenstance reversal of things does not vary no matter where you are.

I'm now in the best of all possible offices: people are bright, there are no kitten-in-peril posters, and the place is not under the thumb of some evil, waddling receptionist who regards us all as a hateful conspiracy to keep her from watching her soap operas. But it's still an office; I still have to spend my day glaring at an evil, life-sucking, radiation-spewing monitor that will probably give me nipple cancer or make my eyebrows drop off. I am required by convention to apply the happy-mask whenever I am there, but given that I can take only so much of office life before my brains run out my nose and ruin the keyboard, it is likely I will have quit or been fired by the time this comes out.

If not, of course, the following ought to force the issue nicely. Let me give you a rundown of a typical day for a certain office worker. First, the ideal.

10:00 Wake
12:00 Hamburger
2–6:00 Reading

6–7:00 Pizza
8–2:00 Writing

Now, the reality.

6:30 Alarm sounds, making one of several noises currently available.

1. Ringing of a bell, which encourages pleasant dreams of hearing the bell signaling the end of a school day, dreams that are cruelly dashed when you open your eyes, note the absence of dinosaur or horse statuettes on your bureau, and realize you are now an adult.

2. Beeping of a garbage truck in reverse, encouraging dreams of being picked up by men in jumpsuits and dumped into the back of a truck fetid with refuse, dreams that are more or less borne out as the day goes on.

6:30–6:32 Sit on edge of bed, staring blankly at floor, combating the awful magnetism sheets exert on flesh, a phenomena some scientists believe is the mysterious "fifth force" that holds the universe together.

6:35 Blindly do what the body insists you do.

6:37 Wake up and discover you are still peeing.

6:40 Go to kitchen, turn on coffeepot. Thank God you put in the coffee grounds and the water the previous night; all you have to do is flip the switch.

6:40–7:00 Watch the news on TV. Bryant Gumble seems vaguely angry that you are not completely awake. Willard Scott shows pictures of one-hundred-year-old women who look as withered and beaten as you feel. Your heart goes out to them. Then again, they don't have to go into the office. Screw'em. Turn the channel. Nothing but robot blondes. Go to get coffee; discover that you forgot to add new grounds and you have twelve cups of pale, acidic water.

7:00–7:15 Warner Brothers cartoons. They provide instructive lessons for the day to come, and you decide that when your boss starts to hector you about a late project, you will respond with the immovable panache of Bugs. Later in the day, when you attempt to say "What's up, doc?" in a cheeky, disrespectful tone, it somehow comes out "You wanted to see me?"

7:15–7:30 Return upstairs, sit on bed, stare at floor, listening to radio news. Wonder why it is that National Public Radio really thinks you care about Zaire's economic plight at 7:21 A.M.

7:32 Begin shaving, aware that you are still half asleep.

7:34 Sponge up blood from around the sink; cauterize wound with cigarette.

7:35 Take a shower. Recall that yesterday you cut open the shampoo bottle, scraped up the last atoms of shampoo with a razor, and reminded yourself to pick up some more. End up washing your hair with cheap hand soap.

7:40 Hair looks perfectly clean, as though you had used expensive perfumed shampoo. Feel sudden resentment toward shampoo manufacturers.

7:41–7:50 Choose pants, preferably pair whose cuffs are not stapled. Vow to actually have some pants taken up before they go out of style. As you knot your tie, realize once again you have no idea how you ever learned to do this. Visualize men in movies confidently lashing a cravat to their throat with a few curt gestures. Get finger stuck in knot. Tie ends up hanging six inches past belt buckle. Try again.

7:54 Select bolo tie.

7:55 Make cursory check of appliances—iron is off, coffee machine is unplugged. (Your mother had a friend who left the coffee maker plugged in one day. Burned the house down. Lost everything.) Turn on TV and radio so burglars think there's someone home. Then again, once they see the un-plugged coffeepot, they'll know different. Leave house with a vague nod to the possessions that might be stolen while you are away earning money to keep up on the payments. Possessions, being inanimate, do not appreciate the sentiment. Feel sudden stab of resentment toward furniture.

7:56–8:28 The walk. Stride purposefully to work. There are no bums. The streets are clean. Your head is clear, your legs powerful. A new day has truly begun, unfortunately.

8:30–11:30 Pretend to work.

11:30 Lunch break. You learned this trick years ago: take your lunch hour at 11:30, so when you come back at 12:30, everyone else will be gone and you can waste a half an hour doing nothing. No one else does this. Amazing. And they call themselves professionals.

1:00–3:00 Pretend to work.

3:00 Break for suicidal thoughts and donuts. Observe the slant of sunlight against the table in the break room and be reminded, for no particular reason, of an afternoon in college, an old girlfriend, summer camp. Be filled with grim determination to do something about your life. Maybe a screenplay about a guy who hates his job. And he suddenly gets involved in a crime. And, he's from another planet. Yeah, that's it. That's your pass out of here.

4:30 Cash paycheck. Buy a lottery ticket.

4:30–5:30 Pretend to work.

5:30–6:00 Drop all pretense.

6:00 Meet coworkers for a drink downstairs. Marvel at their relaxed sense of well-being. Conclude they lead uninteresting lives, and look desperately for evidence. Find none; order second drink and appetizers.

8:00 Leave bar. Your stomach is full of popcorn kernels bloated with whiskey. The city has a not unpleasant list to it; the sidewalk gently pitches and rolls beneath your feet. The city is a ship. Your career its cargo. Unfortunately, its name is the *Lusitania*.

8:21 Get into cab. Driver loathes you and is listening to a cassette of his favorite band, Smite the Infidel. He is silent the entire trip, despite your best effort to reach some common ground ("So! How about that planetary mass being sufficient to give us just the right amount of gravity!") Overtip him because you feel guilty because you take cabs and he drives them.

8:44 Enter house. Look around. Home is intact, but a nasty, acrid stench from the kitchen gives you pause for alarm. Discover that you didn't unplug the coffee machine and the unconsumed cups have boiled down to a thick viscous sludge. Wrinkle nose in disgust.

8:45 Wonder what that sludge would taste like with a little scotch.

8:47 Fix joyless dinner. Realize that your culinary skills can be summed up in your ability to rotate dish halfway through heating.

9:14 Start to make notes for screenplay.

9:15 Remember there's a really good movie on TV. Decide it can be counted as research for your script.

11:30 Iron clothes for next day. Decide there's a metaphor in ironing you can use in the screenplay. Yeah, that's it. A close-up of ironing. Man's struggle to bring order out of chaos, if not wrinkles. Shots of steam to indicate pent-up sexual desire. Hey, there's something here. Feel unaccountably perky.

11:45 Make coffee for the next day. Plug in the pot so all you'll have to do in the morning is hit the switch. Wonder why it is that it's all right to leave the pot plugged in all night but not okay to leave it plugged in all day. Decide to work a coffee-maker fire into your screenplay. Steam, fire: this is looking good. Maybe you should call in sick tomorrow and work on it.

12:00 Go to bed.

(Repeat until fired.)

Not that I actually live this pathetic life. Oh, no. Hoping to escape a miserable office life by writing screenplay about an office worker from outer space who gets involved in a crime? Please.

My main character is from Des Moines.

On Fire

WE WOKE UP THE OTHER DAY TO FIND THAT CANADA HAD SENT its entire atmosphere to us via overnight delivery. It hit suddenly, killing squirrels as they leaped from tree to tree; my street was littered with squirrels in mid-leap, shaped like Greyhound bus corporate symbols. The wind felt like a blizzard of thumbtacks.

On an average winter night our house is cold. When we watch TV, we can see the breath of the actors. We have a heat pump, which is a clever invention that draws in cold air, gives it a Dutch rub, and blows it out a tiny grate with the dimensions of a postage stamp. The result is air that is, theoretically, warm. But often the thermometer says eighty when in fact it is so cold that my wife will have a finger snap off while she sews, and we have to move the sofa to find it. On cold nights we sleep so closely together we wake to find we have grafted to each other, which adds a full hour to getting dressed for work. If she never gets promoted, it will be because her personnel file contains the entry "husband often accompanies her to work and has hand stuck to her inner thigh for duration of day."

So when the cold snap settled in, we made a fire. On the way home I stopped at the store for a cord of wood. This would be the night we inaugurated the fireplace.

12

This is not something we do often, as you'll see.

First of all, I don't trust fire. Of the four elements, fire is the psychopath. The shifty, untrustworthy element. Air? Everybody's friend. Can't have enough of good old air. Water we respect, mostly because it has those oceans hanging around like big, nasty brothers ready to show you who's boss. Earth we kick around like a dumb loyal dog. But fire is all malice, all spite and bad intentions. Put a lump of earth in your fireplace, and it sits there. Place a glass of water on the coffee table, and it behaves. Fire is always looking to go someplace you don't want it to be. The world is fire's buffet table, and it's all-you-can-eat.

Naturally, we build an honored place for fire in our living room. Might as well install a special closet for a serial killer.

Our fireplace has a flue that is only slightly less wide than a thermometer. On a cold day, it's also as frigid as Pluto, and getting smoke to go up the flue is like giving an enema to a person who's sat in wet cement and is glaring at you with their tongue stuck out. Smoke cannot find the flue. It wanders around the house, poking up faucets, nosing at the smoke alarms, which shriek like robots having an orgasm. We spent the first few fire-building attempts fanning the smoke back at the fireplace, like we were shooing birds out of a barn.

Of course, you have to warm up the flue first. This requires holding a flaming torch of newspaper up the flue, feeling like a villager who has gone to storm Dr. Frankenstein's castle but inexplicably got his arm stuck in the fireplace. After the flue is warm—this only takes fourteen hours, after which you are sleepy, or spring has arrived—you put on the wood.

As noted, I buy my wood at the supermarket, which sells cords of wood—a unit of measurement based on "more than you can comfortably carry"—in shrink-wrapped plastic. But they were out, leaving me with only varying brands of prefabricated logs. The supermarket had its own brand of fake log, which made me suspicious; most house brands consist of products that a manufacturer is simply too ashamed to put its name on. This item was called a MULTICOLORED FLAME LOG and sold for a dollar. "HOURS OF COLORFUL BLUE AND ORANGE FLAMES," said the label, "AND

ALMOST NO CHANCE OF ASPHYXIATION FROM ODD CHEMICAL COMPOUNDS. REALLY." The label listed the ingredients: Wax. Sawdust. Multicolor enhancer. There was a little picture of a laughing devil on the wrapper.

The instructions were simple: put it in the fireplace and set its shroud alight. Simple, convenient: a fire for the latter twentieth century.

The caveats, however, took up most of the label. Don't use for cooking. (It will make your burger turn blue and orange.) Don't use in an unventilated area. (You will be found by the cleaning lady with your eyes bulging and your hands at your neck.) Don't poke the log. (It will leap from the fireplace and tear at your throat.) Don't argue religion or politics in the presence of the log. Stay fifteen feet away from the log at all times. Do not take stairs two at a time when carrying log. Dial 9 and 1 while lighting fire and have another person prepared to dial the final 1 as the log catches fire. DO NOT ASK WHY. Failure to use log properly MAY RESULT IN A CATACLYSM THAT WILL CONSUME ALL WHO STAND IN THE PATH OF ITS HIDEOUS, PITILESS FURY.

Sounded fine. I lit the sleeve of the log and set it in the fireplace. Five minutes later the smoke alarm went off, as it always does; smoke alarms are like children who hear the grown-ups having fun downstairs and cry to get attention. Unlike with children, however, you deal with alarms by standing up on a chair and punching them until they quiet. At least, I hope that is not how you deal with children. After I had torn the smoke alarm from its bracket, I went back to tending the fire. The alarm continued to give strangled dying bleats of protest, but it finally decided I deserved whatever I got, and it shut up. The fire was burning nicely now. The log was burning perfectly.

Perhaps too perfectly.

An hour later, it was burning as steadily as ever. Colorful flames danced from its perfect log-shaped contours. A cozy glow spread throughout the room; it was finally warm in the house. The log hissed as the wax and sawdust and mysterious chemicals combusted.

"Bricks in warm jello," said my wife. "Enveloped by well-nippled garbanzos in creosote."

"Rippling surges of fortuitous glue?" I replied. "Fine."

I got up and made us both sandwiches. And did so as if in a dream. We ate them hungrily, frequently missing our mouths. My wife attempted to place the last morsel in her ear, and I watched this attempt with distant interest. The smoke alarm gave a weak cry of alarm from its place on the kitchen table, miles away.

"Thirty weasels might crease my elbows," I said, a look of unease on my face.

"Lick the woofer, Harvey," she said, nodding vigorously. We opened a window and let fresh air pour in. After a few minutes our heads cleared.

"I think there's something odd in that log," she said. I agreed. It was still burning perfectly, its mass unchanged by an hour of combustion. She went to the fridge and fetched a box of baking soda. "This will put it out," she said.

I poured the entire box on the log. The fire would duck, flame up, subside, then roar back.

"Poke it to death," she suggested. I took the poker and stabbed at the log. It broke into several pieces, each of which, like the brooms of the Sorcerer's Apprentice, bloomed anew with twice the vigor.

"We're damned," I said. She agreed, and said that if she was damned, she was at least going to get a good night's sleep. And off she went.

So that was how I spent my night: shivering in a room with all the windows open, staring at a fire that refused to go out, listening to the occasional disembodied remonstration from the smoke alarm on the table. After an hour the log was burning as hot as ever, and I decided I could take no more. I found my insurance policy, put it outside in the car, and went to bed.

When we woke, it was freezing in the house. Cold air was marching down the flue, poking into every corner of the house. The log was gone. No cinders, no charred hunks of waxy sawdust. Nothing to indicate we had probably engaged in some dark and timeless ritual that meant the forfeiture of our eternal souls.

And that is something I will have to explain in the afterlife. When asked if I did indeed burn one of Satan's Multicolored Flame Logs, I'll 'fess up. When St. Peter affixes me with that stern and horrible gaze and asks, "Why?" I'll need say only two words.

Heat pump.

And the gates will swing wide. Heaven will be a good place. I imagine the flues are wide, and the logs always catch. There are no smoke alarms in Heaven, of course; they're all down in Hell. And you can't turn them off.

I'll Take Humility for $500

~~~~~~

ANSWER: IT'S A PERFECT EXAMPLE OF SOMEONE GETTING THEIR employer to foot the bill for a trip out of town to do something they've always wanted to do—namely, try out for *Jeopardy!*

Question: I am brilliant, a genius of our times. Or so the evidence suggests. Every night I watch *Jeopardy!* and win hundreds of thousands of dollars. I crush the sweating nebbishes on the show; I make reckless bets, answer devilish questions, and reap vast fortunes. If the IRS ever decided to tax hypothetical income, I would be in trouble.

My wife has long suggested I go on the show, but I have resisted. They play by incredibly stringent rules—for example, you're actually penalized for wrong answers. Players are not permitted to leave the set and watch another channel if the category is unfamiliar.

Here's the painful truth: Going on the show would strike at my own deep suspicion that I am not brilliant but a glib, shallow generalist. I do not want to show up and be not only confronted with categories such as "Mulatto Circumcisionists" or "Forty-Syllable Flemish Palindromes" but surrounded by people who can answer them.

A few weeks ago, however, I saw that trials would be held in Atlantic City, which is reasonably close. Why not try? If I

17

passed, it would prove I was hypothetically brilliant. And I could always come up with a good excuse for not going on the show. I could drool during the personal interview or clutch my privates and shout "MIMSY ARE THE BORO-GOVES!" at inappropriate moments.

The *Jeopardy!* tryouts are held at a casino—a profane act in a temple of stupidity. Absolutely no feeling of *Jeopardy*ness informs the event. No bouncy theme song, no bright blue and red *Jeopardy!* colors, no cutouts of Alex Trebek blessing the postulants. Gray, joyless casino employees herd us into a small room and give each of us a sheet of paper and don't smile because it's the union's rule.

A recorded announcement tells us we have three minutes to answer ten questions. We must score seventy percent. I'm tempted to ask how many questions that is just to make everyone else in the room feel better.

I flip over the sheet. The first two questions are absolute stumpers. They might as well be Flemish. Maybe they're palindromes! I read them backward: no good. I get the next question, a softball about the author of *Charlotte's Web*. Easy. (I am unsure of Dr. Doolittle's first name, however, so I don't try.)

Then I hit two more left-field queries. I'm dead. I'm cinders. I feel that high, screeching panic familiar to examination day, the sensation of your brain geysering out of your skull from every pore, surrounding you with a fine, gray mist of failure. I answer the rest of the questions, fake the ones I don't know, and leave. I am certain a big pink sign reading FRESHLY CERTIFIED IDIOT is flashing over my head. This being a casino, someone will see the flashing sign, stuff quarters in my fly, and yank my arm.

The woman at the door tells me that the results will be announced at five thirty on the casino floor. Fine. I kill time in the casino, and just to reassert my newfound identity as an idiot, I play the slots. I am playing a one-armed bandit—actually, it's now called a "physically challenged bandit"—when the results are announced. The names roll past. I am not among their number. As the voice concludes listing the honored few, my slot machine belches out sixty quarters. I look at my winnings with revulsion.

Hours later I am in the casino bar, having my cerebral cortex pureed by an overamplified lounge act. Next to me are two women who took the *Jeopardy!* test. They won. "Which test did you get?" one of them asks me. "You get the hard one or the one with the *Charlotte's Web* question?"

We compare answers, and I discover that I was correct on seven out of ten. In other words, I passed. I am mystified. I go back to the board where the rules are posted and learn that the results for my test group were announced at two thirty, not five thirty. They'd given me the wrong time. In other words, I made it.

Not only had I passed, I wouldn't have to worry about going on the show. I was still hypothetically brilliant. End of story.

Wait a minute, I forgot. I must phrase it in the form of a question. Okay:

Wasn't this a great excuse to get out of the office?

Final Exit: The Marketing Campaign

~~~~~~

WHEN *FINAL EXIT,* DEREK HUMPHRY'S GUIDE TO KILLING yourself, hit the best-seller lists, self-help authors all across America sat back and smacked themselves on the forehead. Of course. Why didn't I think about that? Here I try to teach people how to fine-tune their emotional carburetors, when what they *really* want someone to tell them is "TRADE IT IN."

I also was impressed by the book's success, as it proved the old adage find a need and fill it. In this case, a simple means of bringing about one's quietus. If I may summarize, here are the salient points of the method:

1. Put a dry-cleaning bag over your head, preferably from a place that always lost your buttons; karma accumulates.

2. Three hours pass. Getting mighty stuffy in here. Take the bag off, consult book again, note your omission of soporific drugs and enjoy a good hearty chuckle at your absentmindedness.

3. Enjoy a fistful of barbiturates, washed down with a good white wine. If you're not all that depressed, it is permissible to wait for Beaujolais season.

4. Reapply bag; secure with rubber band; settle back; try

not to think about biblical strictures against suicide or Dante's description of suicidal souls whirling around Hell in incorporeal frustration.

5. Feel drowsy; choke back instinctual desire to make sure the alarm is set.

6. Wonder if you should proofread your note a fifth time (applies only to newspaper copy editors); decide that any typos will reflect the depth of your despair (see previous exception).

7. Hope the coroner has nice things to say about your teeth and gums; wonder if badly bitten fingernails warrant a closed casket.

8. Feel yourself leaving body and floating; note cobwebs in corner of ceiling.

9. Enter a tunnel with a bright light at the end; wonder distractedly if this is truly the entrance to paradise or merely the sign of a brain closing up shop; note the letters *GE* on the light and its tendency to flicker like a fluorescent, and feel creeping sense of unease.

10. Shove off; shed this mortal coil; earn your harp and halo; vault the clouds; high-five St. Peter; dip a toe in the sulphurous pool (this offer applies only to Catholics, although certainly not for a limited time only); i..e, die.

11. Become an insensate slab filled with happily munching microbes who, frankly, cannot believe their luck.

This is not to demean suicides, who undoubtedly have an advocacy group somewhere lobbying on behalf of the rights of the Mortally Challenged. I myself have known deep, black despair and mentally shopped around for tall bridges from time to time. In college it was fashionable to obliquely allude to suicidal intentions to impress the rest of the poetry class; there was no better way to spend an evening than to listen to fifteen self-penned eulogies, particularly if wine was served afterward. Surprisingly, there was no rush to throw a rope over the beams after half a jug of Chianti; by then I was off in a corner trying to flatter a young woman by complimenting the way she rhymed "hope in vain" and "opened vein."

Inevitably I assumed the standard attitude toward death,

which is to bow gallantly at the waist and say, "After you."
Suicide is not the answer, no more than a car wreck is the
answer to a request for directions. I can imagine hastening
my end only if in the dry, tight grip of some hideous disease.
In that case I would go out by my own hand only if I could
rig up the coffin so that it issues a hearty Bronx cheer upon
opening. Given the number of Italian in-laws I have, I'd like
to be posed in the box with one hand grabbing my privates.
Yo, Death. I got your sting, right here.

That said, there is still something pernicious about *Final
Exit*. Death is something to be cheated. A maître d' who will
seat us at the worst table no matter how much we offer to
pay. We all have a reservation, of course, but the point is to
show up as late as possible. Giving the permanently sad some
advice as to how to be first in line for the ferry that crosses
the Styx is probably not a good idea.

But it *is* a profitable one.

So there's no reason to stop with a book, when merchandis-
ing opportunities await. Sequels and other spin-offs. In case
Mr. Humphry isn't feeling too chipper nowadays (and incidentally, I would have loved to see the royalty payment
schedule for a how-to-suicide-book author; if the company
was smart, they stretched the payments out over ten years),
I offer the following suggestions.

The *Final Exit* Page-A-Day Calendar

Every weekday is a Monday. Every weekend day is a
Wednesday afternoon. Each page has an inspirational quote
or interesting fact about suicide, such as:

"324 B.C.: Marcus Sentorius discovers the parallel incision,
breaking with the traditional perpendicular slashing of the
wrists."

"It's the birthday of the plastic bag, invented in 1953. *A
votre santé!*"

"Most suicides occur around the holidays. Here's a kitchen-
tested recipe for Seconal fruitcake."

After October, each day will simply read "Are you still
around?"

The Final Exit *Cookbook*

Sumptuously illustrated, with easy-to-follow instructions for all sorts of fascinating dishes, such as:

Laudanum Flan
Bad-Clam Casserole
Spaghettini with Nightshade Pesto
Thousand-Aspirin Salad Dressing
Quicklime Pie
And, of course, that old favorite, Careless Betty's Church Picnic Cole Slaw—ingredients: cabbage, carrots, mayo already past the expiration date—Instructions: Chop and combine all ingredients. Put in a poorly sealed container and place in trunk of car. Drive to picnic. Leave car in the sun for four to six hours. Remove cole slaw. Serves: 20. Kills: 14.

Final Exit Action Figures

It's a hard, tough world, and kids have their anxieties too; dolls can help them resolve their fears and learn to cope by assisting their dolls in "play" suicides. For the boys, there's Rock 'm Socrates; he drinks his hemlock—and wets, too, showing how all involuntary muscle control is lost when you pass on. There's the glamorous movie star, Misunderstood Marilyn, for the girls; they'll spend hours applying smeared mascara and getting her disheveled hair just so. (Available with an optional President's Friend doll, who can put the realistic diary into his jacket pocket.) Best of all, she talks! Pull the cord, and no one believes her.

All accessories, such as the Empty House With No One Due Back Till Monday, are sold separately.

The Final Exit *Save-the-Earth Guide*

Includes fifty ways you can help Mother Earth, such as:

- Use plastic bags that break down in sunlight.
- Eat to stock yourself full of nutrients much prized by grubworms.

- Make Sure the Air Conditioner Is Off! The smell will dissipate; ozone, meanwhile, is irreplaceable.
- Flipper Weeps, But Not for You: having your ashes scattered at sea sounds romantic, but the metal in your fillings can kill fish.
- If you don't plan on being discovered for a while, check those washers: over a gallon a day can be lost.
- If you must arrange lighting fixtures for that dramatic spotlight to highlight their discovery, exchange those bulbs for energy-saving fluorescent.
- Composting, Zoning regulations, and You.

The *Final Exit* Video Library

Here the *Final Exit* ethos is interpreted by America's premier video self-help heroes. Included in the series are Jane Fonda's *Flatter EKG Lines in 30 Minutes a Day* and *Looking Natural: Firming Up for That Last Makeover.* Richard Simmons weighs in with a merry, heartwarming video called *Croakin' to the Oldies,* in which weepy, mid-tempo teen-suicide ballads are played at increasingly slower speeds. (Includes Simmons's Deal-a-Last-Meal system, where special menu cards help you plan a final banquet that won't require your burial garments be let out.) Turner Broadcasting offers a special version of *It's a Wonderful Life,* which gets to the scene where Jimmy Stewart throws himself off the bridge and then cuts to the credits. Perky Germanic sex maven Dr. Ruth offers a tape for couples engaged in an assisted suicide ("Be honest vith each other. If you vant to say, 'I am embarrassed to put zis needle in your vein,' say it. But do it.")

Each of these is available on audiocassette as well, for those who spend most of their time stuck in traffic and haven't time to get around to this month's *Vanity Fair,* let alone killing themselves.

Final Exit: The Board Game

Fun for up to four players. (Four more can watch and help.) Race around the board, collecting the means to leave the game. Oh, oh—doctor suspicious about your claim that you need one hundred barbiturates to help you sleep; back two paces. Hmm—you've landed on a Shaky Motives space. What will the card say: unlucky in love? teen angst? heavy metal music? Good news—societal attitudes toward doctor-assisted suicide soften! Oh, my, it's a Tip the Balance card, one that will give you a reason either to stay alive (and lose the game) or to stay in and keep playing. What will it be: intervention of loving relatives? (lose one turn), read an article about how it's not your life that's messed up, it's your brain chemistry? (trade in game piece for another, start again). No! It's the appearance of *Final Exit* in your local bookstore.

Proceed directly to Go!

Press 3 to Keep Reading

VOICE MAIL, WE ARE NOW BEING TOLD, IS THE WORST THING ever to befall civilization. American productivity plummets while we languish on hold. People suffer crippling nerve damage from the repetitive motion of pushing buttons or else are wounded by painful splints of plastic when they slam their cheap receivers down in frustration and the damn thing explodes. Why, it's so bad that the network news programs have all done a story on its horrors, right in that slot they reserve for Proof the World Is Going to Hell, right before the uplifting little-girl-with-leukemia-gets-her-horse slot that ends every program.

The news the other night carried a story of a company president who did not realize the horrors of voice mail until he tried to call one of his managers and got a machine. Whereupon the scales fell from his eyes with the clanging sound of manhole covers, and he decreed that the next time he got a voice-mail machine, he was going to have one less manager. We were expected to applaud this. But what it means, of course, is this poor Dagwood is forbidden to stray from his desk lest Mr. Dithers seek his counsel, and the man will no doubt be found dead with a burst bladder and uremic poisoning.

I'd suggest that it's not the concept, but the execution.

Good voice mail should be helpful but stern, like a policeman helping a drunk get home. Bad voice mail leaves you with the feeling that you are staggering down a labyrinth culminating in a Minotaur who will eat your message and cut you off.

Examples.

Good voice mail.

"Thank you for calling. If you'd like to leave a message, press 1. If you want an operator, press 2. If you don't do anything, a device attached to my belt will issue a painful electric shock and I will be compelled to take your call, but I can't guarantee I'll be civil about it. That is all."

Bad voice mail.

"Thank you for calling 911. In order to serve you better, your call is being routed to the police department, fire department, hospital, or mortuary best able to help you. If your home is being broken into, press 1."

(Pause)

"If the intruder is armed, press 2."

(Pause)

"If the intruder is in the room from where you are making this call, press 4."

(Pause)

"If you are attempting to avoid detection and have turned off the lights, press 23392092383, followed by the pound sign."

(Pause)

"That is not a valid number. Please try again."

(Pause)

"You have not entered the number. If you have been attacked and are dazed and unable to recall long strings of random numbers, press 1."

(Pause)

"If you are bleeding, press 4. If you are bleeding all over the rug, press 5. If you would like the number of a good cleaner, press 7. If you want more options, press 1776-star, in honor of the choices opened up to humanity by the American revolution. If you want to know the choices in other states, press 1776 followed by the number of stars that would indicate the order in which that state was admitted to the union. For a listing of the order of admission, press 4. To repeat this message, press 2. If you are still bleeding, press down hard on the wound."

Bad voice mail, in other words, is like a poorly plotted novel. ("If you want to be reminded how the crazy beggar's taunts remind the heroine of her father, press 8.") Even if well done, critics insist, it removes the human aspect. To which I say, Thank God.

Consider the vast, unpleasant boiler room of directory assistance operators. When I call directory assistance in New York, I can feel the tension and misery of the entire city come howling down the line, and I'm never quite sure if the place isn't being robbed as I speak. I frequently become so unnerved by the brusqueness of the call that I dial directory assistance in calm, content North Dakota and ask the number for 911 and spend a pleasant minute chatting with the operator while she looks it up.

Truly helpful operators are rare; most appear to have been interrupted while sketching notes for their next symphony and are peeved at yet another interruption from the trivial world. They are doubly angered by the fact that you are standing in the way of another call, a call yet unanswered but undoubtedly far more important, a call from the one person for whom they would gladly put down their quill and staves and devote the rest of their day to helping.

Rare are the voices who seem genuinely pleased that I have called. Mind you, I don't expect sincerity—when someone spends their lives slurring the name of their employer into a small plastic tube hanging from their ear, they are seldom expected to bring deep joy to the prospect of saying the hated mantra for the seven-millionth time. But neither is the dullness of their trade a reason for abrading my mood with their unhappiness. Please lie and act happy.

This of course is not to denigrate the fine receptionists who are helpful, saintlike, conscientious and number in the low dozens. It is simply to say that voice mail is here for a while, and we had best learn to employ it correctly. Rail if you like against the mapless dolts who lay down its little electronic roadways. But press 1 if you have a better idea.

Press 2 if you want to talk to the woman at the front desk

with boyfriend problems, a full bladder, and nails so long she cannot hold a pen to write down your message but merely pretends to take your message.

Press 3 if you would like this message repeated.

(Pause.)

Thank you!

Voice mail, we are now being told, is the worst thing ever to befall civilization. American productivity plummets while we languish on hold. People suffer crippling nerve damage from the repetitive motion of pushing buttons or else are inflicted with painful splints of plastic that shatter when they slam their cheap receivers down in frustration. Why, it's so bad that the network news programs have all done a story on its horrors, right in that slot they reserve for Proof the World Is Going to Hell, right before the uplifting little-girl-with-leukemia-gets-her-horse slot that ends every program.

The news the other night carried a story (CLICK)

Surplus Lincolns

ʊʊʊ

MOST AMERICANS WHO HAVE VISITED THE LINCOLN MEMORIAL and gazed upon that weary, noble face have the same emotion: man, he was an ugly cuss. Gaunt and stringy, with those odd vacant eyes—if he hadn't been president, you might think his memorial was something built to honor the Unknown Drifter. If he came at you, you'd cross the street. Unless he said, "Hey! It's me! Lincoln!" And then you'd relax.

Lincoln, or at least his vestigial organic remnants, was in the news last week. Scientists—and I am not yanking your chain about this—are planning to clone Lincoln from strands of hair, bone fragments, and dried blood. It's a gee-whiz story, something that belongs in a supermarket tabloid, except for them to run the LINCOLN CLONED story they'd have to retract the LINCOLN STILL ALIVE AND ADVISING BUSH story they all ran during the Gulf War.

They won't clone the whole Lincoln, mind you, just a side order of DNA. They're looking for evidence that Lincoln suffered from Marfan's syndrome—an affliction that makes people tall, sunken chested, and twitchy. Lincoln having been all those things and more, scientists want to pick apart his molecular instruction manual and see what caused it.

This raises some interesting issues. Such as What do you do with the cloned Lincoln DNA once you're finished with it? Throwing it away seems vaguely disrespectful. Putting it in the back of the office fridge and waiting until someone gets fed up and posts a note reading PLEASE CLEAN YOUR LINCOLN BITS FROM THE FRIDGE wouldn't be respectful. Placing it on a chair in a balcony in Ford's Theater would seem rather pathetic. Reburying it with presidential honors would seem to be the proper thing, but then the DNA would have to lie in state in the rotunda, with people passing by to peer in a microscope and daub away tears.

Perhaps the scientists could clone a whole mess of the stuff and sell it as souvenirs, much like they did with the Berlin Wall. An asbestos-laced rock that once kept dour East Germans from becoming slightly less dour West Germans is one thing; an actual scrap of a president is another. Street vendors could move it easily. ("Lovely fresh Lincoln, just in.") DNA embedded in plastic paperweights and key chains, little Lincoln Memorials under glass that snow tiny bits of floating DNA when you shake it. I'd buy it.

This, of course, dodges the real issue: Why stop at cloning one cell's worth? Why not just grow a whole Lincoln? Obviously, the technology does not yet exist. It's not like Sea-Monkeys; you don't pour DNA in a bowl, add water, stir, and get the sixteenth president. But it's only a matter of time before the bright folk in the lab coats figure it out. Say they unveiled a walking, talking Lincoln. What might the results be?

- Republicans less likely to throw around the phrase "the party of Lincoln" as often if they knew he was sitting in the gallery, taking notes.
- Unseemly spectacle of people trying to get Lincoln to endorse Brady Bill.
- Possible embarrassment over surrey trips taken at public expense.
- Unavoidable implication of an immortal Nixon.

If they can clone one, of course, they can clone a dozen. Or a hundred. In fact, I think they ought to turn out about fifty thousand Lincolns, let them loose in Washington, and see what happens. I believe we'd be better off if the population of any city was ten percent Lincoln. We could have a special police force made up entirely of Lincolns, their strongest weapon being weary moral disapproval. They could stand in a line in their special black Kevlar frock coats and stovepipe hats, shaking their heads in sad regret. "Un-oh—here come the Abes!" criminals would say, and flee.

The problem would be that fifty thousand Lincolns would dilute his legacy, as a certain percentage would go bad. If they cloned a variety of other dead presidents, and some of them started misbehaving, you'd have the unseemly sight of Lincoln, Jefferson, and Eisenhower having loud drunken arguments in the park about states' rights. Or down-and-out packs of rogue Hoovers shaking down people for pocket change. It would be hard to keep one's respect for this nation if you passed a newsstand and half the men in the girlie mag section were Ben Franklin, adjusting their little glasses and grinning like the picture on joke money from the novelty store.

Maybe this is all a bad idea. Perhaps we should just let sleeping DNA lie. We may think we'll profit from cloning Lincoln—just as people in the next century may discover a disease that causes perpetual five o'clock shadow and want to clone Nixon. That would be disrespectful.

Unless, of course, they decide to clone Agnew and sell the matching set as lawn ornaments.

Puh-lease, Mr. Postman

〜〜〜〜〜〜〜〜〜〜〜〜〜〜〜〜〜〜〜〜〜〜〜〜〜〜〜〜〜〜〜〜〜〜〜〜〜〜

I HAVE A SURLY MAILMAN. GIVE HIM A LETTER WHEN HE SHOWS up, and he looks at you like he's hauling cinder blocks and you've just handed him another brick. He talks to himself and spends a long time in his truck and for two years has been under the delusion that a man named Guzman lives with my wife and me instead of a block over. I think he is a few months away from the point where mail carriers go mad and start burying each day's load in their backyard.

So you will understand why the recent announcement that the post office might cut back mail delivery to four days a week did not exactly make me wail with alarm.

I may be alone here. Businesses no doubt want delivery every working day, and kids waiting for a breakfast-cereal premium will no doubt be disappointed by the decision and, kids being what they are nowadays, will shoot up a few post offices. But most of us could live with it. Adulthood, after all, begins when you realize you no longer look forward to the mail.

Think about it. Here is what makes up the daily deposit in most mailboxes:

- A thick bill from the power company, including a detailed listing of fluctuating kilowatt-hour charges, written in

33

five languages and printed in a type ants would use for the bottom line of their eye exam, also, a forty-seven-page brochure on how you can cut energy costs by mummifying dead family pets, dipping them in pitch, and using them as torches.

- A thick bill from a department store, with an ad for luggage and a perfume insert so pungent that all your nose hairs fall out and flutter to the floor.
- A magazine you haven't time to read, which, for all you know, could be filled with blank pages or perhaps a story on you, including grainy, furtive-looking photographs and comments from your neighbors, none of whom, it turns out, really likes you.
- A bill for your subscription to that very magazine.
- An appeal for money from the United Eel and Tapir Preservation Fund. ("Dedicated to Unattractive, Skittish Animals in No Particular Danger.") Enclosed: pictures of eels in need of adoption. ("Inch for inch, your best charity bargain.")
- A catalog from Brawny Splinters Outfitters, full of jut-jawed brutes modeling ugly clothing you couldn't possibly use, and a catalog from Tender Slivers, their lingerie division.
- Political mailings from all the people who want your vote. No matter what party, they're all talking about the deficit and the importance of getting the nation back on an even fiscal keel.
- Seventeen preapproved credit card applications.
- Seventeen notices of credit card cancellations. Hey! it all evens out.

That's the standard load, at least around our house. No wonder the mailman is surly: he knows he bears a load of woe. No doubt people blame him for bad mail, the same way they blame the local weatherman for inopportune rain showers. (Except that the weatherman rarely sends us storms meant for Mr. Guzman.)

So do we need two fewer days of mail? Well ... perhaps. As noted, we don't want to provoke—sorry, disappoint—the nation's youth. I recall spending weeks in tortured suspense waiting for my Quisp Magic Ring to arrive and was heartily disappointed when I opened the mailbox to find nothing from Quisp, just letters spelling out the terms of my college loans. (The ring didn't come until I'd left home, and I blame flunking physics on it.)

But there are perhaps more important reasons for keeping mail delivery at its current schedule. What defines Sunday, but God, football, and no mail? You don't look at the mailbox on Sunday; you don't even think about it. No bill can touch you, no circular can petition for your attention. The world doesn't dare get near you on Sundays; its rectangular troops are held at bay.

This probably won't happen. It strikes me as a ploy for attention, a pistol to the temple that will end in a hasty approval of higher postal rates. We are, after all, used to that. When I was a kid, the raising of postal rates came infrequently and seemed to be a dark portent of unassuageable change. My father talked about postal hikes with the same tones used to describe the decision to give the Catholic mass in English. And we were Lutherans.

In our profligate age, however, we are accustomed to spiraling rates; we'll pay anything to keep the mail coming. Even if it is mostly bills. Because the mail is our line to the world; the mail is the tap on the shoulder that reminds us we're connected to something bigger. We'd be lost without it.

I know this is the case for me. How Mr. Guzman has made it this long without his lingerie catalogs, I can't imagine.

Wring out the Old

𝔳𝔳𝔳

HOW A DOZEN ROSES BECAME SYMBOLIC OF VALENTINE'S DAY, I have no idea. They are expensive, don't last very long, and can be picked up on the street corner—more appropriate for National Hooker's Day, really. Likewise, candy. What compels us to give candy to show our love? It's not like candy is some rare and valuable substance. Plutonium: now there's a way to say I love you. No matter how much you may mutate, I'll always care. There's more of you to love! More arms to hold me, more eyes to wink fetchingly!

And why candy, but not, say, cheese or bacon? Is it just the sugar content that does it, and if so, then why not give a bag of beets? They're red, and they don't make you gain weight.

Whereas candy requires women to perform a complex series of calculations. Holiday cookies plus upcoming Easter candy, divided by the number of aerobics classes they could feasibly attend if they quit work every day at ten A.M., multiplied by the sense that it's a pointless battle. When you give candy with skimpy lingerie, you add another variable: huge irritation that the man has been panting over the lingerie catalog and actually expects all women to be mopey, moussed-up sticks with industrial boobs and pouty bellybuttons. Does he realize women cannot spend all day lounging around in bras with their eyes closed? Does he know what the heating bill would be like? The jerk. The boor.

Whereupon the woman eats the entire box of candy and retires early, depressed over the prospect of summer and swimming suits.

You're safer with beets.

I overgeneralize. My wife is nothing like this at all, which is why she is my wife and the various old flames alluded to above are not. My wife does not expect candy and flowers, which is why I get them anyway—partly to follow the traditions of the season, partly in the hope that my frequent statements about not expecting a 27-inch TV for Valentine's Day will some day bear fruit. I no longer buy lingerie, however. I have bought her enough lingerie to open a brothel. It is cheaper to stare intently at the catalog for a full minute, then quickly look at my wife: I see a ghostly image of the garment, and it lasts as long on her as the real thing would. And I have learned to ignore the price code that floats over her shoulder.

But I observe this holiday only because I have to. Because the calendar says it's time to go dopey. One feels dull and churlish making a stand against the national day of love: the point of it is laudable. But it's all so banal. In the neighborhood store there are placards of bears hugging pink hearts. This is not love to me, no more than pigs hugging livers or ferrets embracing adrenal glands. Maybe if you're in high school, it's cute.

Adult love is generally not cute. It is not all pink hearts and bubble baths. It is also about who cleans the bathtub afterward. For example, it took my wife two years to train me to wring out the sponge after I swabbed the tub. In her hands, a sponge is eternal; in mine, it is a useless, brick-hard husk after a day. Because I love her, I learned to wring out the sponge.

Learning what drives the other person nuts and changing your actions even though you personally don't see the big deal: that's love. It is also characteristic of life in totalitarian governments, but that's coincidental. Show me a card with a bear hugging a sponge.

I'll buy it.

Prettyism

∿∿∿

THE LEFT NEEDS NEW SCRIPTWRITERS. NOW THAT *RACISM* AND *sexism* have been used to castigate everyone not sufficiently worshipful of all things multicultural, they have lost their power to inflict even the trifling wound. And so we have new conditions of sickness, such as heterosexism. An example of heterosexist speech: referring to your wife as your wife, instead of "partner."

Duly noted. I'm sure my WIFE will be interested to hear about that; it's the sort of thing my WIFE finds amusing in her WIFELY fashion. WIFE WIFE WIFE. *HUNKA HUNKA* BURNING SHE-THING: WIFE.

Have I offended anyone? I doubt it. In fact, I put this issue of heterosexism to a gay couple I know, two fellows long settled into de facto marriage (minus the tax breaks, regrettably) and was met with rolled eyes. "I couldn't care less," said one of the guys. "Although my wife might." But more important, if I have offended anyone, I truly do not care. I cannot micromanage every utterance so that each syllable salves the nerves of someone who holds a contrary opinion. We indeed may be judged by the words we use, but failure to use the Official Approved Words does not mean one is racist/sexist/statist/Trappist/hostess-with-the-mostist, etc.

There are people who go into the world each day like a

vast slack sail, waiting for the winds of injustice to fill them up and hurl them onward. You can never say the right thing with these people, and it's not worth it to try. Occasionally, they find a small legislative body—usually a college committee composed of glowering, overheated students with delusions of glandeur, or a small California town council—and get them to do their bidding. The most recent example is a bill before the Santa Cruz town council that would ban . . . lookism.

Lookism is just what it sounds like: discrimination on the basis of physical appearance. The bill would make it a crime to deny someone a job or an apartment based on appearance. The authors of this bill note that people with purple hair—I'm serious here—have had problems getting jobs and housing. Another social abrasion in need of the clammy poultice of governmental intervention.

I don't doubt that this happens. Note the absence of four-hundred-pound myopic men in feed caps and Confederate-flag T-shirts working the Victoria's Secret cash registers. But I've noted that people generally work where they fit in—at a place where the dress code is either so loose it falls off when you bend over, or so tight that it makes the Amish complain.

For example: There is a record store in the building where I work; as far as I can tell, they do their hiring exclusively from the Society for Creative Self-Mutilation. In addition to the requisite shabby black clothing and hanks of hair that look like an oilworker's glove, half the staff sport lurid eructations of color and nightmarish imagery tattooed into their flesh.

This is fine when you work at a temple of thumping inanity where people want the presence of sullen, indelibly painted nonconformists to validate their countercultural experience. But if I, say, had an apartment to let, and someone with a large hairy spider indelibly inked on their shaven skull showed up, I couldn't help but wonder, If he does this to his skin, what in God's name will he do to my walls?

In short, what this bill would do is forbid people from making snap superficial judgments based on appearance. Making such judgments may be wrong; they may be stupid.

But forbidding it is wrong. Personal appearance can be an instant reference check. An immediate aptitude test. Show up for a job interview wearing a greasy T-shirt that reads NO FAT CHICKS, three days' beard, and fingernails that suggest you are a part-time topsoil smuggler, and you say much about yourself, every other word of which is unprintable.

The bill's supporters say that it would not keep an employer from enforcing an appearance code after employment—you could force the purple-haired to get a dye job and a trim after you gave them the job. ("Welcome to your new job as a Mormon usher at the Mormon Tabernacle Choir, Stig; now, perhaps we can talk about that tattoo of the horned skull.") This seems an awfully long way to go to protect the right to not have to check the mirror before you go job-hunting.

Behind all this is thought control—the notion that you don't have the right to make judgments on people based on their choices and actions. The focus in expanding and securing rights ought to be placed on those conditions truly irrelevant to a person's character and ability, such as race. But this puts hair color and skin color on the same moral plane. It's like putting the physically disabled on the same level with someone who gets drunk and tries to retrieve a bottle opener from a howling garbage disposal, or equating the mentally handicapped with someone who plays Russian Roulette with a nail gun and spends the rest of his days twitching and gibbering in a small room.

Let's review the facts. There are some things you can't or shouldn't change and that should not be a basis for discrimination. Such as:

- skin color (except Michael Jackson)
- sexual preference (did you decide to be heterosexual? Really? Was it fun?)
- glandular malfunctions that make you very large
- glandular malfunctions that make you Sean Young

There are things you can control.

- number of Day-Glo colors streaming from your scalp
- number of dinner-plate-sized loops impaled in your nostrils
- number of foot-thick slabs of fudge inhaled before noon

Clip and save. This is just the beginning. Next up: Quickism, which is discrimination against the dead. Hey, just because they're gutted and embalmed doesn't mean they don't have feelings.

Great (Ignored) Americans

〰〰〰

A WHILE AGO, *LIFE* MAGAZINE UNVEILED ITS LIST OF THE "100 Most Influential Americans of the 20th Century," prompting people all over the nation to say, "Who asked them? Did you ask them? I didn't ask them." The next thing many people did was to scan the list for their name, in the hope that perhaps they had been sleepwalking one night, stumbled down to a nearby laboratory, and invented the semiconductor, and forgot all about it.

I have the list before me now, and no, I am not on it. I'm in good company, though. None of the presidents, for example, made the list. Not one.

"Every president is important to us. That's the nature of the job." So said *Life* editor Mary Steinbauer, quoted in a news story run by several newspapers normally reluctant to publicize contrived, self-serving magazine articles. In other words, since all presidents are influential, by virtue of their ability to kill people and raise taxes—to name just two items on the job description—why put them on a list of influential people? That would be so obvious, like drawing up a list of influential religious figures and including Jesus Christ, Buddha, and Mohammed. I mean, like, *duh.*

Who did make the list? Lots of worthy folk. Marlon Brando, who inspired an entire generation of actors to become grossly obese and produce dangerous offspring; Ernest Hemingway, brilliant author and inventor of the two-barreled method of flossing the back molars; General Douglas A. MacArthur, who singlehandedly revived the moribund corncob pipe industry; the Wright brothers, who, like they say in the record club ads, are a double album that counts as two selections.

It's all subjective. Three choices, however, I insist on refuting.

Bob Dylan
Dylan's a guy who not only sings like a chicken choking on a lungful of helium, he plays the harmonica so poorly you're actually glad when he stops playing and *starts singing again.* He's on the list, and FDR isn't. In other words, this raggedy warbler is more influential than the man who redefined the role of federal government and led the nation to beat Hitler, and did it all sitting down.

Frank McNamara
Inventor of the credit card. McNamara, I believe, received the Nobel Prize for Inventing Something That Someone Else Would Have Got Around to Inventing, Eventually.

Jackson Pollock
Inventor of "action painting," which is to painting what a bloody car wreck is to defensive driving. Pollock produced art so ugly it required twice the usual number of art critics to explain it, and he influenced about thirteen people, all of whom were immediately derided in the art world for being imitators of Jackson Pollock.

This sort of dispute, of course, is exactly what *Life* wants to provoke. They want people to talk about the list, buy the magazine, argue about the list, buy the magazine, and, incidentally, buy the magazine. Well, since that is the point, let's sell some newspapers. Here's my list of People Who Should Have Been on *Life*'s List, Because They Really Influenced *Me*.

Ernst P. Schtiek

(1880–1938) German-born mechanic and vending machine pioneer. Was working at a garage one hot day, underneath a customer's car, when the jack slipped and pinned him under the car. He was trapped for half a day, during which a leak in the crankcase dropped hot, stinking oil into his open mouth. Schtiek, in his autobiography, *Time on My Hands, a Buick on My Chest,* wrote that during this time, his mouth full of steaming, undrinkable fluid, he conceived of the notion of Vending Machine Coffee.

Madeline Hoover

(1924–1988) Inventor of the loose subscription cards designed to fall into your lap when you open a magazine. Died of multiple paper cuts when she inadvertently stepped in front of a machine that blows the cards into the magazine. Appropriately, when her body was taken to the morgue, she fell off the slab every time they opened the drawer.

Peter Blugner

(1912–   ) Inventor of the stereo-system remote control with three hundred buttons so tiny it cannot be used unless you have several dozen trained ants on hand. Blugner, who has no arms and communicates by typing with a toothpick held in his teeth, has said in interviews that he doesn't know what people are complaining about.

These are people who've made a contribution to life as I know it. There are more. The poet who first wrote "Be kind, rewind," for example; because of his guilt-inducing doggerel, I spend half my life standing over my whirring VCR, wishing I could whip it into rewinding at a faster speed. The unknown man who decided that beer should come in packs of six, so you can feel virtuous when you leave that last one for later. Let's not forget the most influential person in American history—the one who decided to boost circulation with a specious list.

Now *there* was an American visionary.

Heresy in the Church of Kirk

∿∿

Are you a *Star Trek* fan? Good. Here's a little quiz.

Which of the following was Captain Kirk's standard procedure for dealing with new cultures?
A) React warily but diplomatically.
B) Find leader, sleep with his daughter.
C) Sum up centuries of conflict in an overwrought, two-minute speech that convinced the natives everything they had ever known was, in fact, wrong.
D) All of the above, week after week.

Which of the following was never spoken by Dr. McCoy?
A) "Dammit, Jim, I'm a doctor, not an escalator."
B) "Dammit, Jim, I'm a houseplant, not an office partition."
C) "Dammit, Jim, I'm a metaphor, not an analogy."
D) "Jimmit, Dan, I'm a spoonerism, not a dyslexic."

Scotty, the chief engineer, was eventually demoted for:
A) Wearing his kilt and doing the Marilyn Monroe pose over a venting grate in the engine room one too many times.
B) Inability to change the laws of physics.

C) Being found guilty by inquiry panel of consistently overestimating the time needed for repairs.
D) Turbolift races.

The occasion for this is the twenty-fifth anniversary of *Star Trek,* a quarter century of exploring the galaxy in tight uniforms. The old *Trek* is long gone, of course; there's a new one in its place, different from the old show in one crucial way: it has been around long enough for you to notice how the actors are putting on weight. The original *Trek* was canceled before Scotty got a start on that kettledrum belly he currently sports, before Kirk lost his hair. (Radiation, perhaps.) The new *Trek* has a couple actors who apparently put their signature on a contract guaranteeing six years employment, turned around, and said, "Waiter? Dessert." This I cannot understand. If I had to appear in a leotard before millions each week, I would live on Popsicles, blades of grass, and saltpeter. (They are tight leotards. You never know.) But in the future, things are different. Astronauts are fat. Perhaps beat cops of the twenty-fourth century are thin, just to show how society changes.

But I digress. The twenty-fifth anniversary of *Star Trek* occasioned the usual media hoo-ha; most of the coverage was gushing and uncritical. It gave one the idea that the old *Star Trek* was, start to finish, *A* to *Z,* one hell of a television program, a *Playhouse 90* with ray guns. They were perhaps wise not to suggest otherwise; hard-core devotees of the original show brook blasphemy about as well as Shiite clerics, except that the clerics do not issue their death sentences in pouty voices that crack with puberty. What everyone seemed to miss in this orgy of *Trek*-licking was that the old show was frequently stupid, and that the new show is so superior that it makes the original look like *The Little Golden Book of Galactic Exploration.*

I offer the following points in evidence:

CAPTAIN KIRK. For those who grew up idolizing Wild Jim Kirk, rider of the nebular pampas, realizing that the man is actually a pompous blowhard is somewhat hard to take. But the more you watch the original episodes, the more the good captain strikes you as . . . excitable. The last time a ship's captain had that gleam in his eye, he was rolling two steel balls around in his hand. Kirk was written to be an adventuresome sort, no doubt, a man of healthy appetites. But played by Shatner, Kirk's meals consisted almost entirely of scenery.

ALLEGORICAL OVERKILL. It's curious how many planets in the twenty-fourth century have civilizations whose major problems just happen to illustrate some telling point about United States culture circa 1967, such as race, war, free love, rebellious youth with electrified instruments, etc. Occasionally, these allegories worked, such as . . . well, the idea was used to fine advantage in . . .

No, come to think of it, it never worked. Granted, *Star Trek* was laudable in addressing subjects that would have had the Smothers Brothers not just canceled but broken up and sent to separate orphanages. But it tended to make you see its point by inserting both thumbs in your eyes. One episode concerned a planet that had been pared down by war to two men—a guy with the right side of his face painted black and the left side painted white, and a guy who had the opposite arrangement. That's right, a *meaningless distinction,* based on color. Surprise, they hate each other.

Yes, yes, it's a daring parable on race relations. But the show consisted mainly of these two psychotic mimes in white tights running around the ship glowering at each other, engaging in fistfights carefully choreographed so they wouldn't smear the greasepaint. The lesson: We should love our brother, no matter how heavily made-up he is. (One of the two-tones was played by Frank Gorshin, aka "the Riddler" on *Batman* and a high-pressure hose of manic energy in his own right; letting him and Kirk act together was like tossing a pair of rabid ferrets in a paint can and sealing the lid shut.)

BAD SPECIAL EFFECTS. People of my age, who grew up while *Trek* was on the air, might recall one unique disappointment: building the model of the ship and finding out it looked more realistic than the one on television.

This is unfair; of course *Star Trek* had neither the budget nor the technology of the new show, and *2001: A Space Odys-*

sey had not yet changed our view of what a spaceship should look like. But it's still tough to look at the bridge of the old *Enterprise,* what with the clunky push buttons, obligatory rows of meaningless lights, and backlit spirograph displays. It's hard to believe that a ship is going faster than light when the lighting shows the elevator doors are painted plywood.

You can ascribe most of this to the constraints of television, but there was a certain failure of imagination at work here as well. The computer, for example, made strange card-punching sounds, as if there was a UNIVAC with rusty relays taking up four floors in the basement. (That's when it wasn't being infected by the spirit of Jack the Ripper, as happened in one episode; then it shouted *"Die Die Everybody Die"* in a Mansonesque cackle.) It's the aural equivalent of the push buttons—something that takes its cue from the present instead of imagining what the future might come up with. The phasers, which sounded like an ostrich being throttled, were okay, but even then, they got a detail wrong: the phasers always left the ship like twin points of a compass, then hit their target as parallel lines. Although perhaps this is a nod to Einstein's theory that space is curved.

HOKEY PARALLEL-WORLD PLOTS. To judge from *Star Trek,* the universe is filled with planets that bear a remarkable resemblance to the Paramount studio back lot. There was the planet that still had a Roman Empire—and called it Rome! (At least they could have called it Reme, or Rame, or something.) There was the planet of the gangsters, the planet of the toga-clad super Athenians, the planet of the Elizabethan witch-hunters, etc. It's one thing to believe, as one still must, that the universe is simply overflowing with people who speak colloquial English. It's another to say that they came up with Cotton Mather hairdos and three-piece suits all by themselves.

One of the worst examples of this was "Omega Glory," a Vietnam parable written by the series's creator, Gene Roddenberry. The planet has been involved in a long—and, naturally, pointless—war between Yangs, or Yankees, and Coms, or Communists. (See? They're just like us.) At the end of the show the Yangs haul out a tattered American flag and a crumbling copy of the Constitution, which they regard as a holy but incomprehensible relic. (See? They're just like us.) The High Yang gives it a read but mispronounces all the words. It's up to a heavily gesticulating Kirk to flail around and teach them the meaning of the words, while reminding us that the words are "not just for Yangs! But for Coms! Too!" The entire scene has the subtlety of a sledgehammer driving a tenpenny nail into your forebrain and seems to suggest that the Nixon administration's main failing was its refusal to grant the vote to eighteen-year-old Vietcong. Great knife fight in the fourth act, though.

Those who love the old *Trek* are probably shedding hot tears of indignation now, and rightly so: the above is unfair and is the sort of thing that tends to grate only after you've seen each episode about 3,354 times. You need to remind yourself that when *Star Trek* was on, science fiction on television was best exemplified by *Lost in Space*, which was essentially a nuclear family driving an interstellar station wagon through a series of bad neighborhoods. *Star Trek* ought to be judged against the shows of its time, which were also frequently clumsy and unconvincing.

But (cut the music) the *Star Trek* story is a powerful message of hope and human progress. We'll get off this puny marble, it says; and once we get out there, we'll meet billions of bipeds who share our desire for peace and democracy. Makes you want to slap everyone in the UN, tell them to shut up and get working on the rockets, because there's something waiting we simply have to explore.

Provided we're not too fat to get out of our chairs.

Putting the Foot Down

I'D LIKE TO OFFER, FREE OF CHARGE, THIS CAMPAIGN ISSUE to either party: the metric system. It is un-American, loathed from coast to coast. Given its foreign origin, its relentless march toward world domination, and its inhuman, scientific precision, it is a perfect replacement for godless Communism. *We will bury you! At a depth of three meters! You will sell us the kilometers of rope we will hang you with!* See? It's all the same.

Granted, most people don't worry about metric conversion. They think the threat has passed, and it's quarts and cups forever. Well, wake up, America, as haggard, irrational conspiracy theorists say. Government is still trying to shove it down our throats. In 1988, Congress demanded that all federal agencies use the metric system, perhaps so that the phrase "foot-dragging" would be replaced by the less accusatory "0.3048-meter-dragging." And Congress, as usual, has accomplices. In 1992, transportation officials from twelve southern states—where you just know folks are crying out for metric conversion—gathered to study the metric issue and figure out ways to make the lowly public love it. They concluded nothing, other than they need to meet and study some more, preferably next winter, in Hawaii.

But it's not just pointless junkets they want, or they'd form the House and Senate Partnership for Mandatory Pig Latin or the Joint Committee to Walk Like Festus or some other useless excuse to get out of town and drink. No, they mean this. *They believe.* This spiny, shiny monster of metricism is still out there, ready to slice up our familiar world into neat little portions. There are many advocates for such a conversion, including:

- The Highway Sign-Makers' Lobby, along with the White-Reflective-Letter PAC
- The Pale, Dour Euroweenies in Shorts and Black Socks Who Come Here on Vacation and Can't Figure Out How Far It Is to the Zoo Lobby
- The Grimly Anal-Retentive Association of America
- The National Center for Making Your World Virtually Unrecognizable
- The French (end of argument)

Here are their standard arguments for the metric system:

- *Everyone else is doing it.* This argument didn't wash when I used it on my parents, and it ought not to wash here. So everyone is doing it. So what? If Belgium jumped off a cliff, would you? And if our trading partners won't trade with us because we don't use the metric system, well, then they weren't really our friends, were they?
- *It's easier.* The metric system is based on units of ten, just like the fingers on your hands, and therefore you always know how much of one goes into the other. This way a man need never find himself with a twelve-ounce bottle of beer and an eight-ounce glass, and have to stand there in the kitchen drinking off those four extra ounces from the bottle. Life will make sense, unless of course you lost a finger in an industrial accident, in which case you will need a neighbor's help to match up the bottle with the proper glass.

Next, we can do something about the day and the year, those utterly confounding items based on twelve, and hence the source of endless confusion.

Normally, ease and ubiquity would be a good recommendation, but not in this case. The metric system has one fatal flaw: it is wholly imaginary. The meter does not exist in nature, whereas I can say with some confidence that the foot does. Try it; stand up. You have just provided twice the argument for our system than all of Europe can give for the metric way.

The foot is imprecise, of course, but it has a connection with culture and tradition. Time was, every nation had their own standards. The British had a curious measurement called the stone, as in "Pictures of Fergie's nude romp revived speculation that her brassiere has been built to withstand loads of up to three stone." Even today, every profession has its measurement system—sailors measure the deep in fathoms, apothecaries count out their potions in scruples and drams, auto repairmen charge by a unit called "labor," which consists of any moment of time in which they actually happen to glance at your car while en route to the pop machine.

You couldn't beat these concepts out of these people. Doesn't matter that it's easier if everyone in the great wide world knows that ten bleckameters equals one glogameter, ten of which equal one spurkameter, which is one-tenth of a cackameter. If you grew up with quarts, then quarts it is. It's in your DNA.

Of course, if it becomes the law, then our heads must bow or roll. I suggest re-education camps for the metrically resistant. Apply the hot lights and rubber hoses. Have people make monotonal televised confessions in which they admit their counterrevolutionary tendencies. *I am guilty of walking a mile for a Camel. I am guilty of accepting an inch and wanting a yard.*

Like I said, it would make a splendid political issue, if only for its potential to breed new political subversion. Somewhere, someday, a new Winston Smith will crack open his diary and write that freedom is the right to say four cups equals one quart. Down with Big Brother, he'll write. How far down?

Oh, six feet under. Imprecise, perhaps ... but you get the idea.

How to Tell You're Irradiated

∿∿

Tips from the humor writer's handbook: When the idea is too flimsy to support prose, write a list; when strapped for a good idea, reach for the Old Standbys. Below is a gratuitous assault on nuclear energy, the Luddite equivalent of Dan Quayle jokes. I actually prefer nuclear power to filthy coal, but when a deadline looms, you defenestrate such subtleties and go for the cheap laugh.

THE YANKEE ROWE—RHYMES WITH *GLOW*—(SEE WHAT I mean?) Nuclear power plant is the oldest in the country and has been told by the NRC to shut down for safety's sake. Reason: the reactor container vessel has been weakened by thirty-one years of neutrino bombardment. Think of a rusty cocktail shaker filled with nitroglycerine and strapped in a paint shaker, and you have an idea of the situation.

Elsewhere, the Seabrook reactor in New Hampshire announced that two thousand gallons of radioactive water was mistakenly dumped into the plant's purified water system, including the little fountains where workers wash out their eyes. This was not brought to anyone's attention until a contaminated worker, sitting down to his evening meal, realized he could see through his hand, his wife, the wall of his house, his neighbor's wall, and his neighbor's oven. At which point he shouted "Fish! We never have fish!"

"I've never known him to complain about what I put on the table," his wife said later. "That's when I began to suspect he'd developed supernatural powers."

Expect more of this in the future. The nation's nuclear plants are aging, and their licenses are up for renewal. Back in the days when nuclear power was a wonder toy, licensing procedures were a bit more lax. Then:

"Turn that baby on. Whoa! *Whoooo*-boy! You can feel it in your fillings, can't you just? Looker that—radiation's plumb off the dial on the Geiger counter. Well, boys—have to get me a bigger dial!" (Hearty round of backslapping.)

Today, of course, it is a different matter. The NRC, stung by the perception that it rubber-stamps the wishes of the nuclear industry—it actually uses a synthetic, rubberlike substance on its stamps—is getting tough. Until the plant comes up for relicensing, however, can one be sure if the plant up the road is operating perfectly? Well, given that nuclear radiation causes strange, hideous mutations—you've all seen those giant moth movies—there are signs that your local nuclear plant may be poorly run.

- Ads for local department store begin to tout comfort and durability of lead-lined underwear.
- Sudden realization that everyone in town is bald.
- Not to mention seven feet tall.
- City council dominated by telekinetic schoolchildren.
- Fuel rods used as batons for high-school relay races.
- Hardware store sells mousetraps the size of dining room tables.
- Garden dies off; plastic plants begin to grow.
- Mortuaries advertise for second-shift workers.
- The last guy to pop a knuckle blew off a hand.
- Hot dogs can be cooked by holding them out the window and counting to ten.
- Rifles sold as a means of controlling the ant population.

- People get unnerved when the civil defense sirens are turned *off.*
- When Uncle Fester of *The Addams Family* puts a light bulb in his mouth and turns it on, no one thinks that's particularly unusual.

We'd like to remind people that far more citizens expire annually from producing coal than from producing nuclear power. If, say, a nuclear power plant melts down and spews radioactivity over a one-hundred-mile radius, well, you just pack up and move. Whereas when a coal mine explodes— well, there's just no end to the dusting and sweeping you have to do. In fact, studies show that if a coal mine exploded, more people would die tripping over the vacuum cleaner cord than would die if a nuclear plant melted down. (Source: Bureau of Small, Identical Albino Nuclear Lobbyists.) It's a dangerous world. Take your choice.

Alas, Alack, Alarms

~~~~~~

THIS WAS SUPPOSED TO BE ABOUT THEFT-PREVENTION SYSTEMS, but someone stole my notes.

Truly. I was standing outside on a fine Washington spring day listening to the sounds of car alarms; for some reason they were going off in all directions, baying to one another like dogs in suburban backyards. After a while I stopped taking notes and put the notebook down, just to listen and ruminate. When I got up later, I left the notebook on the bench. About twenty feet away, I had that vague sense that something was wrong, the sense that makes you check your fly, wonder if you left the iron on, or realize it's your mother's birthday. Then the brain, ever helpful, flashed a picture of the notebook. I dashed back. I'd been away all of thirty seconds. The notebook was gone.

If that notebook had been designed to my specifications, it would have done two things.

1. Emitted flaming phosphorescent warning flares the moment I walked more than fifteen feet away.

2. Exploded the moment someone else tried to pick it up, shredding him with a thousand painful paper cuts while a specially designed pen clipped to the notebook then squirted him with a fine mist of lemon juice.

Personal alarms of all sorts are popular nowadays, what

with the high quotient of sticky-fingered sociopaths that fill our cities. Two examples come to mind.

HOME ALARMS. Most home systems are designed to tell the burglar his presence has been noted. (The predecessor of such systems was called "a dog.") My neighbor bought a system with, literally, all the bells and whistles. Should a window be breached, his dwelling lets forth a lamentation of shrieks, whistles, and ululating sirens. The general idea seems to be to deafen the burglar so he can't hear you coming with the baseball bat. The house is also surrounded by motion-activated floodlights, and they too are a nervous wreck, interrogating every leaf, gnat, or mote that swims before their twitchy eyes. The other day I watched fireflies set it off—and considering that fireflies light up to attract mates, it seemed a rather cruel thing to do, like a bully kicking sand in the face of the ninety-eight-pound weakling and stealing his girl.

My neighbor's house has not been robbed. He was, however, held up outside of work.

I have motion detectors as well—portable plastic devices secreted under pieces of furniture. They can be disarmed by picking them up and dashing them against the floor and are designed to not just slow down the burglar and make him edgy but to alert me to his presence, giving me precious extra moments to cower under the blankets and attempt to summon a gun out of thin air by concentrating really, really hard. The detectors came with warning stickers, but I have never found these too comforting. My neighbor has many stern stickers on his door, and they say, "WARNING! PREMISES PROTECTED BY DATATRON SECURITY INC.! VIOLATORS WILL BE PROSECUTED!" That's very nice, but most thieves are illiterate and see REJNLEW! EOFSLEFF SEFMSMOOE YM ESOMEWOEP DOEVCURW NMS!

This might frighten Latvians, but it does nothing for the burglars around here.

CAR ALARMS. There's a car in my neighborhood that has quickly moved to the top of the Most-Likely-to-Be-Stoned list. Its alarm consists of a greatest-hits medley of irritating noises, one after the other, like someone screaming HELP in ten languages. Its owner parks it outside my building and then leaves this hemisphere for weeks at a time. The car gets lonely and calls for him, whereupon he returns and gives it a loving wash-job while blasting reggae music from its one-hundred-gigawatt sound system.

It does not take much to set the car off. The pat of a toddler's hand on its bumper. A car door slamming a block away. The change in air pressure occasioned by a police helicopter passing above. The moon exerting a tidal pull. But the alarm also subscribes to a Gandhi-like theory of brotherhood—if any car is being burglarized, it is being burglarized. Nothing else explains the causeless torrent that pours every twenty minutes. One weekend I was printing off a book, a tedious chore that demanded I spend entire days watching the printer to make sure it did not jam and print entire chapters as one wet black line. The alarm went off all the damn day, to the point where I memorized its various whoops and hollers, its cadences, the precise moment when it shut up. A month later I was becalmed in a shuttle bus in the parking lot of an airport in Houston and heard an identical car alarm; without thinking, I began to hum along, conducting the song with my index finger, grabbing fistfuls of air like Bernstein as the racket rolled to its climax. People looked. Then the alarm went off again; this time I sang harmony. Madness has its compensations.

I have come to believe that we need more alarms. Klaxons for every minor act of thievery. Such as:

Ice Cream Alarms. In our household, domestic aggression is not played out with proxy wars over ice cream. One of us buys some ice cream, both eat it: end of story. Never any conflict about leaving only a few spoonfuls or finishing off the container without waking the spouse or calling them at work and giving them veto power. But my wife is occasionally prone to episodes of flavor mining—following the rich vein of fudge down the side of the container, leaving what looks like a mole hole burrowed in the ice cream.

An ice cream alarm would sense whether pressure was being applied equally on all sides of the container, scan for continual pressure in any particular area, adjust for minor flavor mining, and then—if the offender does not desist—the carton would explode.

Because if *I* can't have that ribbon of peanut-butter fudge, no one can.

If you could dissuade someone from stealing the flavor ribbon by detonating the dessert, why not discourage car theft by inventing an alarm that would actually destroy the car if anyone attempted to steal it? Wire a bomb to the ignition, complete with sticks of dynamite and a loud ticking clock. You'd lose a few thieves at first, but after a few weeks in which the air would be thick with smoke and crook-bits, word would get around. It would cut down on drunk driving as well. ("No more for me—I'm defusing a bomb tonight.") And if someone did attempt to steal a car, there wouldn't be the hour-long shriek—just one big *kaBOOM,* a tinkling shower of glass, the gentle *plosh* of atomized criminals hitting the pavement, then blessed silence.

The idea, while drastic, is good. The more we rig our possessions to bleat like gut-stuck sheep, the more valuable we make them to thieves. Only when we blow them up with cavalier disdain will we dissuade criminals from desiring them.

Note to home-alarm inventors: Don't use motion detectors to trigger the home-bomb systems.

Although it *would* make for some interesting hailstorms.

Quiz for Budding Sociopaths

〜〜〜〜〜〜〜〜〜〜〜〜〜〜〜〜〜〜〜〜〜〜〜〜〜〜〜

YOU MAY HAVE HEARD OF A NEW SURVEY THAT FINDS NINETY-one percent of Americans lie routinely. (The remaining nine percent were campaigning and unable to respond.) You may have been appalled to learn that nearly half of all married people don't love their partners, and that sixty-nine percent of America lies to their spouses. Which means that a certain percent of America is quite up front about not loving each other. If any of those people are among the thirty-one percent who are having an affair, it must be an interesting time around the dinner table each night.

These and other statistics were culled from *The Day America Told the Truth*, a rather scarifying new look at the nation. There's a whole lotta prevaricating going on, if this book is to be believed. The authors asked a random sample of folk to fill out an eighteen-hundred-word questionnaire in complete honesty. And honest they were. The admission that made many eyebrows elevate was that seven percent of Americans would kill someone for ten million dollars. At first this would suggest they had stopped an inordinate number of professional boxers, who get not only ten million but a percentage of the gate. Or perhaps they interviewed a disproportionate number of Mafia hitmen, who regarded the question as a job offer and have been sitting in a hotel room chain-smoking for the last six months, waiting for the phone to ring.

60

But no, that's seven percent of everyday America. It shouldn't be a surprise; in my neighborhood, the removal of sentient beings is often performed for under fifty dollars, with bystanders winged free of charge. Factor out the wide-eyed sociopath, however, and you still have a ravening pack of killers, waiting for the right opportunity. Are you one of them? Take this handy quiz, and see if you'd commit murder under certain circumstances.

Would you commit murder for

A) Ten million dollars?
B) A peek behind door number two?
C) Jodie Foster?
D) A peek behind Jodie Foster?

Would you commit murder for ten million dollars if there was a slight chance you might be identified? If no, why not?

A) I am J. D. Salinger.
B) I would be inundated by favor-seeking relatives.
C) I have *LOVE* and *HATE* tattooed on my knuckles, and I realize this is now a cliché; I would not want nation to know about it.

If yes, why?

A) There's a good chance an attractive actor might play me on *America's Most Wanted,* thus leading to more dates.
B) Life on the run offers the opportunity to sample many interesting regional cuisines.
C) The opportunity to compose taunting letters to the police might help me break this writer's block.

Would you commit murder for ten million dollars if there was a great chance of being caught? If yes, why?

A) For the opportunity to see a really good lawyer at work close up.

B) If sent to gas chamber, I will get chance to break Houdini's record for holding one's breath.

C) Do you know you can get anything for your last meal? *Anything?*

Would you commit murder for five million dollars?

A) Yes, if you toss in expenses.

B) Hell, no; after taxes, there'd be nothing left.

Which of the following rationales for shooting someone works best on a judge?

A) "I was doing research on the single-bullet theory."

B) "I mistook him for Pontius Pilate. It was the light."

C) "He made a threatening motion, indicating he had a spatula."

For ten million dollars, would you kill someone you knew?

A) I don't know anyone. Drat the luck!

B) Can we really *know* anyone? Given that we all hide our true selves behind a wall of smiles and words, is it possible to truly grasp the singular reality at the core of any individual? No. So can I pop the new guy with bad breath in my car pool? Please?

C) Yes, but I'd offer to split it with them, first.

For ten million dollars, would you murder a member of your family?

A) Sorry; I already did that.

B) Here, Spot! Here, boy!

C) Do I count?

Which of the following is a very, very bad rationale for murder:

A) Dinner was late.
B) Dinner was Spot.
C) Book authors used your bankrupt morality to make money and didn't split it with you.

If you answered C, shame on you.
But we understand.

Painful Elimination

∿∿

"I WILL ELIMINATE TWO HUNDRED FORTY-SIX PROGRAMS. SOME of them have noble names, but all are not indispensable."

With this one rhetorical flourish, the President established the criteria for eliminating federal programs: noble names and dispensability. Instantly everyone in Washington scurried to their copy of the budget—in this town it shows up at your door just like the phone book—and sought out programs that filled the bill. After a night of furious searching, a grand total of four programs were deemed both noble and useless:

APOLLO (Association of Potholder Owners Loaning Leaves to Others) Received a $2.8 million grant to help rural housewives assemble a national database of table leaves, to be used when company unexpectedly drops over for dinner and you can't find that thing that extends the size of your table.

ENDIVE (Experimental National Division for Inordinately Vibrating Elves) This program annually dispensed $1.6 million for the study of the physiological response of very short people placed on vibrating beds in cheap motels. The program, an Army research effort, had been defended by the Pentagon as being essential to determining the effects of such motion on the body, in case the nation ever has to fight a war with an army of midgets during an earthquake. "Plus, it was fun to watch the little fellers bounce around," said one wistful spokesman. "But no more, I guess."

NFFNF (National Foundation for National Foundations) This organization, which received $296.7 million per year, dispensed money to organizations whose charter was dedicated to "giving money to organizations." Intended as a short-term aid to struggling endowments, given on a first-come, first-served basis, the organization had in recent years given all its money to the National Foundation of National Foundations (NFONF), an umbrella group set up by private endowments to provide efficient distribution of the moneys. The money was usually given away by January second, and the NFFNF spent the rest of the year free to pursue other interests; an OMB study recently concluded that sixty-four percent of the game show contestants and ninety-three percent of talk-radio callers were actually NFFNF employees on their lunch hour. (NFFNF employees are permitted up to three weeks for lunch.)

Closing down the NFFNF will not only save millions but allow the government to put its sprawling, ten-story marble building to other use.

IPS (Institute of Pointless Science) If Bush eliminates funding for this project, it will truly demonstrate a willingness to cut the budget regardless of partisan concerns. The IPS has for years supplied the nation with tales of ridiculous research expenditures, for the sole purpose of giving congressmen something to complain about. Some recent examples:

- $19 billion to study the cola preference of a frog.
- $276 million to study the reproductive habits of a Thermos.
- $76 million to determine what, if anything, is worse than a poke in the eye with a sharp stick (results inconclusive so far, although all-commercial-radio shows promise).
- $3.1 billion to study the digestive tract of the chatterbeak hummingbird, a rare species that eats only sugarcane and coffee beans.
- $874 million to walk slowly around a pig while rubbing one's thigh and exclaiming, "Oh! Matilda!" Purpose of

study: determine whether the pig will eventually be forced by evolutionary pressures to develop the capacity to shout, "What the hell are you doing?" Results to date: inconclusive, but project is slated to run for additional one-hundred-thousand years.

If the IPS is cut out, Congress will no longer have an easy target to hit when making popular speeches about waste of public money.

This one will face tough scrutiny on the floor.

Swing and a Myth

TIME FOR THE LARDBALLS OF SUMMER. TIME FOR THE SIGHT OF lumpy, grinning millionaires irrigating plastic grass with streams of tobacco juice. Time for the inevitable footage of umps bumping guts with managers and exchanging mists of spittle over whether or not a grown man touched a bag before another man touched his shoulder with a small, hard spheroid. Time for editorial-page writers with the muscle tone of a slack strand of spaghetti to rhapsodize on this, the Ultimate Sport. Time for—yawn, snore—baseball.

I know—heresy. All Americans are supposed to love baseball. All good little boys are presumed to have spent their youth with a frog in one pocket and a slingshot in the other, staring at a baseball game through a knothole. Well, not me; in fact, I was a pasty little slug whose contact with baseball was limited to the occasional ball thrown through the library window by one of the grinning illiterates on the playground. What I remember about baseball is that the people who liked it also liked to beat me up. This explains my heresy. Don't take it personally. Don't hit me, either.

I like the *idea* of baseball. I like baseball movies, where the dramatic moments happen in slow motion. It wasn't until I actually attended a baseball game that I realized *everything* happens in slow motion. If it happens at all. Baseball seems

67

little more than a bunch of guys waiting around for something to happen, and if I wanted to see that, I'd go down to the corner in my neighborhood; at least there, when someone swings a bat, the cops show up. Forget your "swing and a miss"; we have "frisk and a pat."

Someone once tried to explain baseball's inherent dullness in terms of chess—the strategy, the careful methodical planning, the pinpoint exploitation of your opponent's weak spots. I could buy that, except

- In chess, players do not check every forty-five seconds to see if their genitals are arranged precisely the way they were forty-five seconds ago.
- Chess players are not allowed to steal squares when their opponent is not looking.
- The chess world is not plagued by huge, grinning mascots.
- Chess players rarely excuse crushing defeat by saying they "lost that bishop in the sun."
- No tiresome purists insist chess will be spoiled by aluminum playing pieces.

And so forth. Baseball is a simple game; that is what appeals to some and bores others to unconsciousness. But it is also what enrages me when I read about salary disputes. The average salary in baseball is over four hundred thousand dollars, not counting endorsements for making stilted, monotone pitches in TV commercials for local car dealerships. Good money for running around in your pajamas.

But then I hear of a guy like Frank Viola, who recently turned down a three-year, thirteen-million-dollar contract. I could not utter the words "turn down" and "thirteen million dollars" in the same sentence without having the speech centers of my brain seize up and start to smoke. I'd take that money for standing at the plate and letting Frank throw the ball at my head every day. Granted, once I got that old all-American baseball spirit, I'd probably want out of my contract, request fifty-two million dollars, and insist on the right to duck.

Not to suggest that money ruins baseball—it does, but that

doesn't really matter. What counts is that enough people look to that green diamond and take pleasure from the ritual that unfolds. You have your Boys of Summer; I have my Thugs of Autumn, namely football. But I do know that when I have a child, I will no doubt haul it off to a baseball game, just to see if the child takes to it. After all, my dad took me out back to play catch, for which I am eternally grateful. I remember the deepening twilight, the sense of timeless ritual.

And I remember the year I refused to show up for spring training unless he hiked my allowance. When he didn't, I engaged in a wild swearing match and went to play catch with a father down the street.

Loyalty, sportsmanship: yes, baseball taught me much.

The Devil, You Say

∿∿∿∿∿∿∿∿∿∿∿∿∿∿∿∿∿∿∿∿∿∿∿∿∿∿∿∿∿∿∿∿∿∿∿∿∿∿

WE ARE PLEASED TO ANNOUNCE THAT A SIMPLE HOME TEST HAS been developed to see if you test positive for stupidity.

It is a simple photocopied flier announcing that on March first of this year, the president of Procter and Gamble got up on the Phil Donahue show, announced he was a Satanist, and that P&G gives large amounts of money to the Church of Satan.

Do you believe it? Then you are stupid. Incontrovertibly brain dead. It is entirely possible you have no brain in your skull at all and should seek employment as a harbor buoy. Do you half-believe it? Then you have antibodies in your brain that attack rational thought, which shows that you are susceptible to stupidity.

If that flier sounds familiar, it should be: this nonsense has been circulating for about ten years. It was thought that the company put a stake through the rumor's heart a few years ago, but here it comes again. If you haven't heard the story, it usually appears in the form described above, with the head of the company announcing he's tight with Old Scratch. The latest flier adds that all P&G products will now carry a symbol of a ram's horns, which somehow form 666—which, as we all know, is the prefix for all the phone exchanges in Hell.

The rumor seems to stem from P&G's corporate symbol—

the Man in the Moon sternly regarding thirteen stars. In his
beard are little squiggles that look like 666, providing you
squint, hold the picture upside down, and have someone hit
you in the head with a hammer and shout "DON'T YOU
SEE THE SIXES?" in your ear. It looks like a typical
nineteenth-century corporate symbol, but that carries no
water with people whose brains are stuck on the fourteenth-
century setting. These folks became convinced that using a
product with this logo would line the coffers of the Prince of
Darkness, and then you'd have Mrs. Satan walking around
town in a new fur, putting on airs. They didn't consider several factors that argue against a demonic presence.

- If Satan made laundry soap, it would not remove tar and
  blood, but add more.
- Lava soap would get rid of the pumice and replace it with
  tiny, painful shards of glass.
- Mrs. Olson would return on behalf of Folgers coffee and
  require desperate homemakers to sign an elaborate
  contract before teaching them the secrets of good
  coffee.
- Comet cans do not say, "Now With the Fresh Stink of
  Sulfur!"
- P&G's toothpaste is called Crest. Not AntiCrest.

Well, say the doubtful, what good would it do for P&G to
trumpet their connection to the Lord of the Flies? None at
all, of course. Which is why it is preposterous to assume that
the head of the company would stand up on a show aimed
at the very people who buy the laundry detergent and say
that the company uses their money to roast newborns and
have intimate congress with talking donkeys.

But back to that logo. Tired of people who phoned to
express fears that they would open their washer and find
grinning imps with horns and hooves spitting on their delicate
unmentionables, P&G took the logo off its products in 1986.
But the rumors persisted, and now P&G has sent the old
Man in the Moon to a hair salon: his beard has been trimmed,
removing those curlicues in which the imaginative found the

sixes. The company insists that this has nothing to do with the rumor. *Mm-hmm.* And Coke brought back Classic Coke because they had time on their hands.

Changing the logo won't prevent the neuron-free from believing the satanic rumor, of course. The new flier doesn't even mention old Mr. Moon. Nor will the company's efforts to quash the story do much good. The estimably decent Rev. Billy Graham has come out against the rumor. Ann Landers has fulminated against it a few times. Doesn't matter. The Pope could put a ring in his ear and make personal appearances on behalf of Mr. Clean, and people wouldn't believe it.

Because people believe in the Devil.

So do I, in a way. He could be nothing more than one of God's staff members, the one who on Judgment Day will take the fall for war, famine, tooth decay, etc. (In fact, "Armageddon" is probably Aramac for "reshuffling the cabinet.") He could be just random badness, the absence of goodness: evil doesn't have to unionize to be effective, you know. Hell is an open shop. Whatever, I just do not believe that old Splitfoot has a hot line to everyone's id and makes us go all steamy with evil thoughts when the fancy strikes him.

As for Hell, or One Sulfur Plaza, as it will probably be called once all the S&L crooks get there, I don't believe it exists to punish fallible humans and reward evil laundry-soap-conglomerate CEOs. There may indeed be eternal punishment, as anyone who's sat through a grade school recital can attest. But a lake of fire? God has more imagination than that.

Hell is probably a photocopy shop, one of those twenty-four-hour joints with bright lights and smelly chemicals and arrogant college students behind the counter. Your punishment will be to copy off fliers touting your specious, paranoid delusions for all eternity.

Incidentally, in Hell, the paper tray jams every time.

Kickboxers in Peril

ONCE AGAIN, IT'S SATURDAY NIGHT, AND YOU'RE PLAGUED BY the restless suspicion that you should be out in the world, sampling new cuisines, laughing at a bar with a curly headed stranger, listening to hot, saucy saxophones belt out their cocky salutes to urban civilization. You have, in short, watched too many beer commercials.

Instead, you're alone, looking for something to watch, something to shove the world into a corner and cover it with a blanket. You've gone to the video store in the hope of finding something made in the last decade, a film whose opening credits do not include the words "And Introducing Bert Convy." As usual, the place is picked clean. Earlier today, there were two copies of that NR-17 movie that featured a washed-up actor slathered in bronzer and pawing at a model-actress, but the staff snapped them both up. (Must have read the same article about the sex scenes and the closed set.) Three hundred copies of the latest must-see feel-good weeper about the trials of southern womanhood were here yesterday, but they were all gone by six o'clock Friday. You could be home crying now if you'd thought ahead; but no, you are standing forlorn in a video store whose New Releases category is so broad that it includes *Birth of a Nation,* unable to find anything worth two hours of your finite life-span. Here are your choices:

Drama

Lick Me Fiercely

A made-for-cable drama about a woman whose agent convinces her that limited nudity is essential for her career development. Unfortunately, one of the actors with whom she does a made-for-cable movie becomes obsessed with her and embarks on a mad campaign of terror: he finds a new way every day to make her feel soiled, so she must repeatedly take showers. Even by made-for-cable standards, this one has an inordinate number of showers; production of the film was reportedly shut down twice because of violations of drought-stricken Los Angeles's water-use regulations.

Action

Kickboxer Wiseguy

Kickboxer films are a subgenre of fight movies. Instead of sweaty, up-from-hunger heroes using their hands to convert other men's faces into a ruined porridge of blood and cartilage, here they use their hands and their feet. *Kickboxer Wiseguy* features an upstart rubout artist who kicks rival mobsters to death instead of shooting them. Best scene: the policeman examining the body of a victim, saying, "From the look of it, I'd say they used an Armani loafer size eight. All the signs of a classic gangland kickboxer rubout." Phrase on box: "Honor. Respect. Tradition. A lot of kicking."

Horror

Slay-Doh II

Concerning the homicidal rampages of a demon made from modeling compounds. It was ordinary clay until about thirty minutes into *Slay-Doh I: The Shaping,* when some teens used it in a ritual to summon Satan, who of course appeared—Satan always returns his calls promptly—and inhabited the clay model of a high school principal. The first movie con-

sisted of a fat, bald, seven-inch-tall career administrator stabbing people and making endearingly evil wisecracks. The film
made money in overseas release, so this led to *Slay-Doh II:
The Hardening*. Here the demonic modeling clay has been
exposed to air and thus is so hard it cannot be destroyed by
conventional religious techniques such as holy-water immer-
sion or even frenzied cross-waving. The plot involves the
clay's attempts to get back in its container before the stiffen-
ing becomes irreversible. Phrase on the box: "Meet the Kills-
bury Dohboy."

Golem III

The return of the creature who has been described as "the
Jewish Godzilla." Like its predecessors, this one is preceded
by a message from a rabbinical authority certifying that all
the slayings in the movie were conducted according to dietary
law. Worth it for the moment when the detective investigating
the killings says, "Well, they may be dead, but at least the
poor devils didn't feel any pain."

Documentaries

All of the interesting tapes are long gone—both of them.
This is the section usually full to overflowing on Saturday
night. Some average offerings:

David Copperfield and the Magic Bullet Theory

Here the famed sleight-of-hand artist takes on the JFK
assassination, showing how it is possible for one bullet to
have taken so many tortuous turns and ended up not only
intact but embedded in Mr. Copperfield's thigh. Highlights:
sawing the switched coffin in half; making autopsy photos
disappear while dozens of people watch.

Faces of Death, pt. 37

A popular series of tapes for people who lack both the
drive and initiative to become serial killers, the *Faces of
Death* series concentrates on the many fascinating aspects of

violent death. There is a limited amount of relevant footage available, of course, so the last fifteen of the series have begun to scrape the bottom of the barrel. Included in #37: goldfish mistakenly transferred to chlorinated water during a tank cleaning; mealworms in a trash compactor; tomatoes freshly picked and hence technically alive being fed to a trash compactor (in color); and a vial of ants sent to an ant-farm owner and delayed in the mail, so that all are dead on arrival.

Sports

Season of Kings

An unsuccessful attempt to document the chess grand-master tournament in the style of NFL films, with the use of heraldic music, portentous narration, and dramatic slow motion for each play. This is a 127-tape series.

Wrestlefrenzy VI: Heroes of Wrestling vs. the Monster Trucks (Featuring the Valvoline Girls)

Various steroid-fed men rip off their shirts and grimace theatrically at the camera while silicone-stuffed women in wet doilies drive big trucks over old cars. Originally aired on pay-per-view. For those so stupid they move their lips while watching the sun set.

Science Fiction

The Octopoid Horror (also released as Kickboxers in Space)

In a spaceship circling a distant planet, a crew of kickboxers grapple with a slimy, ferocious beast with eight legs. Don't miss the zero-gravity kickboxing scene, where the momentum of those kicks regularly carries the fighters across the room and into the wall. Phrase on box: "In space, no one can hear you get kicked really hard."

The Kickboxers vs. the Soap-Bubble People

Has its moments, but seems a mismatch. Phrase on box: "The masters from *Kickboxers and the House of Cards* are back!"

Comedy

The Nutty Periodontist

Early Jerry Lewis film, rarely seen. Lewis plays a bumbling pinhead with thick glasses and buckteeth who, through a series of zany mix-ups, goes from being the gardener of a New York hospital to being its chief oral surgeon. Not released in States due to wildly negative audience preview reactions. Phrase on box: "It's laughter in spades—and hoes!"

The Nutty Single Gunman

Another Jerry Lewis film, intended as the comic version of *The Manchurian Candidate.* Here Jerry is a bumbling buck private with thick glasses who is brainwashed into assassinating a popular drunken, philandering pop singer, played by Dean Martin. The film was withdrawn from circulation after *The Manchurian Candidate* was withdrawn after the Kennedy assassination; this has fueled speculation that *The Nutty Single Gunman*'s portrait of a conspiracy against a Sinatra-like character was too close to the withdrawal of *The Manchurian Candidate,* which starred Sinatra. Now reissued with a restored print and commentary from the director.

Le Goat

A tired, leering French sex farce, in which a middle-aged couple try to keep their infidelities from their mate. Contains many scenes of the flabby, infantile husband hiding his young nubile lovers in the closet when his wife comes home unexpectedly. Imagine the surprise when the young nubiles eventually asphyxiate from overcrowding! Also released as *Les Visages de la Mort, pt. 36.*

Sex and the Single Girl in the Valley of the Easy Riding Supervixens

Perhaps the worst cheap movie made in the sixties, this incomprehensible pastiche aims to be a swinging, with-it romp, complete with beaded curtains, groovy organ music, swirling amoebalike blobs of color, and bouncing Swedes in thigh-high boots. Plot: A single girl learns how to be "liberated" by appearing in a happening, with-it movie and submitting to the advances of its groovy, swinging, over-forty producers (playing themselves). Notable only for a cameo from a somewhat confused Al Jolson (his last film appearance).

Sex and the Single Gunman

Sequel to aforementioned swinging, early sixties, with-it romp. Concerns a young stewardess (Lee Grant) and her affair with a loner (Peter Fonda) who happens to be planning the death of the President (Jack Lemmon). Lacks the experimental edge of its predecessor; remembered for its sultry Nancy Sinatra theme song, "He's Leaning out a Window, Aiming at My Heart."

Kickboxing Nerds

A mid-eighties coming-of-age comedy, in which five socially awkward virgins gain respect and girls on spring break by kicking their handsome, sexually adept rivals in the face. Second-biggest grossing film of 1983.

Classics

There's been a resurgence in the reissuing of old forties movies, due mostly to the public's willingness to rent anything whose box features a black-and-white photo of tense, dramatically lit, hat-wearing people. This has resulted in some bottom-of-barrel rereleases, such as:

They Mowed by Night

Perhaps the ultimate in film noir. The story of blind, second-shift lawnkeepers whose lives are turned upside down when a gang of criminals abduct them. Adapted from the stage play; takes place entirely in a shed. Reportedly stars George Raft (the lighting in the shed is a little dim).

Incontinence

Forgotten Hitchcock movie. Stars Cary Grant (woefully miscast) as a barrister whose life is turned upside down when he meets a beautiful woman with a strange, shameful secret. One snowy night he attempts to follow her home; it isn't difficult.

The Big Knob

Hard times in a tough town when a gang of criminals holds a hardware store owner hostage. Adapted from the stage play.

The Big Beard

The only Hassidic film noir movie. Rereleased in the fifties as *Forelock Holmes, Detective.*

N

Fritz Lang's unsuccessful sequel to *M,* the story of a child murderer, and his only Hollywood comedy. This one finds the sordid killer—played here by Lou Costello—stalking the Bowery Boys.

Enjoy. And please rewind.
Given that you probably stopped watching in the first half hour, this should not be an undue burden.

A Brief History
of the Economy

ᘛᘚ

For all the recessions we've had, you'd think we'd understand that they are part of the normal business cycle, and that when your economy is running at full tilt for eight years, chances are good it will eventually fall down, hit its head on a rock, and lie there twitching for a few quarters. But no. It is impossible to handle a recession with equanimity anymore, because the TV news every night opens with the fact that the recession is still happening. (Eventually the news announces that things are looking good again, giving the impression that the entire economy picked up in the last twenty-four hours.) The true depth and effect of the last recession I leave to the experts; I offer only these excerpts of columns— notes from the trough, arranged chronologically with the embarrassingly wrong predictions carefully excised. Let's start with December of 1990, when we had half a million folks in the Gulf and about three in the nation's stores.

By Christmas Day, Americans will have spent approximately $32.94 on Christmas gifts. That's for the nation as a whole and significantly down from last year's amount of $280 billion.

Why? Nasal-voiced, bow-tied economists on TV give several reasons. The first is THE BIG SCARY RECESSION THAT'S IN THE CLOSET AND WILL EAT US WHEN THE LIGHTS GO OUT. The second has to do with the rising crime rate—twenty-seven percent of Americans are broke from posting bail. As one man interviewed on the news put it, "I'm facing life for murder; my wife is being arraigned on bank fraud; and the kids are all up on weapons charges. So yeah, we'll be cutting back this year."

But the third reason often cited, to my complete mystification, is "uncertainty over the Persian Gulf situation." It is stated matter-of-factly, as though no exegesis was needed. As though when I am standing in the lingerie shop, debating which item produces the most sin for the dollar, I should consider the likelihood of a land war on the other side of the globe.

Maybe the clerk would be able to help. "This item is lovely and comes in teal and peach, but there have been hints today that Iraq has fortified the Kuwaiti border."

"Ah. Well, given that retreat can only be seen as losing face, I think silk is out. Show me something in cotton."

"There's always the possibility of back-channel negotiations, though."

"You know, you're right. All right, show me a lace G-string."

I don't see the connection. Wars, especially long and hideous wars, tend to be good for the economy. Perhaps people fear that any war will be short and decisive. Maybe on the cutting room floor of a news show a woman is saying, "I'd be happy to spend more this year, if it weren't for our overwhelming air power." Somehow I doubt it.

Whatever the reasoning, Americans are not shopping. They stagger around the malls like zombies, hands slack at their sides, fingers reflexively clutching for bags that are not there. This couldn't happen at a worse time.

Our economy is driven by shopping. Half of our GNP

comes from the sale of pointless kitchen utensils that spray serrated pieces of cucumber onto salads; one quarter comes from wages paid to the people who make them, and the other quarter comes to the lawyers who represent the stupid people who stuck their fingers in the blades. We cannot afford to not shop.

Nor can the stores. Most of our stores are tottering on the brink of insolvency as it is. Given the go-go consumerism of the eighties, in which people reached for their wallets so often that half the nation developed repetitive motion injury, it would seem impossible to be broke. You would have to be criminally stupid to be broke.

Well, I've seen the annual reports from retail business, and I quote, "DUHHH."

Retail companies, we now know, found ingenious ways to wreck hitherto profitable companies. Everyone's favorite was leveraged buyouts, in which they borrowed billions of dollars, repurchased their stock, and invested the remainder in Dick Tracy clothing. The idea was that the board would work harder, since they owed the money. The result was that when the store failed to make interest payments and the banks refused to accept five thousand gross of unsold yellow trench-coats in lieu of cash, the owners had the deep, abiding satis-faction of knowing that for a period of three months, they had owned the doors they were now locking up forever.

This is where we are today: up the creek and a week behind on our payments for the paddle. Like all good chin-stroking columnists who presume to know what is good for the nation, I have drawn two conclusions.

1. It serves the retailers right. Does anyone presume that our holidays will be darker because there are fewer needless gewgaws under the tree? Yes, little Johnny will pitch a fit if he doesn't have Nintendo's latest illiteracy-inducing Super Mario Bros. Vs. the Extended Attention Span game cartridge, but we adults really need little. Perhaps this year we can show that this season is not just a wan bleat of consumerism but is a chance for my wife to show her love by getting me just the espresso maker and not bothering with anything else, like the matching cups. Although they would be nice.

2. It serves the retailers right. The markdowns they are having now are proof that their prices are inflated so high it's a wonder that Macy's doesn't float a buyer down the street in their Thanksgiving Day parade. Maybe if we don't buy this year, they'll take out ads that say, "We're sorry. We don't know what came over us. But we lay down for a while and we feel better, and we promise hereafter never to charge more for a tie by calling it 'a complete neckwear system.'"

I plan to shop on the last days of the season, when the merchants will have marked things down to eight hundred percent of their cost, and then I plan to go home, get cozy with my wife, and sit in front of the fire. Watch the steady, inexorable, all-consuming flames.

Provided, in other words, war has broken out. If not, we'll turn off CNN and just put some logs on. Peace on earth. No payments 'til January.

—December 1990

Ssssh. Quiet. Listen. Hear that?

It's the recovery from the recession. Most recoveries announce themselves like Julie Andrews climbing the Alps to belt out "The Sound of Music," but this one is considerably more restrained. It's an old man climbing the stairs, pausing between steps. The closer his wheezing, the sooner the recovery.

Not that I notice it: I was broke before the recession, and I am just as thoroughly broke now. I am not contemplating any "big-ticket items," which apparently are things like dirigibles, Saturn V rocket boosters, offshore pleasure islands. Nor am I in the market for durable goods, which the government defines as things that go a whole three years before disintegrating. My consumer confidence level is best expressed by a 3-D postcard of Don Knotts, the kind where if you turn it from side to side you can see his knees shake.

The recovery, they tell us, will be shallow and sluggish. (Apparently it will take place entirely in a sports bar at four in the afternoon.) But it will happen. Already we see evidence: TV news shows report a twenty-six percent increase in stories that predict a recovery. A survey of newspapers indicates a heartening three tenths of a percent increase in government spokesmen who predict a recovery and are not authoritatively rebutted by dissenting economists—the third straight monthly rise in that figure.

The only disturbing statistic—a two percent jump in the number of long, unreadable pieces about how the banking crisis will result in every American living in a tin shack and boiling meals over fires made from ripped up railroad ties—turns out to be a decrease, if seasonally adjusted. (The season being used to adjust it is Fall 1226, before the invention of movable type; this tends to bring down the average.)

All very heartening. But coming on the heels of a war that the assembled punditry labeled "the first video war," this strikes me as the first video recovery. Whenever I see an economist testifying to the good news, I expect him to cut away to grainy film—say, something taken from the nose of a convenience store security camera, zooming in on someone buying something. And not holding up the clerk.

Do you feel recovered? I don't. I feel dead broke. I'd feel better if I had cable, where there are encouraging stories about the economy twenty-four hours a day, but I can't afford cable.

In other words, this recession—sorry! this miraculous, vital, fire-breathing, heathen-slaying Hercules of a recovery—is different from its predecessors. For good and bad. Here's what differs.

• The lessons of the Great Depression are not applicable to today's economy. No one today has the attention span for a ten-year recession, for one thing. After one year, we'd ask the great, burning question of our time, "What Else Is On?" Besides, the Great Depression came about because durable goods were just that, durable. They made the mistake of selling hot-water heaters that did not rot out nanoseconds after the three-hour warranty had expired. Of course we're in the market for durable goods again: the basement is knee-deep in water.

• The banking system is not in the shape it should be for a recovery. Normally, it works like this: Banks have money.

They lend it out after a great deal of scowling and deep sighs. You pay it back with interest. They take the money, loan out one fourth, use a fourth to commission oil paintings of fat scowling bankers for the boardroom, and convert the remainder into gold, which they bury in Switzerland with the instructions that the Swiss should shoot them dead if they ever so much as request a sliver of it before the year 3000.

Not so anymore. Starting in the seventies, banks began to be run entirely by Bolsheviks who led the boardrooms in reverent salaams before a portrait of Lenin. They just looked like bankers, and that's why we trusted them. Alas for us; their goal was the utter destruction of the American banking system. What they did was take all the petrodollars gushing their way in the seventies and hand it over to third-world hellholes so corrupt their government officers have extra-tall desks to make it easier to pass money under the table. The money, ostensibly loans for cement factories, was never paid back, the cement factories never built. And good thing too: enough money was loaned in the seventies to build 479,394 cement factories, the combined output of which would have added enough weight to the planet to slow its orbit and increase gravity to the point where Luciano Pavarotti would have to get around by limo, because he would weigh too much to walk.

But it was mere priming for the eighties. When banks realized they could get away with giving money away to nations with the credit rating of a guy in the street holding a paper cup and a sign reading HUNGRY, they decided they could do anything. So great shovelfuls of our money went to the most unscrupulous fools of the century. The following is a sample banking conversation:

Developer 1: "I want to build a one-thousand-store shopping mall."

Banker: "Okay. Here's a bag; there's the vault. Shovel's in the corner."

Developer 2: "And I want to build a one-thousand-and-one-store shopping mall right next door."

Banker: "What makes you think you'll succeed?"

Developer 2: "We'll have more stores."

Banker: "Okay. Here's a bag—whoa! Fresh out of bags! It's been a busy day, I guess. Hold on, I'll go get some more."

The result: Writing off bad loans has caused eighty-three percent of American banking presidents to develop debilitating hand cramps. There is no money in any bank. This is a problem when it comes to sparking a recovery. But it's not as bad as the thirties, when banks simply went bust. Today we have the FDIC, which stands for Federal Developers' Insurance Corporation; this takes money out of our pockets and repays those who are owed money for building shopping centers we cannot afford to shop in.

So relax!

—March 1991

Well, I certainly enjoyed that recovery. Did you? And to think I almost missed it. We'd planned to go to a movie that day, but instead we stayed home, and thus got to see the recovery as it passed by. It looked a lot like a float, with bunting and flowers and pretty girls, all waving and throwing out massive bound volumes of government economic statistics to folks on the street.

Then it vanished. False alarm. Turns out someone in network news was playing with the graphics generator.

So now we're back in a recession again. For the next year or so you can expect the nightly news to open with shots of a fifty-year-old man in a plaid shirt who has just been laid off from the tool factory. Same man every night. They can't afford to find another example.

If it's a depression, then I'm ready. I learned all the important lessons about depressions from my mother, a frugal woman who could pinch a nickel until it wept dimes. Nothing was wasted. To this day she not only washes and dries coffee filters but irons them to put the pleats back in. She has been making coffee with the same paper filter since 1965. The box of filters will be a family heirloom, passed down through the generations.

But it doesn't stop there. The rubber bands that came with the newspaper? Into the drawer. The paper bags from the grocery store? Under the sink. String? Added to the ball the

size of a sumo wrestler in the garage. This, you see, is how
you combat the depression: you fill up paper bags with rubber
bands, tie them closed with string, and whip them around
your head until economic activity picks up. Then you go inside for a cup of coffee.

Superstitious, perhaps, but odd enough to work. Think of
it. President Bush's advisers are already worried that he is
losing touch with the middle class. If at every campaign stop
the President was met by thousands of silent citizens, grimly
twirling paper bags full of rubber bands over their heads and
saying not a word, Bush would probably end up insane.
What's with the bags? What's with the bags? We'd all intu-
itively get it, but no one would be able to put it into words.
Then during the first televised debate, the Democratic candidate would answer a difficult question by solemnly producing
a bag and twirling it, making Bush utter a pained squeak and
pass out on the spot.

—April 1991

Times are tough; money's tight. Yet in the last six months I
have purchased thirty-seven ties. Am I some madcap top-
hatted spendthrift, tossing money away on cravats while my
table wants for food? No. Let me tell about the three-dollar
tie, and why it is a lesson on how to get the economy moving.

First, a recap of why we remain mired in a slump, or
slumped in a mire, or whatever they're saying this week. Anyway, here are the recent developments in the economy:

• The White House is doing nothing. Was there ever a
more heartening sight than President Bush responding to the
stock market drop by going golfing? And not just hitting the
links, but dropping nation-fortifying comments like "Nothing
to worry about" and waving his golf club around. If he'd said,
"Don't worry, because I have this magic club and when I
wave it three times everything will be happy again," I'd have
felt better; at least it would mean he had a plan.

I know, I know, it's all the Congress's fault. Even so, if
Bush had his clubs and wanted to hit something small, round,
and white, he could go to the Hill and whack a few congres-

sional skulls. Make them enact his fifteen-point plan for reviving the economy, which is:

1. Get mad whenever you talk about the capital-gains tax.
2–15. Repeat step one.

I think a capital-gains tax cut is a good idea, but I have a hard time believing the absence of it keeps this nation from bursting the surly bonds of penury. Particularly when the economy is so poor that the words "capital" and "gain" have not appeared within hailing distance of each other for some time now.

• Naysayers are dragging down the economy. This is the new tack being taken by the rosier elements of the chorus— that we are talking ourselves into a recession. Again, I see the point. Given the choice between HOMELESS OPIUM-ADDICTED SPANISH-AMERICAN WAR VETS FIND JOB OFFERS DWINDLE IN TIGHT JOB MARKET, and ABSOLUTELY NO ONE IN FARGO, NORTH DAKOTA, GOT CANNED YESTERDAY, the media will run the former every time.

No doubt this has a psychological toll. But it is hard to blame a slumping economy on insufficient production of happy thoughts. (Unless there is a tax on happy-thought gains, of course; if so, I call on Congress to cut it immediately.) Whenever one of those graveyard bandleaders starts doing the nothing-to-fear-but-fear-itself routine, I immediately commence to fearing. A recovery should be like the risen Christ: the radiance should blind you, and you shouldn't have to stick your fingers in the wound to believe.

• Retailing is still in the dumps. The holidays are approaching, and the retail industry is upset because we are not demonstrating the wretched frenzy for rectangular, foil-covered boxes that is supposed to symbolize this season of peace.

Which brings us back to the three-dollar tie. They are sold all over Washington on the streets, coming in various degrees of hideousness, although no uglier than ties costing fifty dollars. The labels say they are "Pure Silk," but if possession of polyester was made a hanging offense, half the men in town would swing.

Cheap retailing is in vogue now. Plenty of stores say they've eliminated the middleman, but you always get the idea they're still passing along the cost of ammunition. The notion of providing good clothes at an affordable price is so unusual, so revolutionary, that surely it can be extended to the rest of the economy.

If I bought those thirty-seven ties at department-store prices, I'd be out $1,665. I actually paid $122.10 That's a savings of $1,542.90, money freed up to invest in the economy, to get it moving again.

Of course, I leave it up to you to do the investing. That $1,542.90 is going straight to the credit card company.

—October 1991

The average TV news interview of a holiday shopper: "Oh, we're cutting back this year. We used to give gold ingots, live emperor penguins, and vast motorized blimps to everyone in the family, but this year I'm just buying bolts, cashews, and half-empty packs of cigarettes. We didn't buy a tree; just smeared some glue on the wall and threw wadded balls of bathroom tissue at it. Nice flocked look."

Typical interview of a small retailer: "Oh, I'd say it's probably the toughest I've seen since the panic of 1892, maybe even the recession that followed the sack of Rome in 455 A.D. I'm going to keep the doors open until Christmas, then I'm going to lock the doors, soap the windows, take the whole staff out back, and shoot them."

Typical interview of a large retailer: "We've been pleased to see how blah-blah the consumer has come to expect blah-blah drone blah repositioning to a moderately priced blah-blah-blah [insincere, terrified smile]."

Typical interview of a sales clerk: "I'm twenty, okay, and it's, like, rilly cool to be all by yourself with all these clothes? But since we're not, like, selling anything, it's rilly rilly hard to, like, take a sweater home, because they notice."

Typical TV interview of an economist: "Actually, there are long-term restructurings of the economy at work here that don't fit in a cheap metaphor appropriate for a seven-second sound bite, but you know, I really want you to call me again for my opinion. So I'll simply say that what we have here is not a dead horse, but it's not a pacesetter. Due to all the debt in the system, you might say the economy has been put out to pasture, and we're paying the stud fees. Whether it goes to the glue factory remains to be seen."

These voices, or some variant, appear on the nightly news each time you turn on the TV. Apparently this holiday shopping season is not so much a seasonal excursion into gift-giving as it is a telethon for fatally ill retailers. Rip off Santa's beard, the stories imply, and you'll find Jerry Lewis, braying for us to crowbar open our wallets and give until it hurts. If the tote board will show sales up 4.3 percent, he will loosen his big red coat and sing "You'll Never Shop Alone" and cry.

I went to a local mall to see what it's truly like out there. Traffic was backed up for half an hour on the road leading to the shopping center, but that proves nothing; people could be so broke they are reduced to looking at goods and will spend Xmas describing what they would have bought if they had had the money. Which of course could cause problems; imagine sitting around the tree, listening to your sister describe the TV she didn't buy you, and realizing you have nothing to describe for her but a sweater and some socks.

The mall was a thin tall structure teeming with people running around bearing packages several times the weight of their own bodies. Only the absence of air holes convinced me I was not actually in an ant farm. (Although there were several strategically placed skylights, now that I think about it.) Everyone had that grim look of holiday duty pasted on their face; familiar tunes wafted from hidden loudspeakers, meant to remind us of the magical holidays of our youth, but providing little more than the dull jab of vague memories of gap-toothed avarice. The music now means BUY, not GET— the merchants' version of a cattle prod. *Rudolph the red-nosed reindeer,* BZZZZZ! *had a very shiny nose,* BZZ-BZZ!

Thus encouraged, I went into a famous and hideously over-leveraged department store, looking for a gift for my wife. (Since she is reading this, I will have to mumble the nature and cost of my purchase.) I discovered a beautiful *mmrgh* selling for *mrrghuhgh.* It was discounted the astonishing amount of *mmrghm* dollars below the usual price.

"How can you make money with these discounts?" I asked the clerk, who clung to me like a barnacle or, for that matter, like any invertebrate operating on commission sales. She noted that if I signed up for a store credit card, an additional ten percent would be hacked off the price, and if I came back for the special sale, called Moonlight Madness, or Daytime Dementia, or Midmorning Twitching, Drooling, and Uncontrollable Blaspheming Sale, an additional *mrrmghm* dollars would be sliced from the price.

This leads to one of two conclusions.

1. Stores have decided that the best way to survive the recession is to lose as much money as possible on every purchase.

2. Prices have been jacked so high for so long that they can hack at them like serial killers and never hit bone.

Hard to tell. I do know that I vowed to shop wisely this year, to be frugal, and that when I staggered from the mall, my credit card was callused from overuse. I shopped wisely, and well; I was, I think, a typical 1991 shopper: neither profligate nor inordinately cheap. Like many emerging from the helium-and-hot-air eighties, I looked for value and found it.

And I was even interviewed by a news crew doing a story on how bad the recession is. I smiled and held up my bags and said I got a wonderful deal on a *mmmrrghgm* for my wife and that the money I saved would go in the bank. That made it on the evening news. But it was interesting to note that they didn't have a clip of an economist saying it was good for me to spend a little less and bank a little more. What they did was take a clip from the eighties of an economist complaining how we spend too much and banked too little.

They just ran the clip backward. It got the point across. And it probably saved some money.

—December 1991

The President recently spent his precious time hammering out a complex trade agreement, whereby American cars will be airlifted to Australia, stuffed with wheat, brought back to the U.S., then filled with rice and sold to Japan. This plan seems to use government involvement to prop up as many failing industries as possible, and thus constitutes a victory for the free market.

Meanwhile, back home, there was the usual conflicting economic news.

• Housing starts, recently renamed housing fits and starts, were up 349 percent. This was much better than economists had expected but is less impressive when you consider the government had recently redefined "housing starts" to include walking up to an empty lot, framing the spot with your hands, and saying, "A house would look good here."

• The Big Three automakers reported that sales were down 5,203 percent for the last quarter. One person who did enter a dealership in Fargo, North Dakota, did so for the express purpose of putting handprints on the freshly shined cars; salesmen stood around helpless, not wanting to antagonize a potential customer.

• Inventories were down, usually a good sign; unfortunately, they had decreased because of the high number of warehouses torched for the insurance money.

• In a survey of one thousand American households, everyone was sitting by the phone waiting to hear about a job, and so they answered the survey taker on the first ring.

• And on Wall Street, the Dow Jones flirted with the four thousand mark for most of the day before making a rude suggestion and then engaging in inappropriate touching. "I could feel the Invisible Hand all over me," the four thousand mark said. "It was awful." The market still closed at an all-time high. As is the new tradition in this odd recessionary bull market, the trading floor was flooded with champagne to a depth of three feet, and brokers spent the evening splashing about in silken robes and hurling fistfuls of gold coins at one another. (It has been this way ever since Wall Street decided it would be better for the market to weld the doors shut with the brokers inside, take the phones off the hook, and play Pretend.)

You can repeat these items every week, as long as the

economy continues to behave like a drunk on the staircase—up, down, side to side. These stories will be accompanied by shots of the President, looking like he is trying hard to recollect the pictures in the *Little Golden Book of Concerned Facial Expressions,* talking about his plans. You will have Democrats on the evening news wearing cheap suits and happy faces, arguing forcefully that it's time to let them ruin the economy for a while. It's like watching a boxing match and knowing that come November the winner gets to leave the ring and pound us in the head.

And you can expect to see the heart-smiting tales of shop stewards in charge of left-handed widget adjusters, now unemployed. "I'm fifty-five years old. Filing grievances on behalf of left-handed widget adjusters is all I know. Who's going to hire me?" Stories of middle-level execs whose jobs are as secure as a Post-It note in a typhoon. Let's face it, until they start hiring at the newspapers and networks, bad news is all you're going to hear.

Some of it is true. But several larger issues seem to be lacking in this daily dirge. For example, we can all agree that banks made many, many bad real estate loans in the eighties, that speculation and overbuilding resulted in an oversupply that currently depresses prices and forestalls recovery. But the money did not go to a wizard in a pointed hat who tottered onto the lot, waved a wand with a star on the end, conjured up a building, and pocketed eighty million dollars.

People built that thing and were rewarded for it. People in the financial sector, in the construction industry. It's doubtful that the guys putting up Sheetrock on the thirty-seventh floor of Needless Plaza or Speculative Centre ever turned to each other and said, "Y'know, we are just sucking off the great teat of borrowed money that will eventually cripple the very economy on which we depend; what say we throw down our tools and quit?" No. And who can blame them? But when you hear the carpetlayers and painters and marble installers moan about the lack of work, you have to wonder, Did you think the good times would go on forever?

Before you snarl that I am just another out-of-touch Beltway drone pontificating on Ignoramus Americanus, let me tell you I'm guilty of all of this. Did I live frugally and save during the boom? Did I ever turn down a pay raise? Of course not. Speaking here *ex cathedra* on your edit page, I steeple my fingers and ruminate on the big picture. But it's the small snapshots of everyday life that really count. And those are as described above: the odd news that tells us we're in trouble, and the seldom-noticed actions that contributed to the whole mess.

We're all in this together: that's what we know. We're all, in some way, to blame: that's what we forget. It is penance time. Bless me, Father, for I have shopped.

Now go say ten Alan Greenspans, and pray.

—January 1992

Dye a Thousand Breaths

~~~~~~

MY WIFE CAME BACK FROM THE DRUGSTORE THE OTHER DAY with the usual purchases: soap (a variety that dissolves after one day and leaves in the soap dish a substance resembling the afterbirth for an albino); toothpaste, to remove stains; cigarettes, to put them back on; Q-Tips, which the instructions insist are not to be inserted in the ear canal, and which I enjoy pushing into my ear until the cotton hits brain matter and I see new colors; the store brand of toilet paper, which the package might as well describe as "New! Now With Extra Abrasive"; and hair coloring.

A very female purchase, that last one. It never occurs to men to change their hair color. But it never occurs to men to cut their toenails until their wife tires of waking with bloody calves, so men's failure in this area of comportment is easily understood: they are too busy ignoring other aspects of personal design to worry about silly things like hair color. But hair hue is of great concern to women, who believe that dying the inert threads of protein that stick out of their skull will somehow change everything. Or, crudely put, they believe that when you give the house a new coat of paint, you increase the resale value.

This is not the case for all, and certainly not my wife, who is the model of rational humanity. But periodically she decides that she needs to dye her hair red. Not flaming, Irish, pinup-of-the-Provos red, but auburn. Russet. She says she wants red highlights, and, well, don't we all? It makes it sound as though her head will burst into coppery sparks whenever life gets interesting, then recede to brown when the moment passes.

Actually, as she reminds me, it means that her hair will not really be red but give the impression of being redder than it actually is. This will presumably go with the dress that makes her look thinner than she actually is and the heels that make her look taller than she is, all calculated to make me look more deserving than I actually am. This is all very nice, but needless: my wife has a perfect figure, is of just the right height, and the lack of implicated hues in her hair is irrelevant to my feelings for her. She need do nothing to make me look undeserving; it is readily apparent to all. But when it's hair-coloring time, there is naught a man can do but stand back, hold his nose, and flee the room.

Because this stuff is dangerous. I have in front of me the instructions, which are so loaded with warnings and disclaimers you'd think you were performing an appendectomy on yourself. In big letters, prior to all else, is a section called BEFORE YOU COLOR. It has to do with allergic reactions and goes something like this:

"Although approximately seventy thousand cute and harmless bunnies have died hideous deaths, their fur soaked in a riot of disparate and unnatural colors, there is no guarantee that this product will not make your eyes swell, your throat close, your skin erupt in a lurid topography of welts and lesions, and your heart burst with an audible popping sound that could easily be mistaken for the opening of the dye bottle if your husband was upstairs, cowering from the smell of the dye. In order to indemnify us against any legal action, we present the following instructions for allergic testing, which we know full well you will ignore:

1. Clean a quarter-sized patch in the bend of your elbow. Use bleach. Stop rubbing when skin appears to be completely gone.
2. Apply a dab of Russet Magic to skin.

3. Cover with bandage; secure bandage with tape commonly used by moving company packers.
4. If still alive at this point, stop.
5. Leave in place for seven days. If at end of seven days limb is still responsive and need not be banged against the headboard every morning in order to come to life, proceed with hair coloring.

The instructions blithely proceed on to the main event, assuming that the user wants to continue. This is not always the case. Women frequently stall at this point, all thoughts of subtle highlights now overtaken by fears of unknown consequences. Such as:

1. A dye job that results in people noticing that you got a dye job.
2. A dye job so gentle and subtle that no one notices you got a gentle, subtle dye job.
3. A color that is not like the hazy picture on the box but something that resembles the hues found on preschooler toys.
4. Damaged hair. (Men have no concept of damaged hair; hair is hair. "Damaged hair" is, to us, a description of a powerful hangover.)
5. No hair. Looks of sympathy from bald men on the street, as well as moist and hopeful looks from same.

When the skin test is done, however, the decision is usually made to proceed. Time for another page of caveats, this one titled BEFORE YOU RUIN YOUR LIFE. There is a brand-new list of warnings, these being even more ominous, such as "To avoid staining, apply petroleum jelly to nape of neck. And do so carefully, unless you want that racing-stripe look so popular in auto-detailing shops. To really make certain to avoid staining, enclose self in a jacket of fresh paraffin and lower yourself into the washbasin through a series of ropes and pullies."

My wife read none of this; she knows the drill. She was perhaps heartened by the toll-free number at the bottom of the page, which indicated that help was available Monday through Friday until seven P.M. After that, presumably, you call the suicide prevention hot line.

Now, the deed itself.

Open the instruction book and put on the enclosed plastic gloves (necessary because it detracts from the feeling of being beautiful when knucklebones start to appear through the evaporating flesh). And then ... put it in, hang out for half an hour, and wash it out. That's it.

What you do while you hang out is up to you. I have seen my wife pace around with the look of dread common to commercials where people have chosen the wrong long-distance company; other times she has calmly sat at the kitchen table perusing a legal brief, deciding the fate of corporations, her hair a foamy mass of white whorls and horns that made it look as if she had been mauled by a washing machine. In any case, it is over in half an hour, and then comes the moment of truth.

There are two possible outcomes.

1. Wife ABSOLUTELY HATES IT.
2. Wife is DECIDEDLY AMBIVALENT.

There is only one possible husband response.

1. Broad smile; wide eyes; *ooh-la-la* murmurings; admonition not to submit to the cozening flattery of men tomorrow; big hug and kiss; furtive wiping of red-stained petroleum jelly off lips.

And that is it. All that remains is for the newly russeted individual to take a deep breath and march off to work, hoping for the best. In my wife's case, the most recent dye job was greeted with absolute nullity the next day: no one noticed. Apparently this dye's highlights were noticeable only if she fell into a searchlight during a total eclipse. No matter; it looks wonderful, and I've come to view russet auburn as her natural color. Not a bad color for our offspring.

It had better be. There's a warning on the package: "MAY AFFECT DNA."

Hear My Thong

EVERY SO OFTEN A MAN MUST BUY A NEW SWIMSUIT—NOT TO inaugurate summer, not to dazzle the doxies at the shore, but because the elastic on the old one is as loose as a gossip's tongue, and the moment you dive into water the suit will be yanked off your body. And then you will find yourself bobbing helplessly, hands clapped over your secrets, snapping at your suit with your teeth, wishing this was not a municipal pool but the ocean, and you could just ride the undertow into merciful oblivion.

Few men suffer this fate; those that have, remember it.

Some men never outlast their suits—they gain in girth between summers and find that getting into last year's suit is a task akin to stuffing a hamster into the finger of a rubber glove. Men who don't balloon over the winter months may fit their suits but find that its condition has not passed wifely muster—they may open the drawer in June to discover that the suit made the magical transition to shoe-polish cloth months before.

I fit neither category. I'm a vain fool who suffers the delusion that this summer will be better than the last *only* if I have a new swimsuit. The days will never be cloudy, the gnats will never pester, the traffic to the beach will be light, and the traffic home will not have the tenor and mood of Napolean's retreat from Moscow. Scientists will discover that reading *The Atlantic* magazine at the beach instead of a trashy novel protects you from skin cancer.

Of course, none of this ever happens, but I can console myself with the knowledge that when I paraded before ten thousand indifferent strangers, I did so in an *entirely different color than the year before.*

So I went to buy a new suit at a store called the Bikini Hut, located in downtown Washington. This being Washington, it was adjacent to the headquarters for a peppery billionaire running a political campaign. The idea of this billionaire in a G-string is enough to roil the stomach and make you head to Sackcloth Hut, right down the street. But I persevered: I needed a new suit.

The store was staffed by a giggly Gidget who, as befits the young-at-heart and dim-of-brain, had the radio set at a level designed to put a pillow to the face of any sensible thought. The store was jammed with swimsuits, lurid spumes of color cresting and crashing everywhere you looked. Glossy photos of models with the body fat of a hummingbird hung on the wall, all staring off into the distance with the look of someone expecting a new continent to pop over the horizon. A couple of them had happy vapid innocent grins: *Hi Mom, hi Dad! I'm darn near naked and poorly paid to boot!* If I were a woman, I would have felt dark, spiky pangs of hatred toward those creatures and toward the store: it was patently unfair to trumpet these tight, taut ninnies with free time and good genes, mockingly flaunting their perfection, as you contemplated swathing your deficiencies in a one-piece made of spandex, elastic, and tungsten steel.

As a man, of course I merely wondered what they would look like *completely* naked.

There was one row of men's swimsuits, in sizes ranging from the poodle-hipped to the zeppelinesque. I started pawing through them and immediately felt a flush of alarm—this was not the typical assortment of swimsuits. No loose, baggy drawstring models here; most of the suits were so tight you'd have to remove them by sandblasting. The most capacious were the small little swimmer's trunks—the sort that always make a man look like he's trying to mail a one-pound package with a twenty-nine-cent stamp. Down the line were some loincloths, for the You-Jane, Me-Shameless clientele. And then, to my astonishment: thongs.

Thongs! *For men!* Had the laws changed? Had *men* changed? I'm not the hippest lad in creation, but I read men's style magazines and have yet to come across an article commanding me to stock up on sunblock, smear my flanks, and slather my fundament because it's Butts Up for '93! I had an instant vision of those awful, lumbering woolly mammoths you see on the beach—the gentlemen with chests so hairy they look like they should be steam cleaned, their furry, white guts hanging low over a swimsuit the size of a demitasse saucer. Now, they're going to be appalling both coming *and* going.

I asked the clerk who possibly wears these things.

"Guys going to foreign countries," she replied.

Ah. Of course. Bound for Pakistan? Don't forget your thong.

I imagine there are women who applaud this sort of thing; in this culture, women are allowed to go loose and gooshy over men's behinds and have it considered an innocent, wholesome indulgence. (Should men find themselves slack-jawed and sweating as they note a passing bottom, of course, we are instant Pigs.) But while the idea of the thong for men might set hearts fluttering, I doubt any woman wants her honey to buy one, let alone wear it. Unless she is half of one of those We-Are-Perfect Nazi couples you see on the beach, who go home and bench-press each other and cannot have sex without the word "repetitions" coming to mind.

I picked out a suit that was reasonably interesting—not too small, but certainly not the typical Hefty bag favored by most men. (See "vain fool," above.) Best of all, it was adjustable. I don't mean that in the sense of the adjustments men periodically make; the suit was not automated to perform a left-to-right realignment of one's personal apparatus. I mean that the front of the suit could be configured for less or more exposure. It made me feel dangerous, this suit: I would have

Options. Should I fall asleep tanning on my well-walled roof deck and wake up teleported to the beaches of Cannes, one quick yank and I would be as nonchalantly immodest as a European. Or, I could tan on my deck with the suit set at maximum exposure; this way, I could look forward to skin cancer in a wholly new location, like the lower hip.

I bought it. But not without some mortification. It was extremely embarrassing to stand there holding this small suit, surrounded by women holding their equally skimpy purchases. I could see them look at it, look at me—the standard nonchalant calculus you perform whenever you witness someone purchasing articles of an intimate nature.

I felt judged! I felt like a piece of meat!

It was going to be a wonderful summer.

I'm Okay, Euro Disney

EURO DISNEY, THE MASSIVE, MICKEY-INFESTED THEME PARK outside Paris, had a typical European opening: terrorists bombed the power lines, the communists called a rail strike to the park, and the intellectual community suffered a collective sprained neck from the effort of sticking its nose up in the air. If I were Donald Duck, I'd wonder how to give someone the middle finger when I had only four of them.

Most nations would be happy to have a four-billion-dollar enterprise set up shop within their borders, but not France. The French are different. The French believe they are superior to other nations. Now, every culture on earth believes this of itself—except Canada, but they have the French-speaking Quebecois to even it out. The French, however, bring such panache, hauteur, and high-mindedness to disliking the rest of the world that you get the impression they have actually accomplished something of significance since 1789.

Examples: One savant labeled the park a "cultural Chernobyl," a jarring image that makes you wonder if people a hundred miles downwind will start to pick up unusually high levels of Goofy in their food. Another described Euro Disney as "A horror made of cardboard . . . and idiotic folklore straight out of comic books written for these obese Americans." Catch the sneer in those last three words? This from a nation whose eating habits virtually consist of lying down behind a cement mixer filled with pâté de fois gras and shouting "Commence!"

What worries the keepers of the French soul is that the youth of the nation might be entranced by the bright, cheerful vision of Disney and forego their own heritage. I fail to see how; show me footage of people staggering off a roller coaster and renouncing Edith Piaf, and I'll believe it. If in twenty years the cafés of Paris are devoid of brooding youths smoking harsh cigarettes over vin ordinaire and extolling communism, well, then Euro Disney will indeed have been the deathblow to French culture the intellectuals fear.

Perhaps there should be a French version, however. Very well.

VichyWorld. Set on a two-hundred-acre plot, VichyWorld recreates, right down to the last detail, the government that collaborated with the Nazis. An enveloping atmosphere of opportunism, moral ambiguity, and gnawing dread. Bring the kids! You'll spend a day with a smile on your face and fear in your heart as you wonder whether your tour guide believes what he's saying or is just going along with the Germans like everyone else. You'll encounter famous historical figures, moving and speaking as if they were alive—like Klaus Barbie, who separates the Jewish vacationers from the rest of you. Not that you complain! (Lucky them—they get to ride the tightly packed monorail to CampWorld.) At the end of the park you'll hear the VichyWorld theme song, "It's a Short Reich, After All"—and be handed badges that insist you were really a member of the Resistance!

No? Is this too cruel? Well, everyone's history is cruel. Every nation has glories and sins. Every culture bears the blurry watermark of evil on the paper where it pens the elegant script of its achievements. America is no different. (Although, of course, our eighteenth-century revolution did not give way to state-sponsored mass-murder and militaristic dictatorship. But I digress.) Euro Disney is an imaginary place, a culture without sin. The fact that America can devise something like that, and France cannot, speaks books about the difference between the cultures.

I do understand the underlying concern: American culture is loud, brash, crude, full of rude animal energy, a monster truck climbing over local folkways and smashing them flat. But Euro Disney won't do anything that wasn't begun long ago. American popular culture never has to argue on its own behalf or get defensive. Let it rip, and hips move, eyes go blank, mouths water for salt and sugar. We have distilled the needs of the world down to pure form and dressed it in a mouse suit. What's more, we've created a perfect world: Euro Disney is as efficient as Japan, as zealous in its authoritarian tidiness as Singapore, as rapturously besotted with fictional bromides as Hollywood. It's a dreamworld—precisely what America is to the rest of the world.

What rankles the French, I believe, is the inclusion of Snow White in the Disney pantheon. One woman, seven men? That's completely backward.

What lessons will their children learn from that?

Lesser Moments in
Promotional History

ᘐᘐᘐ

My subscription to a particular news journal lapsed
several months ago, and the magazine has only itself to
blame. When I signed up for a trial run, the magazine sent me
a telephone—or an "Ultronic Telecommunications Response
System," as they like to say. The phone was so cheaply made
that I was certain it was disposable—make ten calls, then
throw it away. The sound quality would have been good if
I'd been talking with the spirit world, but in normal business
conversations people ought not to sound as though they are
attempting to penetrate the barrier between the living and
the dead. And it emitted periodic clacking noises while you
spoke, making it seem as though you were conversing with
an agitated lobster. The 1 button refused to work after a day
of use, meaning that when a burglar came in, I'd be unable
to dial 911, and when the police used the phone to tell my
parents in North Dakota that I'd been murdered by an intruder, they wouldn't be able to make a long-distance call. A
typically useless piece of modern consumer electronics.

It was on this phone that I took a call from the magazine,
begging me to renew my subscription.

I resisted their sales pitch—actually, I couldn't understand

a word of it—and the magazine soon ceased to appear at
my house. But I wish I'd renewed. Recently this magazine
inaugurated personalized ads for its nine million subscribers.
Through a combination of computers, advanced printing tech-
nologies, and advertising's unending desire to reach out and
yank so hard on your lapels that your neck vertebrae separate, lucky subscribers will be able to open up the magazine
and see their name printed in a car ad. The ad will also list
the address of the nearest car dealer, for those who are
daunted by the complexities of the Yellow Pages.

They may say this is the dawn of a new age in advertising,
but they're lying. I happen to know that advertisers have
been experimenting for years with new, unusual ways to get
your attention. Most of these stories have been hushed up.
But here's what they've been up to.

In August of 1988, *Newsweek* experimented with placing
small air bags in each issue. Upon turning the page, the bag,
imprinted with the advertiser's logo, would billow from the
spine of the magazine and hit the reader in the face. The
plan was abandoned after a magazine delivery truck hit a
speed bump and triggered 4,662 issues of *Newsweek*. The van,
which eventually attained an altitude of three thousand feet,
crashed and burned in Lindhurst, New Jersey.

In the early eighties, *Vogue* experimented with using genet-
ically engineered mites to direct the reader to particular ads.
The mites were bred to open the magazine to a certain ad
whenever the magazine was left unattended and then, by
sensing the body heat of the subscriber, to move the magazine
to a place where it might be noticed. The plan was deemed
unsuccessful when it was determined that current DNA technology was incapable of developing an insect undetectable by
the human eye yet large enough to move an average issue of
Vogue. In addition, market research showed that consumers
expressed an extreme dislike of seeing their magazine moving
slowly toward them across the floor. The mite technology was
later adapted by *Reader's Digest,* who programmed the mites
to move the issue into the bathroom as soon as it arrived.

In June of 1989, advertisers commissioned a study to determine which scents would put subscribers in a mood to make

needless purchases. Research found that men were most at-tracted by the scent of fresh steel-belted radials, while women went cross-eyed for the smell of tissue paper that had spent six weeks in a box wrapped around new shoes. This was an outgrowth of scent-strip technology, which allowed every magazine to smell as if a five-dollar hooker had fallen into the vat where they make the ink.

The idea was to add a universally attractive scent to the glue that bound the magazine and make the casual browser powerless to resist the magazine. Whether this was actually tried is uncertain, but it is instructive to note that in the month of April 1991 the highest selling magazines in the country were *Stubbs! The Magazine for the Pathetically Endowed* and a women's magazine whose cover story was about how to marry impoverished, sexually repressed religious zeal-ots. Draw your own conclusions.

In late 1986, several magazines got together with the mak-ers of telephones and agreed to give away shoddy, inferior telephones as subscription gifts. The readers would then see the ads for superior telephones, and make additional pur-chases. This campaign, never publicized, is believed to con-tinue to this day.

In fact, they've expanded it. A week before *Time* an-nounced it would be running personalized ads for Isuzu, they called me up and asked if I'd like to subscribe. No free phones, no cheap stereos. Now they're offering me a car.

Or, as they call it, an "Ultronic Quadro-Wheeled Driving System."

How to Destroy Crucial Brain Cells

〜〜

WHILE RIDING THE TRAIN THE OTHER DAY, I FOUND MYSELF talking to two high school students, only one of whom was a chain-smoking pathological liar. The other was an intermittently befuddled young woman who explained the new drug culture in her high school.

"Gasoline is, like, really big," she said. "And other stuff too. I had a friend who went into convulsions 'n' stuff from inhaling Scotchgard. His eyes rolled up and everything."

Gasoline? Aerosol fabric protector? Yes, these are the new drugs. You get a can of gas or Scotchgard, pass it among your friends, and breathe the fumes. The result is dizziness, disorientation, and nausea—thereby bringing back those innocent, carefree days of riding the playground merry-go-round until you threw up. From Toys "Я" Us to Convulsions 'N' Stuff.

I had the usual thought: this is awful, a sign of societal breakdown, and how can I profit? I considered dashing off a TV movie, *Ethyl Is a Harsh Mistress,* which would concern a man who started inhaling only the finest no-lead at parties but was soon reduced to the crudest low-octane varieties available. DT visions of leering sheiks, angry dinosaurs. Second act: He realizes he has hit bottom when he wakes in a strange garage, nose in the gas tank of a lawnmower. Obligatory uplifting ending will have him admitting he is powerless against petrochemical distillates.

Nah.

I began to wonder how someone first gets the idea to sniff gas and propellants. The old saw about learning it at home doesn't seem to apply here. I can't imagine Dad filling the family sedan and taking a big whiff off the nozzle. And few kids find Mom sprawled in the living room, dust rag in one hand, empty "lemon fresh" Pledge can in the other, a glazed smile on her face.

No, this is an idea so brainless it had to come from the newly minted minds of teens themselves. Clearly, we need drug education. And by that I mean a program to teach children what is and is not a drug.

Drugs:

- Dry green vegetation that, when lit and inhaled, makes you dopey, stupid, sleepy, and eventually grumpy and destroys your ability to go off to work, hi ho.
- White powders that make everything seem really keen until your heart bursts from your chest, hits the wall, and flaps around in the corner, at which point someone who's been smoking dry vegetation freaks out and stomps it to death.
- Tiny pills that expand your mind and let you experience a whole new range of understanding, which, unfortunately, is of limited utility in the world; you may find it enlightening to understand that tiny, glistening strands connect everything in the world, but a prospective employer will certainly be unimpressed when you comment on their presence in a job interview ten years later.

Not Drugs:

- Anything whose container says, "Contents are under pressure." It's you that's under pressure, not your drugs.
- Anything that has to be shaken vigorously before consumed. (IMPORTANT EXCEPTION: MARTINIS. IF UNSURE, LISTEN FOR TELLTALE RATTLING BALL-BEARING TO DETERMINE IF IT IS A MARTINI OR SPRAY PAINT.)
- Anything that can be purchased from a guy with his name embroidered on his shirt.

For the point of drugs is not to make you throw up—that may be in the cards, eventually, but en route is a curious thing called pleasure. The main reason people take drugs— and listen closely, kids—is because they make you feel good. Hence the popularity of drugs and the unpopularity of, say, salmonella. (If the latest thing is to sit in a darkened room and lick raw chicken, I don't want to hear about it.) Drugs are fun, at least for a while; that is a clue to their continued popularity. When adults tell kids that the first time they smoke marijuana they will instantly flat-line their brains and become a drooling lump their parents will have to chain to the radiator upstairs whenever company comes, adults are making a big mistake. If kids are going to learn about drugs, they need to know that they are fun and exciting—just as embezzlement, infidelity, income tax cheating, and fishing over your limit are fun and exciting. And a very bad idea.

Behavior-modification ads on TV are obviously useless; if they worked, no one would be on drugs, drive drunk, or get pregnant. (And everyone would be in the army.) Antidrug ads have a special problem. In order to get the point, you have to be sober, which is like making radio ads for the hearing impaired. We need ads that terrify drug users on their addled terms, make them think they are losing their mind. There is no reaching some; you could invent a drug that makes one of your limbs fall off, and some fools would take it four times. But the vast majority of drug-taking youth continue to cheerfully pollute themselves because they have not yet seen any real consequences. So we have to make them think they are going insane. This would require that adults be forewarned; perhaps fliers could be put in laxative packages, warning us in advance that the nation was going to scare the drug users straight. Then have a day when everything is aimed at scaring the holy bejesus out of drug users.

Alter television. Have a soap commercial that looks completely normal, except that the music is played backward, barking noises come from the mouths of the actors, lizards gush from the washing machine, and a gurgling baby turns to the camera and says something cryptic like "Kevin, listen! Hell is full of purple hats." If nothing else, I guarantee the commercial will have a profound impact on any Kevins watching.

Have everything on television play in slow motion, and everything on the radio play at twice the speed.

Have everyone in suits walk crabwise.

Enlist record stores to replace their entire stock with a compact disc by Julie Andrews for that one day. In every bin: Julie Andrews.

Pay the homeless to wear pink body paint for the day.

That sort of thing. It would work. I stopped smoking pot a long, long time ago because I developed a sense of paranoia so acute I could feel other people's hallucinations judging me. I noted that when I smoked pot, I kept close track of my behavior so no one could tell I had smoked pot. After a while I discovered a brilliant shortcut: *don't smoke pot.*

And they say the insights you have when you smoke the stuff are nonsense.

Lament of the
Crash Dummies

DEMOLITION DERBY FANS ARE NO DOUBT ENJOYING A NEW commercial on TV, the one that is supposed to illustrate the consequences of higher mileage requirements for American cars. It shows what happens when a big car—an asphalt-eating, God-fearing piece of Detroit iron—ploughs into a small, tinfoil-and-cardboard auto. The result: The big car absolutely devours the driver's side of the little car, and the small car's crash-dummy driver commits ritual suicide by spearing himself on the steering column.

I draw two conclusions from this.

1. Always be the passenger in a small car, or better yet, stay in the backseat, where you won't get splashed on.

2. Crash dummies are ripe for a good union organizer.

These are not the lessons we're supposed to learn. Not according to the Consortium of Craven Auto Manufacturers or the Council for Evading Corporate Responsibility or whoever paid for the ad. They want us to write our congressman and insist that the new fuel-efficiency rules be eased back, because—as the commercial clearly demonstrates—the only way Detroit can meet them is to build papier-mâché cars with balsa-wood bumpers.

That's the spirit, boys! That's the old can-do spunk!

They forget that all the congressmen drive armor-plated road yachts that could cave in the front end of a Brink's truck while still in first gear, so Congress is not likely to care if the rest of us whiz around in flimsy go-carts. But the automakers still persist. It's not as if they're against clean air, oh, my, no. The only reason they're fighting the government's regulations is—well, son, (the automaker squints at the sky) there's one thing a man don't cotton to (hitches up his belt) and that's his gummint (spits on the ground) telling him what he already knows he has to do. T'aint right.

I don't buy it. For all automakers cared, you'd use up a tank getting out of the garage. That's fine, providing gas costs a nickel a fill, and we can buy a brand-new atmosphere down at the Planetary Supplies aisle at K mart. Given different circumstances, I'm happy that the feds are poking them to improve gas mileage and disheartened by the latest failure of the American auto industry to get off its dead, wide duff and make a car I want to buy.

It all started to go wrong in the seventies, when designers started making cars that looked like the offspring of a slide rule and a refrigerator. Big, stupid, boxy things that had the wind resistance of a file cabinet. Paramount in that miserable decade were AMC's Gremlin and Hornet—cars named after things that annoy you. You kept waiting for the AMC Nettle. It's amazing no one came up with the Dodge Period, with commercials full of women leaping up and shouting that since they got their Period, life has been fabulous.

Only the auto industry could figure we were stupid enough to want to drive something called a Pinto and then—after the Pinto started leaping ten feet in the air on a column of flame whenever it got a swat in the rear—think we'd want a Nova, named for a star that has just exploded.

My first car was an AMC Pacer, a pumpkin-colored bug with a big broad butt and ten acres of glass. It was widely reviled for its ugliness, but in truth it was years ahead of its time: it actually had curves. People were so used to cars that looked like bank presidents' desks that curves were . . . were . . . *immoral.*

The Pacer, of course, was nothing but a Miata with cellulite, but it was an honest attempt to build an interesting car and was thus roundly reviled. It wasn't until the Taurus deigned to throw us a few round edges that we started getting back to good-looking American cars. But they still can't get it right. The new Saturn has all the hallmarks of a car designed in the late eighties: so many meaningless curves it appears to have melted slightly in transit.

All this and wood-grained plastic too.

If you really want to know what American car manufacturers are content to make, drive a fleet car. These are the cars they make when they know no one's watching. No one complains about fleet cars. They have weird names like the Chevy Posthumous or psuedo-sporty names like the Dodge Balk. They either handle like grand pianos or are so underpowered you can't pass a paperboy without red-lining the tachometer. The instrument panels are fabulously ugly and devote much space to "control centers" that give you useful information like "GLOVE COMPARTMENT LIGHT IS OUT," while neglecting to tell you that your bumper fell off and clattered away about thirty blocks ago.

I know, I know; this is unfair. America still makes good cars. I drive a Ford Probe, which looks like a Pacer after an elephant sat on it. I love the car and have the speeding tickets to prove it. Compare it to my best friend's Saab, built with antiseptic Nordic precision. Sure, he can beat me two days out of three in a race, but happily those two days his car is always in the shop because the pistons have slipped by the width of a molecule and rendered the entire machine unusable.

For me, it all comes down to the Miata. You've seen this car. A curvacious little hellion, built for go-to-hell blondes and middle-aged men desperate not to appear to be middle-aged men. And it works: the warranty for the Miata actually covers impotence. The fact that Americans designed it for the Japanese makes it even sadder—you think of the scrap metal we sent over in the thirties that came back as bullets. Except this time we used fax machines instead of ships to give them the ammunition.

Why couldn't Detroit have built this car? It doesn't have

to go a hundred miles an hour; the doors could sound tinny when you slammed them, the body could have been made of corrugated cardboard covered with shellac, and I'd have kicked orphans out of the way to get one. It's easy to make a car like this. Take a boxy monstrosity and start sanding it down. Quit when passersby stop and kneel and propose marriage. That's all it takes.

But what am I thinking? Why do something dramatic when your market share is still in the majority? Hand out the bonuses, jack up prices to exploit the short-term profit, throw billions into new cars that are just as underwhelming as their predecessors, and try to guilt America into buying your wares. Watch while sleek little go-carts erode your profit. Resist attempts to meet them on their own turf.

And if the crash-dummies unionize and demand air bags, well, fight it. Air bags? For dummies?

What makes them think they're so special?

Light It and Run

〜〜〜〜〜〜〜〜〜〜〜〜〜〜〜〜〜〜〜〜〜〜〜〜〜〜〜〜〜〜〜〜〜〜〜〜〜

LIKE MOST AMERICANS, I PLAN TO FIND MYSELF STARING INTO the sky on the night of the Fourth, a smile on my face and a crick in my neck, watching fireworks bloom in the sky. At some point, as always, I will wonder: How much of this can one take? Half an hour of explosions, well, that's wonderful. But two hours? Five? At what point would people start looking around for their things and start to drift away, or would everyone feel some indefinable obligation to stay?

I first thought this during a fireworks exhibition in Minneapolis put on by a Japanese company that had recently purchased a local firm and was anxious to get on our good side. The fireworks began with the sort of explosions that usually signal the end in most displays, that oops-dropped-a-match-in-the-box type of all-out pyrotechnical carnage. It went on and on and on, as though they had a pipeline to China, where dutiful factory hands were shoveling the stuff in as fast as they could make it.

What if this never ends? I wondered. I imagined the bleachers full of onlookers after three straight days of nonstop fireworks—emaciated, dehydrated, staring with jaded eyes into the sky, praying that the next spectacular explosion be the last.

And I'd have been one of them. I am powerless before

fireworks. I regret I live in an age when, in many states, fireworks are kept from the hands of the citizen. I grew up in North Dakota, which at the time was enlightened in these matters: any tot with a fistful of nickels could readily buy all sorts of high explosives. The shacks that sold them appeared on the roads at the edge of town, lean, slightly disreputable places that looked like a carny should be leaning out of them, offering you some crooked delight.

Well, they weren't all like that. Not my dad's shack, anyway. For a few summers, my father ran a fireworks stand at his gas station. In retrospect it seems a dangerous combination: a shack stuffed with gunpowder, next to huge underground vats of gasoline, all overseen by employees with lit cigarettes dangling from their bottom lips. If it had all blown up, it would have lifted half the state of North Dakota about three yards in the air.

When your dad runs a fireworks stand, of course, you get to shoot off what doesn't sell. You have either the worst Fourth or the best. I remember limitless fireworks, though; so business, thank heavens, must have been awful. People seemed hesitant to buy the immense rockets my father sold— big evil things the width of a milk bottle, strapped to a piece of wood the size of a policeman's baton. They looked like they would fly so high you would not actually see the explosion when it happened but read about it in the paper the next day. Perhaps people in nearby towns would commission you to fire this rocket. Whatever, we had plenty of these left over.

We set them off from a pipe hammered into the ground. They flew up with a hideous shower of flame, climbed out of sight, and just plain blew up. No artistic flowers, no cascades of colors: they simply hurled themselves into the sky and spat out a bang. Big deal. We soon learned that the smaller and more inventive items yielded greater entertainment value. Here were the various tools of the child's arsenal, which I repeat now for upcoming generations deprived of fireworks.

From lesser to greater:

Sparklers

Still around. Bogus fireworks, really: they didn't explode, and hence were considered kiddy stuff. That a wire coated with chemicals that burned white-hot and threw off a shower of crackling sparks was considered kiddy stuff ought to tell you about the attitudes toward fireworks in those days.

Ladyfingers

Small firecrackers. Dainty. Ladylike. Only good uses: lighting it in someone's back pocket or putting it in a soft-drink bottle and having gunfights. Bottles were thicker back then. I think. I do recall the look on my mom's face when she saw me loading firecrackers into a pop bottle; it was a look that said Explosion + Glass = Blindness = Guide Dog = Messes on the Rug. So we laid off the bottles. It was hard work explaining why the back pocket of your jeans had been blown off, however.

Black Cats

The real stuff. You did not fool around with Black Cats. You lit them and you ran. They looked incredibly cool, from the snarling beast on the label to the nasty black 'crackers themselves. They were also a good source of raw gunpowder; if you had infinite Black Cats at your disposal, as I did, you could pour out the gunpowder and conduct interesting experiments, such as blowing the lids of baby food jars fifty feet in the air and watching them hit a car on the way down.

Cherry Bombs and M-80s

There was some dispute over which of these was the most explosive, but both were bad news—not so much fireworks as dynamite junior. Cherry bombs had a certain cachet, due to their shape—so innocent!—and their being waterproof. (Drop 'em in a pond. Instant fish!) M-80s, however, had sheer murderous reputation going for them: drop one of them in a trash can, and you'd think a gas main had erupted.

My cousins out at the farm found an additional use for M-80s: thinning the frog herd. They'd catch a frog, stick a lit M-80 in his gullet, and let him go.

Hop.

Hop.

Hop. *POOOMPH*

Cruel, but kids have to learn anatomy some way. Even if it means picking it off the nearby trees.

Bottle Rockets

No Fourth was complete without the mosquitolike whine of bottle rockets past your ear. They came in two varieties: one type whizzed around and blew up, the other flew up and fell strangely silent, almost reprovingly. We sent up many payloads on bottle rockets, usually an insect taped to the side (but only on the type that exploded), legs waving in protest. These made a dramatic appearance in my second year of college, when my dorm had bottle-rocket wars with the fraternity house across the street, making the neighborhood a sort of Beirut Lite.

Roman Candles

If you haven't had a Roman candle duel, you haven't lived. One of these days I am going to write a story about children imbued with a nineteenth-century code of honor: after a slight insult, one of them slaps the other and says, "Candles at dawn, if you please," and strides off.

We did this only once, and no one caught fire. But it was a stupid thing to do, and we knew it. But I can still feel that little kick of the candle, hear the *PHOOMP* of the flaming ball as it discharges. They make for terrifying weapons, and it's a wonder gangs don't use them. Drive-by candlings would make quite an impression.

Whirling Metal Blades

I'm amazed these ever made it through customs. They went under varying aliases, but the basic design was always the same: a sharp little pinwheel of tin, powered by a furious charge of explosives. They had that thick fuse that said, This one means business. You lit it, ran like hell, then turned around in horror to behold the thing rising up, spinning, shrieking out a droning moan that sounded like a bug that had gorged on jalapeños. It came after you like it knew you. Like it had some unfinished business. But it always died and fell back to earth before it reached you. They were awful. Naturally, they came in packs of twelve.

Any sensible person might wonder where my parents were during this. They were watching, of course, which is why I got only halfway through that famed Showdown at the Roman Candle Corral. No one was ever hurt. When we count our memories on our fingers, we can make it to ten.

Fireworks are banned in more and more places nowadays, and what's permitted are usually elaborate little peacocks that hiss and spit sparks, and that's it. That, and sparklers. In my day, that would have been the stuff we exploded on July third, just to get primed. But that's all forbidden now, and all I can do is go to one fireworks display after another, watch it with other serene and careful adults, and recall when the punk was once in my hand.

And if you believe that pious nonsense, think again. I have a whole box of the stuff in the basement. All ready. Just waiting. Any one up for some Bottle Rocket Tag? Any Cherry Bomb Hot-Box? (Bring your asbestos glove!) Hand me that punk, and damn your ordinances: it's the Fourth of July, and I say, Let's light it. And run.

Driving Misfortune

∿∿

EVERYONE THINKS NO ONE KNOWS HOW TO DRIVE, EXCEPT FOR them.

Everyone is wrong, except for me.

These thoughts are not the product of spending a few days driving around with my wife. Oh, no. Not at *all*. But we were discussing my driving the other day, and, as I selected the chisel that would pry her fingers from the car door handle, we hit upon the aforementioned mystery of life. She regards my driving as a form of serial murder with insurance; I believe that her driving skills are those of someone who believes that somewhere in the world, a light may be turning yellow. My wife has an excellent driving record, although this is due mostly to the fact that I become so impatient with her preferred speed that I leap from the car, jog ahead, and alert her to any trouble spots via walkie-talkie.

Each other's mode of driving is not a problem with us, unless, of course, we are in the same car. But even then, it doesn't trouble us: I am busy swearing, and she has her hands full, what with hyperventilating and clawing for the door handle and wiping my spittle off the windshield so I can see, so we rarely argue.

I'm prepared to accept that none of us are capable drivers. There may be one lone human being on earth who has mas-

tered automotive travel, and he is in all probability stuck in
a mile-long pile-up in Calcutta, weeping hot tears of fury
because he was not born in Switzerland, where at least they
signal their turns.

More than likely, no one knows how to drive, period.

For the last two years I haven't driven much; I walk as
often as possible, or trust my life to the vigorously suicidal
cabbies of Washington, all of whom were probably expelled
from their home countries for vehicular murder and who jab-
ber into their two-way radios elaborate plans for sending me
through the windshield. But recently I began to miss driving—
the dance of the pedals and gears, the merry jousting of city
traffic, the hard glory of keeping last-minute mergers from
darting in front of me, the gentle thud of bicycle messengers
bouncing off my hood, the melodic tinkle of their spokes on
the pavement.

I got in the car and nosed back into the world of Other
Drivers ... and then it all came back.

Fact #1: You, you, and, in particular, you, are a wretched
driver. Most of you zoom along clad in a frangible shell of
tin and diffidence, secure in your immortality. Some of you
seem to have wired your fuel injectors directly to your testicles; your purpose is to get other drivers to roll over on their
backs and present their throats in submission. A few of you
are too pure and good to drive the speed limit, poking along
like you're the pace car for a molasses viscosity test, believing
that the slower you drive, the more the rest of us can read
your anti-nuclear-weapons bumperstickers and absorb their
deep, life-changing messages. (Telling indication of bump-
ersticker efficacy: No one has ever, ever parked their car,
strolled up to the first person they met, and said, "Come to
think of it, you really *can't* hug your child with nuclear
arms.") All of you are bad drivers.

Fact #2. So am I.

I know the first because I nearly end up eating taillights
each time I drive; I know the second because my wife tells
me so. Through her comments on my driving—if a terrified
peal of blurted monosyllables can be called a "comment"—I

have come to understand that I am a worse driver than anyone else.

This is a shock to me. Like most men, I have long regarded myself as a skilled operator. Back in Minnesota, I was able to hit an ice patch, shift gears, steer out of the skid, light a cigarette, replace the lid on my coffee cup, and change the radio station in a car without my heart rate changing.

I always presume that oncoming traffic is nuts, but not unreasonably nuts. Sure, he might make a left turn in front of me, in which case we would both fly through the windshield. But he probably won't. There's no need for me to reduce my speed to three mph and send up warning flares everytime I approach an intersection. If we hit, we hit; at least let's have enough speed so we can pass in the air, perhaps exchange pleasantries.

My wife, however, seems to think my driving philosophy has one simple rule: *If you can't read my mind, you deserve to die.*

As a modus vivendi, it has its merits and an almost Stalinesque clarity. But it is not the case with me. I know people can't read my mind, as the roads are not filled with people who have pulled over and knelt as I pass. If other drivers could read my mind, they would not pull alongside with their windows down, playing bass-heavy music that sounds like rhinos copulating inside a timpani. If they did get in front of me and turn on their left-turn signal, they would know enough to throw the car in park, run back, and thrust money at me to compensate for the inconvenience.

But they don't, so I have to believe they are all idiots. (And thus deserve to die.) This, I always thought, was a good assumption and made me a good driver.

I now know the truth. As a driver I am incapable of determining the correct amount of idiocy present on the road. That is set by the battlefield observer in the passenger seat, who is busily toting up sins and noting infractions.

Since we all know for certain that everyone is a bad driver, it is clear that all driving should be left to the passengers, who obviously know best.

We must retrofit our cars with the following accessories:

- A passenger-side brake
- A passenger-side public-address system to warn everyone of our approach
- A passenger-side air bag that unfurls the moment you turn the key
- Passenger-side controls for spraying handwritten letters of apology for that sudden lane-shift

Only this way can we be safe. Of course, we could always stop every few miles and exchange cars; we'd be more hesitant to make a sudden stupid stop if the car behind us was ours. But then we'd have to exchange passengers too. If I bolted from my lane and the guy driving my car smacked into me, I don't know who I'd be more angry with—him, for hitting me . . .

Or my wife for not warning him.

Take My Money—Please

IT WAS NOT UNTIL I MOVED TO WASHINGTON THAT I MET A
species of humanity foreign to the Midwest: a banker who
does not want your money. In the Midwest, you showed up
with money, and the banker smiled, thanked you, took your
cash into the back room, and immediately began to shave off
service charges. Not here. Big-city bankers seem to have
made an uncomfortable discovery: when people deposit
money in your bank, *they may someday want it back*. And so
they have developed a brilliant system designed to keep the
ordinary citizen from opening an account.

I'm here to report that the system works.

The neighborhood bank I visited was undergoing renova-
tion, and the waiting room was now a dingy niche reeking of
cleaning chemicals. My seat was bolted to the floor, just in
case anyone took the injunction to "Have a Seat" too literally. I passed a dry hour studying the posters on the wall;
they were the usual cheery gobbledygook, with big shiny pictures of people balancing their checkbook and beaming so
hard you feared the tendons in their jaw would snap and the
top of their head would loll backward.

I cannot imagine smiling when I balance my checkbook,
unless the monthly statement came with a little pouch of
ether that erupted when I opened the envelope. For that

126

matter, I cannot imagine balancing my checkbook at all. I did it once, discovered that I was in the hole, and never tried it again: couldn't see the point. I don't pick fights I can't win. For the last decade I have kept track of my checking balance solely through intuition, the amount of money a vague, amorphous blob that is either Comfortingly Big, Alarmingly Tiny, or Just Right, depending on how I feel about my spending. My ideal bank statement is a postcard that reminds me to get out the Magic 8-Ball, shake it hard, and ask, "Am I Overdrawn?" (And if it says "Cloudy; try later," isn't that the occult version of "The Computer Is Down?")

It's my way of dealing with money, but not one that strikes me as all that sensible. I am an adult now; it was time to round matters down to the nearest hundred. This new account would be my fresh start. I would break all bad habits. No more would I have three checkbooks going simultaneously— one wearing the respectable plastic cover, the other two naked and dog-eared, hiding in coats or drawers or glove compartments. No more panicked round-ups of all active checkbooks when the account dropped by a thousand dollars in one day, and I was convinced that one of them had been stolen. (It was rent that did it.) (Usually.) From now on I would deduct everything diligently, note all service charges, and grin hideously when I did so. My jaw would snap off and my head fly back, I would be so happy. Cruel kids would play tiddlywinks into my windpipe, but I wouldn't care. I would know my balance down to the last penny.

As I sat in the waiting room, plotting my bright and brave future, I considered branching into other financial vehicles, preferably ones that would keep me from spending my money. Preferably forever. Not just a long-term CD. Something like a Dead Sea D—a certificate of deposit that was placed in a dark cave, buried, forgotten, and unearthed five thousand years later. Your descendants would get the interest, if anyone could decipher the terms. (Substantial penalty for early disinterment.) I liked that idea. I could feel thick, rich financial probity coursing through my veins. Once I had my new account, I was going to be a new man.

Then I heard my name. I got up—and found myself staring at the woman in charge of turning down new accounts.

She had a face so hard that an air bag would probably blow from her nose if you tried to kiss her. The posture of a bulldog having its temperature taken rectally. She led me over to her desk, pointed to a grim metal chair that looked like a Bauhaus thesis statement, and bade me to sit. I told her I wanted to open an account and watched her face twist into a rictus of dismay.

"Do you have any identification?"

I said I did and reached for my wallet.

"The rules specify that we need *two* forms of ID."

The way she said *"rules"* made me think of something slim and golden in the back room, lit by a single spot, surrounded by kneeling tellers. I produced a Minnesota driver's license, a work ID, an expired passport, and my original Social Security card, an ancient document as thin as my chances of ever seeing the money I've paid into Social Security. She looked over the documents, then slowly raised her eyes to mine.

"Anything the matter?"

"A major credit card?"

I didn't have one. If I'd had a credit card, I wouldn't have any money to deposit. I'm not responsible enough; I'd charge everything and end up paying eighteen percent interest on Slim Jims.

"I, ah, don't have one. My wife does. Sometimes she lets me look at it."

Frowns. "I'm afraid that without a second piece of identification, I can't accept a deposit."

Second piece? There were four pieces there. I could get into the Army with less identification.

"Well, to begin with," she said, "I can't accept the work ID. That is not acceptable identification."

Oh, of *course* not. "What name would you like to go under this time?" is such a common inquiry employers make when they hire you. A work ID, naturally, proves nothing.

"This Social Security card isn't acceptable; it doesn't have your picture on it. And—" she added with a special scowl, "the signature is quite different from the signature on the other IDs."

"I was fourteen when I got that card," I said. Irritation was starting to scratch at the back of my neck. "Handwriting changes after you lose your virginity."

Oh, it did, did it? *How did you get this card,* her eyes said, *and what did you do with the little fourteen-year-old virgin who owned it?* I pointed out that the signature closely matched the one on my passport.

"And that is expired, sir." *Don't plan on going abroad again? Bounce some checks while running guns in Bosnia, is that it?*

"It has my picture." There was the seal of the government stamped into the left side of my face, the words UNITED STATES GOVERNMENT appearing to rise from my flesh, *Exorcist*-like, as though I had been possessed by a Federalist.

"An expired passport is not acceptable identification."

"Look, what's the point of this? To prove I am who I say I am, right? Let's use some deductive reasoning. The Social Security card has no picture, but it has a signature, which matches the passport, which *has* a picture. Granted, an old one, with a far more robust hairline, but that's me. See the scowl line on the picture?" I pointed to my forehead. "See the scowl line here?"

"Sir—"

"Now look at the driver's license and the work ID—both have my name, picture, and scowl-induced wrinkle. Cumulatively, it's all spells *me*. Either that, or I have been engaged, since the age of fourteen in a complicated scheme of duping employers, state licensing agencies, and federal agencies with the sole objective of one day coming here and tricking you into giving me a savings account at a poor rate of return. If that's the case, call Interpol; I'm probably wanted in five countries for trading dollars at below the posted exchange rate."

No good. She shook her head with the slight firmness of one who does not make the rules, but merely enforces them with a great deal of pleasure.

"I'm sorry. But I must have a current license, a credit card, or a current passport."

"Do you believe I am who I say I am?"

She admitted, lips tight, that she did.

"That's not the point, sir. It's a matter of procedure. Today I have had to turn down six people for the same reason; it wouldn't be fair to them if I bent the rules for you, would it?"

Fair! Good God, seven people had come to her today and attempted—nay, begged—to hand over piles of money. Here! Take this! Loan it out at a higher interest rate than what you're giving me, and hey—*keep the change!* Even more, charge me needless service fees for the privilege! I don't mind!

"Sorry," she repeated. "It's just the rules."

I found another bank, a New York–based concern heavily involved in South American loans. Their slogan: "Yo! Over Here. We're Hurtin'." I gave them the same forms of ID, and the clerk waved them away. "As long as your money's green," she said, "it's all right with us."

I looked at my travelers checks.

"Actually, my money's blue. Blue-green. Almost turquoise, really."

"Close enough," she said. "As long as the signature matches." She verified this by consulting my Social Security card and passport.

I got my first statement a month later. It was not, of course, a suggestion that I consult the Magic 8-Ball. This bank is far more up-to-date. They use a Ouija board.

I only wish *Overdrawn* wasn't such a long word to spell out.

Bow Wow

∿∿∿∿∿∿∿∿∿∿∿∿∿∿∿∿∿∿∿∿∿∿∿∿∿∿∿∿∿∿∿∿∿∿∿∿∿∿∿

I'D LIKE TO BEGIN WITH A PRAYER FOR NEXT YEAR'S JUNIOR high graduation. I'll try not to offend anyone.

O Bigger-Than-Us, we—and by "we" I mean several of us but not, by any means, all—beseech you to hear our words and then ignore them completely. In fact, forget we called; sorry to bother you. Unless you don't exist, of course. Amen.

This ought to pass Supreme Court muster, wouldn't you think? It's nondenominational, in that it's addressed to Bigger-Than-Us, which could be God, Montana, or the Empire State Building. It is respectful of those who don't believe there's anything up there listening to prayers and who cannot be asked to bow their heads and fall silent without hearing the sound of the Bill of Rights being hacked to shreds.

No, it still isn't good enough. Last week's Supreme Court decision banning prayer at school graduation ceremonies made it clear that no matter how gaseous you make the prayer, it cannot be performed in a building whose very existence is due to taxpayers handing over money that says, "In God We Trust." Go figure.

It was the correct decision to make, in the sense that giving your wallet to the man holding a gun to your temple is a correct decision. Whenever the court is backed up against the wall on church-and-state matters, it has to come down on the side of separation. We don't want the establishment of a state religion here, as in Saudi Arabia, where the religious police are permitted to whip with sticks any woman not modestly attired. There aren't enough trees in North America for the necessary sticks. You'd have to level Yellowstone just to deal with Madonna. Best to leave religion to the private realm and be content with that.

Having said the nice civil-liberty litany, however, I have a piece of advice for the folks who saved the nation from the plague of nondenominational prayer at graduation: Next time, shut up. Let them pray.

I don't say this as a practicing God-botherer hot to turn every public event into an eye-rolling holy hootenanny. I rarely pray; I figure that one of the benefits of being lorded over by an omnipresent being is that you don't have to address Him directly. (If He's taking notes, then I assume He consults the transcripts from time to time.) I mention this only because every professional chin-puller who's applauded this ruling has preceded their comment by expressing how precious their faith is and painted themselves as a pope-without-portfolio who is nevertheless pleased that thousands may no longer pray in a long-accustomed fashion.

Well, I have no particular attachment to any religion and have thus spent most of my adult life bowing my head and being commanded to pray in a variety of situations where I had nothing metaphysical in mind at all. If there were a thought balloon over my head, it would read idle thoughts about where we were going to go for pie and coffee afterward. But I put my head down because it was the thing to do. And it cost me nothing.

The position of the plantiffs, of course, is that prayer in a civic setting is different. Coercion is involved, the insidious twisting of young minds. That's a valid objection to prayer in grade school, but by tenth grade, any incipient agnosticism is not likely to buckle and snap after one public prayer. As for coercion, who says you have to pray as directed? If you're of a different religion, consult your version of the top boss. If you're an athiest, contemplate the existence of a fifth force, which scientists believe may be the stuff that holds the universe together and is probably lint in God's pocket. Whatever.

This, I know, is philosophically unjustifiable in our secular government. The right not to have to bow your head is an important one. But unless there are grim matrons with crosses on their sleeves boxing the ears of anyone who does not tilt their head to the federally mandated angle, there is no coercion. There is the persuasive force of the majority—you don't want to stand there unbowed, looking like a godless heathen. But it should not be difficult to make the moral calculation and decide that bearing a slight inconvenience is of nominal consequence to yourself, whereas summoning the iron hand of the state to swoop down and muzzle those who innocently toss off a thank-you note to the architect of the galaxy is far more destructive.

It is a difficult concept nowadays, but we need to be reminded of it: Live and let live. Or as the book of Moderations has it, "Sweat not the small stuff shall thou, until seventy times seven." Let 'em pray. And look for me with my head bowed and an expression of beatitude on my face. Pie and coffee: two of God's greatest gifts.

Up, Up, and Awry

~~~~~~

YOU CAN'T SMOKE ON AIRPLANES ANYMORE. IT OFFENDS PEOple who do not want their air sullied by secondhand smoke, or, as we smokers call it, "Previously owned smoke." Frankly, I believe that when you are at thirty thousand feet in the heavens, you ought be grateful for whatever air you can get. As it is, I cannot get any air when I fly; I am too busy hyperventilating. Only by a good, satisfying pull on a cigarette can I get anything into my lungs at all. And that is why I hate to fly: since they banned smoking, I worry I'll die of asphyxiation.

The ban on smoking was the only change I noticed when I broke my six-year hiatus and returned to the skies. Everything else was pretty much the same: the planes still refuse to do the sensible thing and taxi the entire way to their destination or at least fly at a level where you could, if so pressed, hop out like someone jumping from a boxcar. They still thunder into the skies with the desperation of a fat man leaping for a ferry that has pulled away from the dock. The captain is still from Macon, Georgia, and unimpressed by anything.

Most of all, the entire experience is still one long howling interval of misery and terror, with free peanuts.

Let me explain. I stopped flying because I had developed a panic disorder that gave me such a morbid dread of enclosed places I had to take tranquilizers to get a sweater over my head. I also have a fear of heights, meaning my idea of Hell was standing on a footstool in an elevator. The notion of being locked—*locked!*—in a narrow hallway with chairs, hurtling high above the earth, is enough to give me lurid hives and a twitching sphincter. I never had nightmares about flying, but only because in my dreams I was too terrified to board; in every dream I am stuck at the door, with arms and feet grappling the side of the plane like a cat being shoved down a toilet.

But even before I went mildly insane, I was a nervous flier. I've never thought it was a good idea. If flying is safer than driving, why don't we fly to the airport to catch the plane? Why isn't the parking lot of your local 7-Eleven clogged with Cessnas instead of Hondas? I'll tell you why: If your engine fails on the way to the store and you're in a car, they will not be picking you out of a cornfield with tweezers. In the air you rarely pass a plane just sitting there with its hood up. If your electrical system goes out, as frequently happens with my car, it's a merry corkscrew into the stony bosom of Mother Earth, with the cabin all aswirl with bad paperbacks and untethered infants, and you *can't even have a last cigarette because you packed them away before you boarded.* Thus you spend your last minute bumming a cigarette from the man next to you, who insists on trying to scrawl a letter to his wife, and big help he turns out to be. Finally he gives you one; you light it seconds before the plane hits, and your last thought is: Oh, great, *it's a menthol.*

The last plane ride I took was an uneventful flight to New York—uneventful in the sense that my heart did not, technically, burst from my chest and fling itself at the door, but it wanted to. I sat in the back, eyes scanning the ground below for the appearance of a huge, acres-wide pillow. Something we could aim for. I spent the entire flight drinking wine—not something I usually do at eight in the morning, but the only other liquor available was a Bloody Mary, which sounded as appealing as a Dental-Records Fizz or an Unexpected-Loss-of-Cabin-Pressure Colada. The stewardess, struggling to convey her displeasure through a death mask of makeup, asked if wine would be all right, and I said it certainly would, prefer- ably in a syringe for more immediate and efficacious applica- tion. I had liquor-spins by the time we landed and was convinced the entire plane was pinwheeling through the sky. *"Hell of a landing,"* I said to my seatmate, *"and a great pilot, considering the plane was making those 360-degree turns."* I got off the plane and fell asleep in the departure lounge.

A few days later, I had to do it again. The memory of the previous flight—during which, of course, nothing happened— had now metastasized into a tempest-toss'd interlude of terror and danger, while the new flight lay ahead as fresh misery redoubled. I showed up early at the airport, proceeded to the bar, tilted my head at the precise angle that renders the gag reflex somewhat inactive, and poured several neat scotches down my gullet. It worked: by the time I got to the gangplank to the plane, it was heaving like a rope bridge in a gale, and I bumped through the crowd to my seat in the middle of the plane. Middle row. People to the right and left, fore and aft: I would never be noticed in the middle of such a crowd. Death would not call on me unless I put my hand up. If we crashed, I would just stand up and walk away.

I made it home safe, of course. But the experience was followed by several months of crashing-plane dreams that, when coupled with an increasing bout of panic attacks, made me so hesitant to do anything that I made Howard Hughes look like a drum majorette high-stepping down Main Street on the Fourth of July. When I had to travel, I did so by train, by sleeper car—the equivalent of traveling in your bedroom to New York. And so I passed from the world of air travel and felt myself all the safer because of it.

Things change, though. The panic attacks passed. I contin- ued to travel by train but grew weary spending large portions of my vacation time in the Chicago train station, where the train has a layover four times longer than the time it takes to fly the entire distance. While the layover yielded unique delights each time—fresh urine stains instead of old ones, an unfamiliar maniac in the restroom, coffee from the cafeteria that tasted like a burnt rat had climbed into the pot—you can take only so many eight-hour layovers before you wonder if there's not a better way. Worst of all, no planes ever crashed while I was on a train, which seemed unfair. I consoled myself by noting that I had not been on any planes; if I had, they would have crashed. But still.

Finally I was left with five vacation days, four of which would be taken up by a train trip. I wanted to go home for the State Fair, see friends, leave the blistering hell of D.C. for the easy green heaven of Minneapolis. If I took the train, I would have enough time for lunch, maybe dessert. It was fly or stay.

I shrugged and decided I'd fly.

My wife, who quite accurately regards my attitude toward planes as proof she will never see Paris, was astonished: *Really? Really? You're going to fly? Really?* Really! Really, I said; leave me alone. Let's not talk about it. You'll jinx the plane. The more we talk about it, the looser the bolts get on the plane I will be taking, the more fatigue will tax the metal. I want to sneak up on this plane. Can't let it know I'm there.

Yes, stealth was the key. I made the reservation in a stage whisper. The ticket clerk played along, and gave me my reservation number, TOQR895882191. *That's T as in Tragedy; O as in Omega; Q as in Quietus; R as in Reaper; 8–9–58 as in your date of birth; T as in Thantanos, Greek god of Death; 2–19–91 as in your flight date and last day on earth. Okay? Thank you for flying Icarus Air.*

Now I had a decision to make: intoxicated or tranquilized? There is something unpleasant about flying pixilated—time passes slowly, you can't read your book, and whatever sympathy you get from the stews when you throw up is negated when they note the platoon of miniature bottles on your table tray. Plus, you arrive bloodshot and insensate, in no condition to appreciate the hugs and handshakes of your friends. Worse yet, you are five minutes into hugs and handshakes before you realize that you don't know these people. I consulted a medical professional and received several pills the size of fruit fly larvae, with the instruction to take half a pill before take-off and half if I still felt anxious.

I took a whole pill when the ticket showed up in my mailbox.

In addition, I was warned not to drink, as that might send me into unconsciousness. My eyes lit up at that: the best of all worlds, here. Then I looked up in a drug encyclopedia the results of mixing this pill with alcohol, and learned that I just might sleep the dreamless sleep from which none shall e'er wake. That was disheartening, but only for a second: I realized that if the plane started to crash, I could knock down a quick one and be dead before we hit the ground. People would envy me: *Look at him. Some people sleep through anything.*

I showed up at the airport an hour early and sat outside on a hill. I was full of a sense of imminent mortality and thus regarded the natural world with a wise and sorrowful eye: O blade of grass. O tree. O cloud—no, skip the clouds. O beetle. I made my peace with the world and chain-smoked the longest brand of cigarette the law allows, then went inside the happily named building known as the terminal.

Pill number one went sliding down the throat when they made the first call. I felt an immediate tap of a hammer on my forebrain, a wand swung by a burly fairy godmother. I was now calm. Unusually so. When I stood, my legs did not quite get the idea and went all rubbery: a good sign. I walked merrily down the tunnel and stepped into an airplane for the first time in six years.

It was as I had remembered. Tiny seats, canned air, muted music playing from hidden speakers. I took my seat and buckled up, put on my headphones and listened to some gaseous New Age music full of peace and mystery. Within fifteen seconds, however, my eyes snapped open like window shades and I was looking for the exit. This was not a deep-down tranquilizer; it merely put a pillow over the face of your anxieties. You could still feel them struggle. I took another. The tap to the brain was, this time, a John-Henry, Pile-Drivin'-Man swing. I fell asleep in seconds.

Hours later, the gentle sway of the plane woke me up. I didn't open my eyes but wondered with a benevolent sense of disinterest where we were. Then the plane stopped. Stopped. Ah, I thought. Some happy perceptual illusion. It only seems like we were stopping. My eyes opened lazily, and I looked out the window.

Still on the Tarmac.

At that moment the engines whined to life and the plane hurtled forward. Panic started up my throat but got lost, faded away, replaced by warm loving trust of the pilot and the Boeing airplane company. I fell back to sleep as we were still climbing, and when I woke again, the towers of Minneapolis were outside my window. Touchdown was as gentle as a kiss. (Well, a kiss after you've been at sea for a year.) I'd done it.

The real test, of course, is the return flight: doing it again. I went to the airport with none of the flaming misery I'd expected, made no eulogies to the world. This was normal. Rote. People did it every day. I still took two pills.

And this time, nothing. The previous trip, I should mention, had been prefaced by a sleepless night, which, when coupled with the tiny white pill, meant a bullet-train ride to oblivion. This time, I was rested. Conscious. Hideously aware. I rode the plane up like a sack of dough, slack-jawed with tranquilizers and misery. Didn't sleep at all, but sat there staring hot holes in the seat in front of me. Eventually the stews came by with the meals, which I ate with dull fascination, unsure what any of it was. When the stew with the drink cart came by and asked if I wanted something, I looked up at her and said the only word present and accounted for in my consciousness: "LUNCH," I said, dully, like Frankenstein shoveling in victuals. "FOOD, GOOD." I eventually got out the word DECAF and was rewarded. Still couldn't sleep.

The flight was without incident, even though the pilot came on the PA system to warn of "light chop" ahead, something that made me fear bright giant mincing knives were about to flash from the sky and crease our fuselage. The landing was unpleasantly thrilling. Only when the plane was on the ground and moving at the speed my mother drives in parking lots while looking for a spot, did I finally relax.

In order for all this to mean something, however, I would have to fly again and do so without chemical assistance. Otherwise, the accomplishment would be no greater than, say, sitting through a Wagner opera while sedated. I am happy to report that I now fly all over the place and actually enjoy it. I've stopped trying to steer the plane from my seat—leaning left when the plane banks right, for example—and I just sit there and take it. Here's how blasé I've become. A while back I was in a plane that was taxiing to the runway when the engines of the plane suddenly ... stopped. The pilot informed us that they'd "ground off a rod," which sounded incredibly painful; every man in the plane crossed his legs. He said we'd have to go back for repairs.

Hey, I thought. That was it. That was the malfunction I'd always feared. The plane crashed, *but we were already on the ground*.

I won!

Tick Tick Tick

〜〜〜〜〜〜〜〜〜〜〜〜〜〜〜〜〜〜〜〜〜〜〜〜〜〜〜〜〜〜〜

IT HAS BEEN A BAD YEAR FOR INSOMNIACS WITH ARTIFICIAL breasts. First, the news that silicone implants may leak and cause all manner of health problems; now, the news that Halcion, the world's most popular sleeping pill, may cause amnesia, paranoia, and hallucination. It's a novel approach to a sleeping disorder: granted, you're still awake, but now it's far more interesting.

Before Halcion: (Yawn) Gee, I wish I could sleep.

After Halcion: Sleep? SLEEP? When I remember the names of the six-foot tall gecko lizards the government sent to get me, then I'll sleep!

Before the lawyers rear up on their hind legs—and dung beetles have two pair—I should note that nothing has been proven, yet. Just because some people take a tranq and get as jumpy as a cat in a roomful of upended thumbtacks doesn't mean the product is generally unsafe. President Bush took a Halcion the day before he deposited an inventory of the day's meals into the lap of the Japanese prime minister, and that doesn't mean that all Halcion users feel a need to woof in the direction of major trading partners.

Nor are the artificial breasts necessarily unsafe. No, there's nothing inherently dangerous in embedding welded Ziploc bags full of Silly Putty in your body, nothing at all. A few, of course, may indeed leak. (Hint: If you have replaced all the washers in your house and you still can't sleep because you hear that maddening drip, see a doctor. Or, of course, take a Halcion.) Dow Corning, the silicone maker, is no doubt kicking itself for not promoting penile implants; even if they went hideously awry, not a man in the land would stand to admit he had one.

No, the real issue is whether or not the companies deliberately covered up studies that showed the products might be dangerous. This may be the case. According to a dozen movies I've seen, devious, evil corporations regularly put unsafe products on the market. Their purpose would seem to be to make a pile of money in the short run, and then, after a charismatic and altruistic team of lawyers and/or journalists discovers their perfidity, to lose ten times the amount they made in lawsuit costs after a moving summation speech to a quietly outraged jury. (Fiendishly clever, these companies.) Here is some sample movie dialogue:

Journalist #1: "You mean they knew that one out of every fifty million *Little Engine That Could* pop-up books might have sharp edges that could cut a child, and they still went ahead with plans to market them?"

Journalist #2: "That's right. I have the document right here. Says that a one in fifty million chance of loss of faith in the little Engine was an 'acceptable risk.'"

Journalist #1: "Those bastards."

Of course, that is how Hollywood sees capitalism. Why an industry whose main product is endless depictions of how to kill people should be so hep on pushing the notion of product liability, I have no idea. But they are vaguely right in their perception of journalists, whose job requires them to dredge up corporate malfeasance and, to impress their overlords, pump up true concerns until the bejesus is thoroughly scared from everyone.

60 Minutes is a good example. About every other week, they give us a Death-Chemical story. Each piece features the same cast of characters. The oily corporate spokesperson who'd shoot DDT down his grandmother's throat with a blowgun if it meant keeping his job. The suburban mother of two on a crusade against immense odds, helped only by her sense of outrage and a flattering portrayal on the most popular news program in the galaxy. The segment usually concludes with shot of the family walking in the park, grimly relieved that little Billy is okay because they stopped feeding him Alar/MSG/Cap'n Crunch/pencil shavings/whatever.

I tend to believe the journalists on these matters, on the stopped-clock-is-right-twice-a-day principle. When you set out to prove that everything manufactured and approved is lethal, you are occasionally correct. But this is no way to regulate public safety. On one hand, we have the media, ever crying wolf; on the other, the companies insisting there is no wolf, and besides, it's safely in a cage.

Isn't there supposed to be regulatory body in the middle somewhere? We've heard for years that the FDA is a rigorous, inflexible body that takes ten years to pass water, let alone a drug. But it now appears that drugs are certified by a narcoleptic with a rubber stamp that reads APPROVED tied to his head. Whatever petition he falls asleep upon goes sailing through to the marketplace.

The solution is simple: every prescription should carry not just the ingredients but the FDA seal of approval (designed to resemble a tortoise with its fingers crossed), the *60 Minutes* seal of approval (a little stopwatch), and a number indicating the volume of internal memorandums the drug maker suppresses. This way we can make educated decisions like informed consumers.

Or we can go back to padded bras and warm milk.

Espressocide

〜〜〜〜〜〜〜〜〜〜〜〜〜〜〜〜〜〜〜〜〜〜〜〜〜〜〜〜〜〜〜

LIKE ALL RIGHT-THINKING AMERICANS, I WATCH THE DRUG raids on the evening news with a grim sense of vindication: this is what their sort deserves. But I also realize that if coffee were criminalized, I would be shoving fistfuls of money through holes in the window screen for my handful of beans, then scurrying off to cook them up over a butane lighter. That is a predictable observation, of course, and wrong as well. Coffee and crack differ in several key ways.

- People lose their jobs because they're always out looking for cocaine, whereas coffee is thoughtfully provided at the workplace.
- Cocaine is more expensive when ground, cheaper when sold in crack rocks; coffee, vice versa. Go figure.
- Crack, to its credit, does not come in amaretto-vanilla flavor.
- Crack does not stain your teeth.
- Coffee-shop cashiers are unlikely to accuse you of being the police and shoot you; then again, crack dens rarely have need-a-penny-take-a-penny cups near the place where you pay.

No, coffee is a drug, and a damn fine one; it quickens the

mind without addling your faculties. It's Lutheran cocaine. I remember as a kid how everyone filed down into the church basement after services for coffee—brewed in huge urns with eggs and pinches of salt. It was the smell of the adult world, the one true Reformation sacrament. This is my java, ground for thee.

I started to abuse the stuff in high school and actually got in trouble because of it once. Coming home from a late night in an Embers restaurant, so beaned up I must have looked like one of those Ed "Big Daddy" Roth cartoons—bloodshot eyes bursting from my skull, tongue trailing from a wide, grinning mouth—I blew through a red light and promptly drew the attention of a nearby policeman. He pulled me over. Asked if I'd been drinking.

"Onlycoffeesir," I replied.

"Coffee doesn't make you go through a red light," he said.

"Itdoesifyou'reaLutheransir," I said.

He let me go. It was my first brush with the dangers of coffee. I have since discovered others.

Frequent Urination

I hate to be indelicate, but there is nothing like coffee for making one feel as though a hot and highly pressurized basketball has appeared in your lower abdomen. There have been several incidents when I have gone to bleed the pipes and been knocked on my tailbone by the force of the stream against the porcelain. I have solved this by means of a leather harness, much like telephone linemen use to keep themselves in place. Once secured, there is naught to do but wait. Shifting from foot to foot every few minutes helps to ward against the formation of bunions.

Sleepless Nights

This is one consequence of coffee with which I have never been afflicted. My wife has an opposite reaction; one cup taken with an early supper, and three A.M. finds her in bed like a wooden two-by-four staring numb at the ceiling, all hopes of slumber abandoned. Whereas I can toss off a pot and sleep the sleep of the just, or at least the just whose pillows have been treated with chloroform. (Soak in five percent solution for one hour.)

One Cup Over the Line, or Nervous Degeneration

I frequently overshoot the limits of my caffeine consumption. On those days my natural temperament, already on the twitchy side, assumes the characteristics of a Scotch terrier getting a jump-start. The world starts to look like one of those TV commercials shot in a fast, blurry, off-kilter style, and I vibrate at such a high pitch that to others, I resemble a poorly erased chalkboard illustration.

Small details. But drinking several quarts of coffee cannot be good for one, and given that Krups has no plans to market a replacement kidney filter for one's kidneys, I began to look for ways to cut down on my coffee drinking. The solution: a substance that would deliver all the punch of ten cups in one quick, potent serving. Espresso.

There was, however, more to the matter than I suspected.

I missed the eighties; no gadgets or shiny toys for me. At best I was able to afford socks in the colors made popular by *Miami Vice*. Now that I had my fingertips on the bottom rung of the punitive tax brackets, however, I felt as though I should have some of the objects that bespeak a certain place in the world. Such as an espresso maker. It's the perfect ostentatious possession: black, full of chrome protuberations, limited in usefulness. The very substance it makes—hot, bitter jumpjuice—is synonymous with pretension. And just to make it perfect, I do not particularly like espresso. *Espresso* has always struck me as a euphonic word for what you get when you leave the pot on the burner for seven hours. And cappuccino, all froth and sugar and milk and cinnamon, is to real coffee what a poodle is to a Great Dane.

In the post-gadget era, such self-indulgent devices are proof that one is out of step with the zeitgeist. Surely the steam from espresso machines destroys the ozone layer. Surely they ripped down rain forests to plant those beans. Surely you know that if everyone drank espresso, homeless people would suffer. (Smaller cups to hold out for change.) People, I have noticed, have taken to dismissing their machine, explaining that it's there for the guests. Well, I did not want the machine to accommodate dinner guests. My guests get coffee with caffeine or nothing, although they are welcome to stick their head under the tap. As a host I have noticed that if you just say, "Coffee?" people will still be satisfied, except for the idiot who will say yes to espresso and no to coffee and would probably be content with hot brackish dishwater if it came in a tiny cup that implied European traditions. (Party tip: Serve your espresso in huge, ugly galvanized tins, with a half-inch of espresso sloshing around the bottom, and see if anyone asks for seconds.)

No, I wanted the machine for what it said about me, the All-Around Man—that I could, if required, perform something both sophisticated and daring. (Fencing also falls into this category.) Plus, I wanted to accumulate those perks of pointless eighties consumerism I had missed. And so at Christmas I gave strong hints that an espresso maker would be welcome. It was under the tree as expected. I opened it with glee and paged excitedly through the instruction book.

And then I put it in the closet and started to nail the door shut.

It is a dangerous machine, I realized.

It has disfigured many people.

It will kill me if I don't use it right.

Let me explain. The machine looked innocent enough, although there was a red decal full of exclamation points on one side. DO NOT OPEN LID WHEN UNDER PRESSURE! it said in traditional crypto-German-English. So much for making espresso during dinner parties, I thought. Then an orange slip of paper fell from the instruction book. WARNING! DO NOT OPEN LID WHEN UNDER PRESSURE! First a decal, now what appeared to be an erratum slip—do you smell the sizzle of innocent consumers staggering back with their heads on fire? Do you detect the faint contours of a heated boardroom decision, seen dimly through opaque pebbled glass, with angry voices castigating the designers in German about how they could allow this to happen and grim resolutions to keep the product on the shelf but add stickers and warning slips?

Perhaps this was just a safety measure, I thought. A preventative step to indemnify the maker against a lawsuit should someone be foolish enough to . . . to open the lid? I went over to my old coffee maker, plugged in and happily burbling out a fresh pot, and opened the lid. Hellfire did not erupt. I read on. The first page was devoted entirely to caveats. Some were sensible; there was the standard prohibition against using the machine outdoors, in a moving vehicle, during a hailstorm (glass may shatter), while slaloming down a mountain, or while landing the space shuttle. I was advised not to use the device for other than its intended use, in case I had any ideas of pouring dirt into a $150 appliance and putting begonias in it or using its milk-steaming feature to remove wrinkles from my clothing.

I was also admonished against immersing it in water; perhaps the bright yellow "Sport" model of the espresso maker would be suitable for poolside use. Nor was it permitted to remove the base, although it did not seem possible to remove it without a bandsaw. And just in case I was in the habit of using a sponge-tipped sledgehammer to do my dishes, I was advised, "Never clean with hard implements." (That has the sound of a maxim. I endorse it. If I ever appear on a talk show, I intend to use it, and tilt my eyebrows sagely.)

The next few pages were given over to little pictures, nice little European scenes of happy folk making happy espresso AND NEVER REMOVING THE LID WHILE UNDER PRESSURE. I expected Tintin to stick his head in the frame and give me the thumbs-up. But then it was back to instructions—four pages of tiny print, with every other section headed ATTENTION! or CAUTION! Let me quote from one innocuous passage, typical of the instructions' occasional careen from carefree to panic-stricken.

> "Technically, one main difference is that the water will come to a boil and will then be forced through the ground coffee. This means that an espresso machine works under pressure and needs special attention. **We therefore ask you**

to read ALL the instructions, CAUTIONS, NOTES, AND ATTENTIONS."

The more I read, the more I was convinced my wife had bought me the Oppenheimer Li'l Atomic-Fission-O-Matic. As far as I could tell, the machine operated by heating water to a temperature of 1.7 bejillion degrees and forcing the steam through an aperture the dimensions of a gnat's urethra. (Unless, of course, you've REMOVED THE LID, in which case pieces of your hand, kitchen cabinet, and roof are blown into low orbit.) I now understood the danger.

But I had to try. Humming the theme from *Miami Vice* (try that sometime) I ground the coffee to the specified consistency, i.e., so fine it cannot be viewed without an electron microscope, and packed it loosely in the basket. I poured in the water, plugged it in, and hid under the bed upstairs. Then I recalled that the instructions suggested using the frothing attachment *in medias res*—if I frothed whilst the steam was screaming at the coffee, I would be assured of sufficient pressure. So I went downstairs and located the frothing attachment (for some reason I thought of a Brooklynite grabbing his crotch and shouting, *Hey! I got your frothing attachment, right here*) and dipped it in the pitcher of milk. The machine promptly exploded like a sailor on leave in a whorehouse, and I dropped the frothing pitcher in panic. There was milk everywhere. Bossie had a grand mal seizure. I tried it again, this time not turning on the frothing attachment until the stem was immersed in milk. The milk promptly frothed. The espresso was nearly done as well. In minutes my wife and I were raising glasses of hot, bitter joyjuice. It took twenty-five minutes to make and a minute to drink.

I did not remove the lid until the next day, and even then, I preceded the operation by bleeding the steam from the machine like a medieval doctor getting kickbacks from the leech concession. Nontheless I wished I had one of those remote-controlled robot arms. All went fine, and I began to trust my machine.

The next time I made espresso was on New Year's Eve, when I was at the point of perceiving the world in triplicate,

so far gone that I was, technically, using the machine outdoors. I made the first pot in a trice, bled out the steam, and
removed the lid without fear. Without thinking, really. It
wasn't until the next day that I realized I had been cavalier
with the steam. Say I'd been hideously disfigured by a blast
of espresso-maker steam. You could get away with that in
the eighties; I imagine it was even chic back then. Now I'd
have to lie and say I was burned dragging babies out of a
fire. Crack babies.

Which reminds me: If my wife drinks espresso while pregnant, what effect will it have on the child? CAUTION! CON-
TENTS UNDER PRESSURE.

Good news: The baby will come out at Mach 2. Bad news:
It will stay awake all night.

Diary of a Book Tour

∿∿∿

WHAT'S THE PHRASE—IT IS BETTER TO TRAVEL HOPEFULLY than to arrive? I'll never know. I travel in a black funk of sweat and apprehension, a fish not so much out of water as riding the conveyor belt to the mincing machine. On such a journey the practice of complimentary snacks does not really help much.

I manage to avoid travel by working a great deal, but the end result of that work is a book, and books need promoting, which means travel. Practicing my ventriloquism and assuring my publisher that I can indeed throw my voice to New York will not do. Nothing sells a book like seeing the author, pale and sweating under harsh lights, stammering out lame synopses of something he wrote a year before and has completely forgotten. So I packed too many pairs of pants and not enough underwear—it always works out that way, so now I just do it on purpose—and lugged myself to the train station.

(The publicist had booked me on many, many airplanes, until I pointed out that the book we were promoting—*Notes of a Nervous Man*—trumpeted my hatred of flying on the cover. There was a pause while he realized I was serious, which meant I wasn't kidding about the various other quirks and tics in the book. Then he came back with the voice you use while backing away from foaming dogs and gave me the number of the travel agency.)

Day 1

On the road. I await celebrating my trip with the complimentary first-class Amtrak Snack Pack. I've come to know it well: warm dull wine in a bottle so small you suspect you've been handed an obscure and discontinued cologne, a selection of rubbery cheeses that appear to be pasteurized modeling clay, and flaky crackers flavored with salt and other exotic spices. My attendant appears and inaugurates our journey by informing me that the snack pack has been discontinued. I consider canceling the tour right then, but it does not seem to be a sufficient reason.

Dinner on the train is the usual horror of four strangers swaying in place while groping about for conversational footing. The dining car steward, with his keen eye for assembling tables of mismatched strangers that will sit mute and vacate the space as early as possible, has put me with three people so old I can only conclude they are taking the train because no one has informed them of the existence of airplanes. The centerpiece of the trio is a gigantic and disagreeable Swede with pendulous ears; he is next to a stolid matron who has had all opinions surgically removed. Across the table is the sort of kindly grandma you see leaning out of advertisements offering a nice casserole. She helps the Swede with the menu, which contains such culinary puzzlers as New York Strip Steak and Chicken.

"Eh? Eh? What's this?" He points to the lasagna, and the woman explains it is a type of pasta. "Eh. Pasta." He waves away pasta and all its evil kin. "Don't like it." When the waiter finally comes, he orders the vegetarian dish, which is, of course, lasagna. The woman attempts to turn him from his course, but he will not be dissuaded. We sit in pained silence awaiting the storm.

Eventually, we talk. Asked what I do, I explain that I write, and I am on a book tour. Blank looks. "I'm going around talking about my book," I say. Images of me strolling the nation's streets, addressing the air and gesturing at the birds, come to their minds. "Radio and TV shows," I explain.

"Eh? What do y'do?"

His temporary helpmeet says that I write books and talk

about them. This earns me a gesture that puts me with lasagna.

"I had a son who wrote. Never made a dime. Not a penny. That was by my second wife. I've had three. The second though, I really liked that one. Yes I did. Son died. Age of thirty-seven."

"An accident?" I venture.

"He had that thing. That thing, what do you call it? People get it all the time."

"Was it—"

"That thing. Starts with a *C.*"

"Cancer?"

"Cancer. He had cancer." He smiles with satisfaction and gets up to use the bathroom, knee bones popping like yard-sticks snapping. He is gone for thirty minutes, during which time his lasagna arrives and congeals into a lurid brick of red sauce and exhausted broccoli florets. We eat quickly lest he return and harangue his pasta.

I spend the evening in the bar car arguing with an old socialist, who instructs me that my usage of the first person plural to describe the actions of the U.S. government is just the sort of misguided identification the bosses want me to maintain. ("It's not *we*, lad, it's *them*. Them them them.") We get around to how socialism would affect the book publishing industry, and I am told that my book would have to conform to the wishes of the collective, and I would not gain undue profit from it. I suggest that this sounds much like the book industry as it is currently constituted and draw large scowls in response. We part in good faith, however; I totter back to the Tool-of-the-Bosses car, and he goes forward to the People's car, where everyone is sleeping with their shoes off and their mouths open.

So far I have not really talked about the book at all. I have no feeling of being an author on tour. Later that night, as I make up the bed and realize I have to spend the night in a stuffy clanking coffin filled with the noxious emanations of my own sneakers ("He died from that thing. Those things people wear. Starts with *S.*"), I realize that this is just like every other trip. Raw, spiky nerves are stirring in the back of my head: you're far from the familiar, miles from home, hearth, and 911. What if I get sick? What if I get a toothache? What if I have an anxiety attack? What if they don't sell the paperback rights? If an author gives a reading and no one comes, does it make a sale? What if no one buys the book— or, God help me, they do and unmask me for the hack I undoubtedly am? The train wheels echo the sentiment: *hack* ety *hack* ety *hack* ety *hack* ety.

I put my sneakers out in the hallway and go to bed.

Day 2

Due to the vibrations of the train, my sneakers have done a two-step down the length of the corridor. I retrieve them before they blister the woodwork. I then perform my toilette, washing my hair in the small basin. This requires I brace one foot against the wall and the other on the window ledge, dunking my head in the water. Not being wholly awake, I neglect to pull down the window shade; given that I am wearing only underwear, I present a provocative sight to the towns we pull through. I realize this when the train stops and I see, upside down through the window, a queue of cars at a crossing. I only regret that the publisher did not equip me with promotional underwear with the picture of the jacket imprinted on the seat. I realize also that with this I have made more of an impression on those folks than I could with anything I could possibly say on tour. Books come and go; wagging buttocks crawling slowly down main street is a sight one never forgets.

Shaving is next, and it is performed over a rough patch of track with fun-house curves taken at bullet-train speeds. I have a brand-new razor and carve several brand-new dimples in my face while shaving. Several of these along the jawline were unstanchable, soaking through every tissue I laid to my face; all I could do was steal an Amtrak pillow, put it over my face, hire an angry Moor to accompany me, and tell everyone I was a professional Desdemona impersonator. Then I dressed from my fine selection of unironed shirts that had spent twenty-four hours crumpled in a suitcase and prepared for my engagements in Chicago.

Well. Not engagements, as such; publicity had not booked me with anyone. My goal was to find my book in stores and sign it, ideally before anyone caught me doing it. But first, a meal. I went to my favorite pizza restaurant, a place I'd not been in five years, and ordered lunch. The first bite was as good as I recalled; I think I closed my eyes, tilted my head back, and savored the reunion. Which explains why I did not see the top of the slice slide off the crust and land square on my crotch. On my light-colored trousers. I immediately ran to the bathroom, face red with shame, and spent a frantic interval daubing at my privates with soaked and wadded toilet paper. This I dried off with the cloth towels hanging from a dispenser, something that required I stand on tiptoe, facing the wall, vigorously buffing myself with the tail of the towel loop. Of course someone came in.

"I'M ON A BOOK TOUR," I wanted to shout, because that, of course, was the reason I was far from home rubbing tomato sauce from my lap, but I knew better. When I looked in the mirror, I nearly wept—my hair was flying all over the place, my face looked like I'd spent the night being nibbled by teething rodents, and my lap looked like I was someone who fed himself spaghetti with one hand, used the same hand to quell a nasty itch, then wet his pants over a particularly crude joke.

Time to go sign books.

Luckily, the book was as rare as a Gutenberg. I prowled through a variety of bookstores, a *Wall Street Journal* held casually over the stain, looking in the *L*s for my opus. Store after store, I grew to resent the authors who inevitably flanked me—one was a big, thick, brawling novel with airplanes thrusting phallically toward the reader, and the other was a thin demure tome by a famous literature professor known for spawning worshipful students and incomprehensible texts. I checked the humor ghetto, filled mostly with books such as *All I Need to Know I Learned From My Vietnamese Pot-Bellied Pig* and various offerings from the franchise humorists; I was nowhere.

By the end of the day, I have found the Book at two stores and have signed all the copies in existence in the city. I do not have writer's cramp. In fact, my writing hand demonstrates the sort of flexibility and suppleness given by constant exercise, such as compulsively jiggling one's change and keys while the clerk looks up your book on the microfiche and assumes a puzzled and sympathetic expression.

Back on the train. Once reunited with my suitcase, I changed into a pair of pants without a prominent groin-mark and take my place in the steerage class: it's only eight hours to Minneapolis. My seatmate and I trade necessary data, and she says she doesn't read much. She proves the fact by hauling out a book with sunbeams on the cover and large simple illustrations of Jesus tending sheep. I suddenly feel as though my entire oeuvre is shot through with irredeemable sin and go back to the bar car. When I return hours later, she is asleep, with knitting work in her lap, presumably for orphans. The reading light shines on her head like the beam announcing divine insemination.

The train creaks into Minneapolis at midnight. I am picked up not by my handler—that's a few days away—but by my best friend, at whose apartment I am staying. It is a small place. The second day of my whirlwind book tour ends on a hard futon on a hardwood floor.

Day 3

I get up and read the papers; Minneapolis is gripped with World Series frenzy, and all things from Atlanta are castigated with vigor on the front page. I think little of it at the time. After a late breakfast I go around to all the bookstores downtown and sign books. The scene is the same everywhere—I bring a stack of ten up to the counter, and the clerk smiles with an expression that says, "Ah! Someone's going to take that stiff off our hands!" A few are disconcerted when I insist on signing them and thus render them unreturnable, but most are happy to have a real author, albeit one with a freshly scarred neck, in the store and signing books. I note that most stores are not putting the book in the window or in a prominent location, so I point out that not only am I a Minneapolitan but Lewis Grizzard, whose new book is piled high in the windows, is from the enemy city-state of Atlanta.

Out goes Grizzard and up goes the homeboy. I wonder what dirt I can get on Thurber and Mencken.

I attend a party that night and consider emulating Dylan Thomas by getting hideously if eruditely drunk and insulting the gross, bland matrons, but they are all friends, so I switch to coffee at midnight.

Another night on the futon.

Day 4

A day off, to let my hand rest from the debilitating effects of writing my name forty times in two days. I sit around the house with my friend watching TV; in an act of manly hospitality, he lets me control the remote. I am so starved for cable that after three hours of channel switching I have carpal tunnel syndrome, and my hand aches. The entire tour is now in jeopardy.

We go out for dinner that evening; I want to tell the restaurant host my name is NotesofaNervousManbyJamesLileks, so when she calls it I can get some publicity, but opt for my last name only: did Halston need more than one word? And like Halston, I have a collection out. Unlike Halston, however, my collection is not being paraded down runways by vacant nineteen-year-olds. And so far it has not been written up by *The New York Times*. While I am considering conducting the remainder of my tour in dramatic yet traditional taffeta, the host calls for the "Leekus party." Many people turn to see who has such a stupid name, and I have the feeling that if there is an author named Leekus, his books will be gone from the stores tomorrow. *Honest, I saw him last night at Bocce's.*

I attend a party that night. First we watch the Twins game, which we win; then I go to the bedroom to argue with an old friend about why I haven't called or written since I moved. I hold up a copy of my book to demonstrate that I have been busy. It is an unassailable argument. Of course, I have to give it to her now, and I have lost a potential sale. I realize it would have been cheaper to drop a postcard from time to time.

I attain a Dylan Thomas rating of sixty-five percent that evening, arguing loudly with strangers about the virtues of vacuum tubes vs. transistors. A stranger gives me a ride home and is amused by my apparent delusion of being an author on a publicity tour. Another night on the futon, which spends most of the early hours throwing itself around the room like a carnival ride.

Day 5

After breakfast in a restaurant full of skinheads and artists, I check in to my luxury hotel, paid for by the publisher. That night, the Twins win the World Series; I grab my video camera and run into the streets, where thousands of lubricated Minnesotans are shouting and laughing and shaking hands with every available biped. I have also taken a stack of promotional postcards, which I scatter as I go; when filmed, I hope, it will appear that a midnight riot has broken out over my appearance. What I get is footage of innumerable feet treading over my jacket photo.

Day 6

The book tour starts in earnest. First, a bleary breakfast happily charged to my publisher. This is one of the true glories of a book tour: eat what you will, and damn the cost. (Although I am still enough of a Lutheran to feel vague guilt and to make sure I clean my plate.) The night before I had made out my breakfast order and hung it on my door, deciding this was one of the true advances of Western Civilization and an apt basis for running one's life; whatever you desire to happen the next day, you merely write it on a slip of paper and hang it outside your bedroom door. *Eggs—a new car—hair on my head—a lifetime's supply of light bulbs.* There is a drawback: two eggs, toast, bacon, a roll, juice, and coffee cost about $348.97, reflecting no doubt the high cost of training someone to go from floor to floor and collect pieces of paper hanging from doorknobs.

At 6:30 A.M. a perky robot in a tuxedo shows up bearing a tray with my food. I sign something, thinking that if the Devil truly wanted souls he would send his minions to hotel rooms at 6:30 A.M. with trays of food; people would sign on the dotted line with no questions asked, and he wouldn't have to give them anything but small pots of marmalade for their souls. I haul the tray into the room and have breakfast sitting on the bed, watching Bugs Bunny cartoons. I have seen them all, so am less disposed to warm feelings of vicarious triumph when Bugs triumphs. Somehow I finish $348 worth of breakfast and shave, opening old wounds and initiating two new geysers on my jawline.

I'm supposed to meet my handler downstairs. Eventually I spy someone else with that blind-date look. She's a perfect Minnesotan: blond, sensible, smart, no-nonsense. We get into her car, a big black 4X4 that looks like a domesticated Brink's vehicle, and speed off to St. Paul. On the way she tells me all the places we can go for lunch and dinner, and I mention that I lived in this city for fifteen years, and she is not obliged to spend the free hours with me.

"Really?" she says. "Some authors just hang on me. *Please don't go.*"

Not me. This is home. Everything has a story here—such as the first building on our stop. It's a public radio station with a big news-crawl at the top—moving lights spell out the headlines, which perambulate left-to-right. You know. Times Square stuff. Once I did a New Year's Eve TV special where we shot the countdown to midnight in front of that building. The lights spelled out the countdown, but went to fractions after 1:

4—3—2—1—⅞—⅚—¾—⅔—½—¼—OK   OK HAPPY NEW YEAR

That sort of thing. While I was yammering at the camera, a number of false news stories scrolled along above me, including news of a fictitious coal-mine disaster in a fictitious Welsh town with forty-seven letters in its name. GROGNAN-GAULAOCHNELORAUTICH ... etc., etc. The idea was to have the name of the town appear on the crawl and keep on coming and coming and coming. (Well, I thought it was funny.) No one told them to turn it off, so the news of that coal disaster, followed by the countdown to Happy New Year, ran all night long on the side of a station that billed itself as the state's preeminent news organization. It was, incidentally, November when we shot that scene. I asked later and was told the station received no calls about it. There are few people in downtown St. Paul after dark; even fewer would seem to be Welsh.

"This is the place," my handler says.

"I know," I reply.

The studio wall holds a map of the member stations and their reach, so I have an idea of how much of the state will be within earshot if I pass out, clam up, swear by mistake. None of these things happen, of course. I have no idea what I said when it is over, but I feel heartened; the day has begun well, and the huge breakfast is not barking at me as I feared it might. Best of all, I haven't run into a woman who works at the station whom I had, years before, unsuccessfully attempted to date; I'd run into her the last time I did that station and had the fear that she'd taken the mike after I'd left and said, "Author schmather, let me tell you, one of the worst dates I've ever had." Off to Minneapolis for interview number two.

This one is at WCCO, the powerhouse of the state. Drive away from the Twin Cities, and this station dogs you like a bored state trooper. Upon entering I meet a young woman I worked with years ago, who announces that there is a twenty-five-pound salted nut roll in the kitchen. I don't know whether she expects me to rejoice or go in and kill it. Then I realize what she is talking about: a Pearson's Salted Nut Roll, a local candy I have been missing since I moved to the land of Goo Goo Pies and other fine Southern treats. I shave off a wedge, devour it with two cups of coffee, and enter the radio studio with the feeling that my hair is on fire. It is not unpleasant.

The interview is genial and wide-ranging. Given that my book is not about politics or science and contains no thesis other than I WROTE THIS, NOW BUY IT, it is rather difficult to discuss any specifics, so I spend my time kicking Washington and lauding Minneapolis, all at rivet-gun speed, leaning into the mike and talking so fast I had chewed the foam from the mike after only ten minutes.

"Can I get you anything?" says a pretty production assistant during a break.

"Coffee'dbenice," I say.

"You're sure?"

I nod so vigorously my head is merely a blur. The rest of the interview goes by *amazingly* fast.

The third interview, at another radio station, is an hour long, and by then the coffee and salt and sugar have worn off; I must struggle to be animated. The interviewer has the gall to ask questions that cannot be glibly turned aside but demand a reasoned response. I am given but one brackish cup of coffee, and the hour is a struggle. After the interview my handler takes me back to my hotel room. I order a pot of coffee, which is only $65.00, and practice what I will read that night. I discover that I hate every piece in the book and cannot bear to read any of them. Well, reviewers had said I worked in the same vein as Thurber, Benchley, and Perleman, and that with forty-nine years' practice and an implant of the DNA of any of those writers, I might be in the same league, so why not just cut to the chase and read Thurber, Benchley, etc., for the audience?

Nah. I finish the coffee and rejoin my handler in the lobby, who, after picking me up and dropping me off three times in a day, looks like she relishes the days of clinging authors. We drive in howling sleet to the bookstore. Yes, if you're going to hold a reading, do it during inclement weather, on the day after the biggest catharsis the state has seen in half a decade. I predict an audience numbering in the high single digits.

And that is an exaggeration. I am greeted by perhaps six people. *Well,* I think, *this will be intimate.* I ask my handler for a cup of coffee—large—and retire to the restroom to obsessively comb my hair over and over in the hope that there is an ancient legend that says people will come to your underpublicized reading if you stand in a stinking lavatory dragging an Ace comb with three busted teeth through your thinning hair. After ten minutes I have reached two conclusions: my tan has completely faded, and there are lines on my face I'd never noticed before. Time to meet my public. At least I am not bleeding.

To my shock, the room is now full. The thing with the comb apparently worked. My handler gives me a cup of coffee, and

I take it with a palsied hand: I am quite nervous. I warm up with a few ineffectual lines not intended to be very funny, to dispel any preconceptions that I expect people to laugh at me, and then launch into a piece. The response is what you would expect from sixty damp Minnesotans: kind, but restrained. I haul out the larger pieces of comic artillery, essays I vaguely remember writing in a happier time, and the response grows with each piece. By the end I am emboldened to stride around gesturing and playing it rather broad, and we all seem to be having a good time.

It is time to stop, but I ask if they want to hear one more, and of course, like good, kind, encouraging Minnesotans, they shout yes.

"Let's see," I say, paging through the book for a piece I don't entirely despise. "You'll probably all leave saying, 'Y'know, he should have stopped before he read that last one; it wasn't as good as the one before.' "

I do believe that's what they left saying.

But plenty file over to the bookstore for autographed editions. And that, my wedding day aside, was perhaps the high point of my life: sitting underneath a large cardboard cutout of my book, watching people drinking wine and eating cheese provided on behalf of my publishers and lining up to tell me that they were glad I was back in town. Of course, no one offered to put me up or spot me a couple grand to help me move home, so I believe only so much of it.

After I sign every book on the premises, I repair across the street with friends for a celebratory dinner. I order coffee, then begin to vibrate with a particular resonance that makes the piano player in the bar stop playing and strike keys at random, trying to place the note I am emitting. (High C.) I tell the waiter to bring me a fishbowl full of ice, a straw, and a bottle of scotch.

The evening ends at the hotel bar, where I am eating pretzel mix and talking with a member of a strange religious sect having a convention in Minneapolis. He explains reincarnation to me; I end the conversation by saying I hope he enjoyed Minneapolis and comes back someday. He says he will, as only a reincarnationist can say it. I find my room and hang my breakfast order on the door and sleep.

Five hours later a starched and unnaturally alert man in evening wear shows up at my door with seven breakfasts. I had apparently confused the time of delivery with the number of people eating. I fear the phone will ring with my wake-up call and a robot voice will say, "It is now bacon and eggs. Have a nice day." I eat and take a cab to the train station. As the train pulls out I set my radio to the station I used to work at and hear familiar friends chattering away. They never sleep and they never go away, it seems; each time I come home, they're there, happily bantering away another crisp Minnesota morning as if such days weren't precious and rare. After half an hour on the train the station fades to static, and that's the moment when I feel the East Coast set its hook in my soft palate and tug, hard. I never remember what the bait tastes like, or why I took it.

Day 7

New York City is precisely as I left it on my last visit five months ago. Although a couple cars appear to have moved forward a few lengths on Park Avenue. I trudge up the escalator into Penn Station, going from the stale electrified-urine smell of the tracks to the made-fresh-daily urine smell of the waiting room. A taxi dispatcher files me in a cab like a bill he has no intention of paying. The cab has accretions on the seat excreted by a creature that lived on chewing gum and old shoe polish. The Plexiglas screen between me and the driver looks like the last occupants were fifteen hot-and-bothered men on the way to a premature ejaculation clinic. I can feel viruses swarming over my skin. My driver coughs out something substantial enough to trigger the horn on the steering column, pulls into the traffic. I give my destination. "Fourth and Fifty-sixth?" he says. "I can take you there." What a nice surprise.

We proceed for one whole block before the street seizes up in gridlock. New York intersections generally resemble a revolving door full of sumo wrestlers, but this is genuinely impassable, probably due to some congestion fifty blocks away that won't disband until the vehicles rust and fall apart and are disassembled by hand. Meanwhile, we wait. The driver turns around to talk. He wants to know what I think about the Democrats. *I DON'T GIVE A GOOD GOD-DAMN ABOUT THE DEMOCRATS* is what I wish to say, as this is precisely the claustrophobic nightmare I face every time I go to New York. My breathing is starting to come in short shallow hitches, and I can feel my heart getting ready for the old jackhammer pump.

"Dukakis, now, I think he can come back," says the cab driver. "Or maybe McCarthy. I think he could win it."

"How long have you been in this country?" I inquire.

"A year. Am from Soviet Union. But I have read much about the Democrats." Not enough, I think, and then I see it! A break in the gridlock! Go, you fool! Go!

The driver notices the gap and lurches forward, enters the intersection, BUT he slams on the brakes as the light—and this must come as a total surprise to the man—turns red.

WHANG! We're hit from behind.

I look at my watch. I have been in New York for seven minutes. I'll be wearing a neck brace in all my public appearances. *Hurt your neck? No, the doctor made me wear this collar to keep me from licking my stitches.* The cabbie investigates the accident and unilaterally declares it to be nothing, then gets back in the cab and proceeds through the intersection. On red. The driver who hit us follows us alongside for blocks—all of a sudden, streets are empty enough to permit angry drag races with fist-shaking drivers, but that's just part of the magic of Manhattan. Some cities are made for lovers.

My hotel was built, I'm guessing, in the early teens. The lobby was renovated in the eighties, probably because they were having new brochures printed and decided that it would be cheaper to do the lobby and photograph that than do the rooms. The lobby is a cramped and tomblike space no matter how you decorate it, but some genius had given the walls an Egyptian touch, so they all slant outward, making the place look like the sarcophagus of a middle-level Pharonic-era bureaucrat. I get in line behind a half-dozen shouting Germans and approximately three million identical twittering Japanese stewardesses. Eventually I stagger to the head of the line, am told that there is a "problem" with the billing, and am bade to wait while a weightless little snit in a dun-colored jacket calls my publisher. He clearly holds me in contempt for checking in to this hotel. He also seems to be under the misunderstanding that switching from groveling servitude to officious condescension in the space of three seconds is something that will earn my respect and admiration. After the "problem" is cleared up I am sent to my room. Second floor. The elevator, whose inspection card lists the dates of inspection, name of inspector, and size of bribe, has so little respect for me it goes straight to three. I get back in and wonder whom I have to pay to make it stop on my floor.

My room is a sty with complimentary mints. The curtain is hanging off its rod; the television has five channels, four of which are devoted to telling me about the late-night soft-core French sex farces I can order if I'm too tired to order up a hooker. In the bathroom there's a little bottle of shampoo ("Specially formulated for our guests!" it says; it smells medicinal, making one wonder just what special formulation guests here seem to require), one bar of soap that devolves into hard, soapy nodules the first time I use it, and towels so threadbare from washing that they would be useful only if you were performing the dance of the seven veils and wanted something gauzy and transparent. Of course, in this bathroom, it would be the dance of the three veils, one washcloth, and a beige plastic nonskid bathmat.

I have to get out of my train clothes. I strip and carefully remove my socks, which after two days on the train, are lethally odoriferous. Slip one over the head of a cat and the beast would die in seconds—stiff, legs out, tail a rod of stark terror. The socks go into the plastic bag with the rest of my road socks; barking sounds come from the bag as I open it. I call housekeeping for an ironing board and take a bracing shower. Clean and attired, I leave the hotel. New York awaits.

After two hours of walking around, I end up at a pizza place, eating a slice that has had all moisture scientifically extracted by some procedure known only to indifferent Italian store owners. I am reading the newspaper and paying no attention whatsoever to the radio. At least until the music stops and an announcer comes on.

"THIS IS THE EMERGENCY BROADCAST SYSTEM," he says. "THIS IS NOT A TEST. THIS IS NOT A TEST." *Beeeeeeeeeeeeeeeeeeeeeeeeeeeeeeeeeeeeeee* ...

—I look up; across the aisle, a man in a bow tie and *The Wall Street Journal* looks up, his pizza sliding from his hand—

Beeeeeeeeeeeeeeeeeeeeeeeeee . . . "THIS IS THE EMERGENCY BROADCAST SYSTEM," the voice repeats. "THIS IS NOT A TEST. THIS IS NOT A TEST."

That's it, I figure. Of course, it makes sense; I finally get a book, the U.S. and the U.S.S.R. finally come to terms, and then some Azerbaijani in an abandoned silo is playing with the launch codes out of boredom. *Let's try this sequence—oh, oh.* And then I get stuck in New York when the bombs fall. Understand that I had spent the eighties trying to figure out a way to survive not a nuclear attack but the claustrophobic effects of evacuation. When I moved to D.C. right before the Gulf War, which everyone secretly suspected was really going to be the Gog-Magog nukefest we'd heard so much about (in fact, when I think about it, it's a surprise retail spending was so low that Christmas; if people had been honest with themselves, they'd have spent like crazy), I had my route planned out of town—sidewalks taken by moped, with a buckknife between my teeth, canned goods, Sterno, gas, and gold coins in my backpack. I had but one rule: If world events turn curdled, STAY THE HELL OUT OF NEW YORK.

And here I was.

Beeeeeeeeeeeeeeeeeeeeeeeeeeeeeeeeeee ...

The tone did not stop. I stood and walked automaton-style out. *"Have a nice day,"* the counterman called after me. Outside there was no panic, no one running to the subway. Yet. No sirens howling. Yet. I strode to my hotel, where people were not being shoveled into shelters. Yet. Took the elevator to my room, and of course the elevator overshot by a floor. Made it to my room and turned on the TV. None of the fleshy satyrs on the all-French sex-farce channels had any idea what was going on. I flipped to the sole local station, and

they were playing a seventies police drama. This is the way
the world ends: not with a whimper, but with a *who loves ya
baby*. No, maybe it was a mistake at the radio station. Yes.
That was it. A mistake.

Then the screen flickered, and the words EMERGENCY
BROADCAST SYSTEM hit the screen. I stood, heart banging, and began to throw things in my suitcase. I could walk
out of New York. Sure. Hoof it.

Beeeeeeeeeeeeeeeeeeeeeeeeeeeeee

"THIS IS NOT A TEST," said a scratchy voice. "THIS IS
THE EMERGENCY BROADCAST SYSTEM. A STORM
FRONT WITH DAMAGING WINDS HAS MOVED INTO
THE NEW YORK AREA. HIGH WINDS AND COASTAL
FLOODING IS LIKELY."

And so on.

"THAT'S IT?" I screamed. "For Chrissakes, THAT'S IT?"
It struck me that New Yorkers were so jaded the only way
you could get their attention was to play the sound that generally meant the end of the world. All this over weather? For
God's sake, in Minnesota when a storm comes along and
dumps four feet of snow in an hour, the TV stations just run
a crawl that says, "You might want to stock up on bread."
This was the equivalent of sticking a flare gun down someone's pants to tell them the mail had arrived.

After I calmed down, I called an old girlfriend and went
out to dinner. Related the above story to mild amusement:
*yes, the end-of-the-world sound; you get used to it living out
here.* At the end of the night I stumbled upstairs and spent
five minutes jamming my card in the key slot to no effect
before I realized I was on the third floor. Then I staggered
back down to my room and ordered up a French sex-farce.
I wondered why the French were considered such great lovers
when the words *sex* and *farce* were so frequently connected
in their presence. It was a bad movie, with fat mustachioed
men panting after vacuous young nubiles when not lying to
tightly wound wives who, eventually, came to forgive their
husband's wanderings because he was fat and French and
therefore irresistible. When it was over, I went back to broadcast TV and saw the Emergency Broadcast System kick in

again. I laughed and turned it off and went to sleep. I told you I was a New Yorker in a previous lifetime.

Books signed: 0.

Books sold: unknown.

Books given away to old girlfriends: 1.

(Note: I had to cancel my next day's appearances in order to rush back home to mediate a domestic crisis. Given that the next day involved live television, which I hate, I couldn't believe my luck; my publicity agent couldn't believe my story, and the TV station couldn't see any reason why they'd want to invite me back again.)

Day 8

D.C. again. Back home, the tour continues. I get up at seven in the morning and do a radio interview with a station in Chicago. Unbeknownst to the audience I am sitting naked in a bathrobe, half-awake, unable to talk about much at that hour. When the host says, "Let's talk about your book," I say, *"Oh, please, do we have to?"* and he replies, *"Of course not."* Hell of a fellow. We spend the entire hour taking calls about who would be a good actor to play James Bond. I hang up and nap, then get ready for another radio interview in town.

"So," says the host that afternoon. *"Notes of a Nervous Man,* eh. Are you really a nervous guy?"

I grin and gulp some coffee. I tell him it's all a marketing tool. Then I plead with people not to buy the book, because if it somehow becomes successful, I will be obliged to do this all again. The host laughs.

He actually thinks I'm kidding.

Gorgeous Decline

~~~~~~

FALL IS THE SEASON THAT REQUIRES YOUR ATTENTION. SPRING grabs you by the lapels, shouts like a happy lunatic; summer is a long sticky embrace. Winter couldn't care less about you or what you think. But fall: this is the season that asks you to lean close, be silent, and learn.

It is easy to lose fall, to call its first half summer and its other half winter. We're loath to see the former go and all too willing to believe the long slog of the latter has begun. After all, the calendar says that summer doesn't end until the twentieth of September. Fall's not here. Not yet.

Of course it is. The calendar says summer begins on the twenty-first of June, but no one believes that. Summer commences the moment you open your eyes on the first day of June, and it ends when you go to sleep on Labor Day. We all know that when you wake on that grim Tuesday, dutiful September has changed everything. The heart steps aside and the brain sets to work. It's the first day of school. Doesn't matter if you're five or fifty: back to class. Sit up straight.

The efficient way to arrange the world would be for winter to follow summer, immediately. Think of it: one irrevocable stroke at midnight. The land changes from a smear of green to a sheet of white without detail or dissent. Instead, the world goes into a dream of gorgeous decline—the trees shed

169

their uniform and improvise melodies of yellow and red; the wind gets sharper, colder, rushing to tell you something, pushing you toward something it wants you to see. The sun pulls away and speaks from a distance. Everything unravels.

We are, of course, too busy to pay attention. There was school then, and there's work now. We see the changes in small doses, and they exhilarate us—not like the promise of spring or the false hope of eternity that summer brings, but something richer, more complex. Everyone's memory of autumn seems to take place at three o'clock in the afternoon, when we were let loose from school to stamp and kick through dry, quiet streets, hearts still running on summer's rules, our heads full of new lessons, new rooms, new clothes, new friends. The end of the world and the beginning of ourselves—these two ideas were fused solid every year, and we never forget the feeling. Decades later, the slant of the sun and the color of the trees bring the same emotions. Hope, curiosity, regret.

But that is the sentimental side of autumn, the part taken in small doses. The harder truths are these: fuel bills, scratchy sweaters, mortality, drafty windows, the end of birdsong and cricket serenades, balky furnaces, empty trees. Fall—idealized autumn—is wonderful. But it lacks a happy ending. There are times when you don't want winter to come, and you wish you could persuade fall to do it again, repeat that part with the leaves, give us another day where the sun was warm and the sky was pale and weightless. Another day of running through the leaves, sweating hard beneath thin jackets.

You won't get it. The very aspect that makes fall mysterious is what makes it bittersweet: this song isn't sung for us. The world is entertaining itself. You see the leaf only in midflight; you never see the leaf turn, cast off from its moorings. Autumn is conducted in private. We can look through the window, but we can't join in. After all, we're alive. Autumn is all about dying.

In my home of Minnesota, the State Fair ends on Labor Day. When it opens, it's August, sticky and thick; the fair rambles through ten days, a great shaggy beast that takes us from the lush grass of summer to the cool stone floor of autumn. There are fireworks at the end. If you stay around long enough, you see the lights of the rides turn off, and the bare metal trunks cease to spin. Stern, polite people guide you toward the gate and shut it behind you.

If you look up, you'll see the clock of the moon turning toward harvest.

And then you join the thousands leaving the fairgrounds and head for your car. You find a radio station that plays the songs you danced to; you join the row of autos, everyone bound for different points, every car blaring a different anthem.

It's cold; you roll up the window. You tap your hands on the wheel to the song. Your breath gathers on the windshield.

You could turn on the heater.

Not yet, you think. Not yet.

Innumeracy

〰〰〰〰〰〰〰〰〰〰〰〰〰〰〰〰〰〰〰〰〰〰〰〰〰〰〰〰〰〰〰〰〰〰〰

YOU HAVE NO DOUBT READ RECENT SURVEYS THAT INDICATE many schoolchildren still could not find Iraq on a map, as well as surveys of Iraqis that indicated that was just fine with them, thank you. But you may have doubted that the failure of our education system is limited to geography. Good news: Our kids are washouts at math too. Little Johnny couldn't put two and two together if you gave him glue and an industrial vise.

Proving the fact is a recent survey of the nation's eighth-graders, which found them all sorely lacking in math skills. Addition they found easy, division less so, multiplication made half of them bust out in hives the size of Frisbees, and when presented with division of fractions, a certain percentage of American children actually blow up.

Perhaps the problem lies in the test questions. Here's an actual question: If a sphere weighs thirty pounds on earth, and the moon's gravity is one sixth that of earth, what will the sphere weigh on the moon?

This is important only if the kid grows up to run to a bowling alley on another planet.

Or, there are multiple choice questions. To the normal child, terrified by the threat of failure, they all look like this:

If $x=3$ and $y=z-2$ and $z=x+2$, then who the hell cares?

A) Your mom and dad! Now buckle down!
B) Your teacher cares! Look busy!
C) No one cares! They're all against you! You'll have to defeat them all with your Spider powers!

This is not how to get kids to enjoy math. You use problems like this:

The rock group Def Leppard had five members. The drummer lost an arm in a really gross auto accident, and a guitarist died of a drug overdose. What percentage of their limbs did the group lose?

Or:

You're at an eighth-grade party. Twenty percent of your hormones are telling you to go talk to those girls. Seventy percent of your peers are against the idea. Forty percent of the girls are wearing training bras. What is the chance you will go home and examine yourself in the mirror for body hair?

There have been the expected wailings from all corners. Lamar Alexander, the secretary of education, said, "This ought to sound an alarm bell ringing all night long." That sounds less like a prescription for better education than a torture devised by the North Vietnamese. Is this what parents want—their children kept up for weeks by the ringing of that maddening bell, until they crack and confess on television that two times two is four, and they harbor no ill will against the freedom-loving prime numbers? I don't think so.

Another expert insisted, "In this age of computers, kids need to learn math." At first glance, this seems ridiculous, like saying, "In this age of bullet trains, kids need to learn how to walk very fast."

But there's truth in that assertion. Rely too much on computers, and you get blithering idiots who cannot make change when the power goes down. Witness what happens when you hand a fast-food clerk a ten for a $9.87, wait until they have punched ten dollars into the computer, and then give them twelve cents with the notion of getting a quarter back. They stare at the coins until their limbs lock up, the scent of an electrical fire wafts from their ears, and an assistant manager has to take them away and stack them in the back closet with the rest.

If kids balk at learning math, they have good reason. If it stopped with the basics—addition, division, subtraction, multiplication—they'd go along. That's just enough to prepare you for real-world things like taxes, kiting checks, and understanding just enough of your mortgage application to know you are being deeply, truly screwed. (If you understand more, of course, you did well in math. You're also the one drafting the papers.)

But kids know that it doesn't stop there. A bottomless chasm of math lies beyond the eighth grade—the whole seething mass of algebra, trig, calc, ready to drag you, and your grade-point average, down. I don't remember a bit of it. I have a grasp of math, but it's slippery; performing complicated division is like writing my name with a garden snake.

I get by. Enough math remains so that I can tell whether something is true or false—when I see that a can of peaches sells for $1.00 for sixteen ounces, and that the two-quart jumbo econo family size sells for $216.99, I know that mischief is afoot. (If I don't bring it up right there in the store, it's because I fear being mobbed by citizens thrusting forth cans and boxes, begging me to evaluate their purchases.) Math ought to describe the arid topography of the world of numbers and then leave it up to you to decide whether you want to proceed further. It's not as if three years of math taught by bitter, frustrated high school teachers is going to give me the ability to look at a bridge and decide that the stress levels have been inaccurately calculated.

Those grad-grinds inclined to get hot and humid over algorithms are welcome to them, so the rest of us can proceed with our lives, merrily toting up sums on our all-knowing calculators. Leave math to the professionals.

Otherwise, you've no defense when you have your first audit.

Live Orbital Goop

NASA RECENTLY UNVEILED ITS NEW, SCALED-BACK SPACE STA-
tion. It will now consist of four Yugos yoked together with
baling wire. There will be no sophisticated communication
systems; data will be relayed by calling *Larry King Live* and
hoping for an open line. As for the mission of the new ship—
previously an attempt of the United States to establish a per-
manent beachhead on the trackless shores of space—now
we'll be conducting experiments along the lines of whether
or not humans can stay in high orbit for five months without
receiving a Publisher's Clearinghouse Sweepstakes offer.

Actually, we might not even get that. NASA's multibillion-
dollar space station was encountering harsh resistance from
congressmen who saw it not as a waste of money but as a
waste of money that would not take place in their district.
Had each state in the space station's orbital path been allowed to float a tollbooth, you know they'd have voted yes.
But these are tight times, and not even the Tinkertoy bucket
described above could pass muster. Our manned space program now sits becalmed. The sole space station in orbit is the
Mir, a Soviet tin box that's seen more occupants than a mining town motel on payday and probably smells just as high.
What they do up there I have no idea, other than eat dehydrated cabbage and pirate the MTV satellite feed. But at least
they're there.

Us? Well, we went to the moon, but that seemed to take everything out of us. After that we put up *Skylab,* whose greatest contribution to national pride was falling out of the sky in the summer of 1979. People spent half that season looking up in terror, expecting something that looked like a soda can hurled from the window of some joyriding celestial giants to come roaring out of the sky and smash them dead.

Sure, we lob a shuttle into the ether every so often, but ever since the *Challenger* disaster it's not the same. We used to watch them go up with fearless pride, like something knocked into the heavens by Babe Ruth's bat. Now we wave at them like someone watching elderly parents back uncertainly down the driveway and head off down the middle of the street. We feel worry and love, mingled with a sense that they're getting too old for this.

It's still incredibly dangerous, of course. And when I watch a shuttle go, I feel more pride than terror. But I wish the missions were a little less mundane. The latest mission, for example, will loft about 2,478 miniature jellyfish into space. I am not certain why. It does not inspire awe. People are not likely to stop saying "If we can put a man on the moon ..." in favor of "If we can loft 2,478 brainless flecks of animate jam into a temporary orbit . . ." Why jellyfish? I read the news stories and find no answers. I have the awful fear that NASA has discovered that a horrible race of invertebrates is heading our way bent on invasion, and NASA is trying desperately to train translators. (When the official flight-crew photo includes a smallish, uniformed Portuguese man-of-war, one tentacle gripping its flight helmet as it poses for the group picture, you'll know we're in trouble.)

If the mission isn't routine, it's classified. Lasers and death rays. Fine by me: space ships need death rays. But let's get people excited with a demonstration. Have a guy stand in the Nevada desert with a cigarette; let the shuttle pass overhead and light it with a laser beam. Or do some wood burning from several miles up. Something to inspire us again.

This, I know, is not fair to NASA. First of all, their planetary mapping satellites have performed heroically, sending back candid close-ups of the planets so vivid in detail it's a surprise Bob Guccione hasn't bid on them. The *Voyager, Galileo,* and *Magellan* craft have done everything but find a Stuckey's on Neptune.

Second, it's not as though the next step—Mars—is all that easy. By the time the Apollo missions were ended, flying to the moon was about as challenging as pulling into a drive-in window. Mars is a year away and requires rockets that possess the explosive power of at least fifty Rev. Al Sharptons. We have to figure out what we do when we get there. Most of all we have to get the money. Lots of money. If only Saddam had invaded Mars; we'd be there yesterday.

But we have to go. We're behind already. It's always amusing to watch those science-fiction movies of the fifties, where everyone wears silver leotards and rides around in big aluminum cigars. They were so wrong, you think. They had no idea. Well, 2001 is on its way, and there happens to be a movie about that year. A movie with a beautiful whirling wheel circling the earth, a bustling colony on the moon. When that movie was released in 1968, it made sense. Surely, that's what the future would look like.

Come 2001, we'll look up at an empty heaven, a vacant moon. We'll see the movie on the Late Show and laugh: they were so wrong.

They had no idea.

Err on a G-string

FIRST OF ALL, I WANT YOU TO KNOW THAT I'M WRITING THIS wearing a G-string and pasties, because that's the kind of guy I am: dedicated to freedom of expression, whatever form it takes. I fully intend to get angrier as I write, so the pasties should be twirling by paragraph eight. Keep that image in mind as we discuss a recent legal decision.

In Washington, the Supreme Court has decided that states have the right to ban nude dancing. In a 6–4 decision, the Court said, "Wait a minute, who's that guy? There's only supposed to be nine of us," after which the Court was cleared, and bailiffs explained to the Vice President that he was only to wear the robe and play Supreme Court Justice when they weren't in session. Then the court reconvened and issued a 5–4 decision, which read, in part:

"My robe is too tight, and my lips are blue."—Rehnquist, for the majority

"Yowsah yowsah yowsah! (*Thud.*)"—Blackmun, for the dissent

Or words to that effect. Justice Souter actually was bold enough to dissent on this one, although his ears burned as he did so—something which, incidentally, necessitated three fire trucks to extinguish. Rehnquist, who is uncannily adept at splitting hairs for a bald man, went on to say that the

Indiana statute in question was not aimed at banning the expressive nature of nude dancing but banning public nudity, period. Apparently there's a lot of trouble in Indiana with public nudity; Justice White noted that the law was intended—and I am quoting here—to forbid people "from appearing nude in parks, beaches, hot dog stands."

Getcher red hots, indeed. Listen, if there's anyone stupid enough to stand naked next to a pot of boiling water and drop hot dogs in it, they deserve what they get.

Actually, I don't believe nude dancing is a constitutionally protected form of speech. If it is speech, it's a form I rarely encounter in daily conversation. I've yet to get in an argument with the clerk at the grocery store and have her strip buck naked and do a dance proving I gave her a ten, not a twenty.

Ah, but speech is not always words, as we learned with that other great crisis of American civilization, the flag-burning issue. Sometimes speech is setting afire a piece of fabric with a specific arrangement of dyes and waving it around to the cheers of other Mohawked simpletons. That I accept. The rule seems to be: If a symbolic action has a political message that makes onlookers want to kill them, then it's speech.

Not so with nude dancing. It's difficult to see what political point is being made, other than "vote for people who let you watch me do this." I don't believe that some great art is being expressed, as with poetry, or you'd see people doing it poorly, and for free, in the basements of local libraries. There are no stripper critics in newspapers; there are orchestra critics, who cannot be swayed if the orchestra comes over and sits in his lap.

One of the justices, the honorable Justice White, quoted the French writer Mallarmé, who said that the dancer "writes with her body." Well, perhaps. I do know that when I write, I do not squat down to pick up a pencil offered by a palpitating businessman. Shall we be very clear? This is about sex. Period.

Which is fine by me. I do not lie in bed at night, eyes wide, my spine a rod of righteousness, inflamed that somewhere, someone is nude in a way I disapprove of. If consenting adults (female variety) wish to part fish-mouthed onlookers (male variety) from their money by walking in front of them wearing naught but perspiration, fine. No one forces anyone to work there or go there.

So the trick now is to find new legal, protected ways to dance nude. Some suggested ideas for ingenious strippers:

- Call yourself Betsy "Nasty" Ross and wear a flag on stage. Remove flag. Burn it.
- Instead of dancing, call it "begging." Beggars who merely shake the cup are entitled to constitutional protection. If nude dancing doesn't qualify as that, nothing does. This way your dance is what it really is: commercial speech. And no one has to bend over backward to defend it. Unless it's you doing the bending, of course.

A final note to dancers: Do not, in the future, expect kind treatment from people whose work clothes extend completely to the ground.

Oh, and one more thing: It would help in the future if you could get those pasties to swing to the right. All the way to the right.

More Useless Entertainment Options, Please

∿∿

IN HIS NEW SONG, "57 CHANNELS AND NOTHING ON," BRUCE Springsteen sings about—well, actually, I don't know what he sings about, because it was a boring video and I switched to the All-Wok-Cookery-Infomercial channel. But I inferred he was complaining about the dearth of interesting programming on cable.

He shouldn't. Cable provides a rich world of endless complexity, and it's about to get better. Soon local cable systems will open the sluice gates on two new pipelines of bewitchment—the Cartoon Channel and the Sci-Fi Channel. That's right: it will now be possible to recline in a happy stupor before a twenty-seven-inch image of Deputy Dawg, while the robot from *Lost in Space* shouts "Danger!" in the picture-in-picture window.

Cynics will sniff that these new channels are just more of the usual bilge that cable has been pumping since its inception. They say that the Cartoon Channel's playlist is heavily larded with the jerky hackwork of the Hanna-Barbera studio. Critics say a pure sci-fi channel will have to broaden its criteria to include portentous Orson Welles–narrated Nostradamus documentaries and will inevitably break the gentleman's

181

agreement that there should never be another *Planet of the Apes* marathon.

Perhaps. But who cares? This is what cable is about: not better TV, but more TV.

In fact, two new channels aren't enough. There ought to be fifty more announced daily, so that the coaxial cable is as thick as an old-growth redwood trunk, and we all have to cut huge holes in the walls. Sure, it'd be drafty at first. So caulk it up! Turn it on! We can't rest until there is a channel for every particular taste in the nation. Here are some suggestions for some new, desperately needed channels:

The Mr. Belvedere Channel

Portly-butler humor, twenty-four hours a day. Belvedere excitement, on demand. Tonight: Mr. Belvedere responds to a family crisis by arching an eyebrow.

The Local Convenience Store Security Camera Channel

Hours of boredom, in which strangers pay for overpriced items of questionable nutritional value, are interspersed with occasional eruptions of violence, observed from a God-like perspective. If you're really bored, why, set your VCR, go down to the store, and wave at the camera.

The Time Capsule Channel

A camera has been buried in a box due to be opened in the year 2020. Tonight: inky blackness. Tomorrow: the suspense mounts.

The Critic's Channel—TV for the Ironic and Self-Aware

This is TV for people who admit they watch TV, but do so from a critical distance. Tonight: *America's Most Ambivalent*. Horrible crimes are recreated, and people are asked to call a special hot line and discuss how the use of camera angles and lighting can simplify complex issues of sociopathology. One can't deny its effectiveness. But does everyone understand the simplification, or are they merely reacting to the vigilante instinct the show so effectively induces? Whatever you believe, it makes for compelling—and repellent—television.

The Questionably Diminutive Cartoon Channel.

Nothing but cartoons consisting of younger versions of established cartoon characters. Included: Tiny Toons, a baby version of Warner Brothers characters, as well as the new spin-offs, Fetal Tools, Zygote Toons, Ovum Toons, and Freshly Metabolized Protein Toons.

The Lazy Man's Channel.

In order to facilitate the indolent and reduce repetitive-motion disorder, this channel mimics the channel surfing of the brain-dead sofa spud, never staying on one channel for more than two minutes. Suggested picture-in-picture combo: **The Steaming Eye-Rolling Woman's Channel.**

C-SPAN After Dark Channel.

In an attempt to make C-SPAN more high-mindedly boring than usual, this channel features static shots of empty conference rooms being cleaned by low-wage Salvadoran immigrants. Contemplate their lot while listening to the music of Vivaldi.

These are only a few of the delights we ought to be able to experience. Of course, it's just a stop-gap measure—the cable of the future will consist of huge data highways, with an exit ramp slamming into your Sony; you'll be able to call up whatever you want in precise doses.

Why wait for the Cartoon Channel to run a Warner Brothers cartoon? Call up the warehouse and bark out an order for all cartoons in which Foghorn Leghorn confounds the Hound in defense of the Maiden Hen. You won't wait for the Sci-Fi Channel to run your favorite *Battlestar Galactica*—you'll simply program your home computer to run a search with the keywords *Lorne Greene, Star Wars, Ripoff,* and *Blatant,* and voilà, entertainment.

It will be wonderful. No more browsing through the channels, looking for a channel that is not playing *Mister Ed* or even threatening to play *Mister Ed* eventually. Control will be ours. And once voice technology is perfected, we needn't even pick up the phone or turn on the computer. We can mutter our requests from the La-Z-Boy. And then we can get on with the pressing business of evolution and get rid of our arms and legs, our mouth reduced to a tiny slit, our eyes as wide and empty as Hula-Hoops.

I know, I know: it sounds wonderful. But beware. This explosion of choice makes vast demands on a finite amount of programming, and at some point it will cease to be profitable to churn out new entertainment for our restless eyes. When we've evolved to the point where we can't leave the La-Z-Boy, that's when they'll yank the plug and plunge us back into the days of network-only TV. We will be helpless. They will show more commercials. They will bring back ALF. They will show *Perry Mason* shows with the reels out of sequence. And we will be helpless, because we will have only vestigial limbs.

Which is why women should never complain about men's proclivity for deep, earnest scratching of the self during televised sporting events. It sounds hard to believe, what with the glorious future before us, but the day may come when we actually will want to turn the TV off. Keep scratching yourselves, men. In the kingdom of the armless, the one-armed will lead.

Providing the batteries in the remote still work.

Walk a Mile in These, Buddy

~~~~~~

LEST WOMEN BELIEVE THEY ARE THE ONLY ONES MADE TO FEEL inadequate by advertising, let me recount the text of an ad that haunted my childhood. It was a placard in the window of a shoe repair shop, right next to the store that sold comic books. For years, every Saturday, I saw the same placard. The top half showed a beaming man adjusting his tie; the bottom had a picture of some shoes that looked as if they had been used as teething aids for a brood of woodchucks.

In between, this phrase: "You're not dressed up . . . if they're run down."

That tidy fashion axiom burned itself into my mind, and as a consequence I have felt dressed up perhaps five times in my life. No matter how sharp the cut of my suit, or flashy the tie, my shoes give me away. The shine is off, the heels slant away, perhaps an indelible scuff marks the leather. More than likely one of the laces culminates in a tiny knot, like a bow for a Lilliputian's gift, because the damn things snapped that morning.

Let me tell you about the four pair of shoes I currently own. One pair consists of sneakers so toxic that I couldn't wear them into Canada without being arrested for importing plastic explosives. I have some brown dress shoes bought when I desperately needed brown shoes, a fact that so depressed me that I could not bear to spend more than was necessary, and as a consequence have shoes whose instep bears the proud words "ALL MAN-MADE MATERIALS." These shoes were not woven; they were extruded. I have a pair of gray shoes, whose origin is a mystery to me; they are the nicest things I own and I cannot recall buying them. They may have been left by Shoe Sprites who took pity on me, but whose kind gesture only went halfway: gray shoe polish is about as rare as caviar in my neighborhood, where most residents are hopeless street drunks whose shoe needs are solved by a vial of VOMIT-B-GON. Finally, there is my most recent purchase, a black pair holding their shine like an unhappy woman with three kids holds on to her memory of youth.

The problem is not that I am unwilling to spend money on shoes; I would be happy to do just that if buying shoes did not require I call my broker and liquidate all stocks, muttering that I am moving my assets "into a leather posture."

For men, it's either cheap shoes that don't last or expensive shoes that last perhaps a day longer. (There is a vast middle ground of unspeakable brown things with soft crepe soles, but for the purpose of this essay we will pretend they don't exist.) Let us first examine cheap shoes.

My neighborhood cobbler is part of a chain devoted to cheap, painful shoes. Roughly a third of the shoes have signs that proclaim them to be "FLEXIBLE," thereby implying that the remainder are the equivalent of wooden slats bound together with vise clamps. On closer examination, the FLEXIBLE shoes are shown to consist entirely of plastic—and this is considered a positive attribute. Sure, they're loose now, but you build a nice fire and wear them around the fireplace and they'll shrink to fit. If you ever want to take them off, just apply a good solvent. Plus, these shoes never need polish; they require only the occasional touch-up with a Magic Marker.

Up the street is another place that sells cheap shoes, but this one carries stylish, night-on-the-town wares. And to judge from the construction, one night is all you get. These shoes are so cheaply made as to be soluble in water. I had a pair once, and when I sat down for a shine the man rubbed them away with ten swipes of his cloth. Simply erased them. He was polishing my socks before either of us noticed. My current pair of work shoes is of the cheap-and-stylish variety, and they have lasted only because I never wear them while actually walking. I trudge to work in comfortable sneakers and then wear the shoes while sitting with my feet under the desk, unseen. I could be wearing scuba fins for all anyone knows, or cares, but in Washington there seems to be a general rule: the president may drop by any minute and ask us to do a handstand so he can inspect our soles, so wear good shoes.

Even though I never actually walk anywhere in these shoes, I have still managed to wear down the heels. (See above, "Not Dressed Up If.") Either the plastic heels are made of the same material used to fabricate biodegradable bags, or the rush of air across their surface as I cross my legs has eroded their edge. In any case, if I stand in these shoes, I instantly roll backward.

I could solve this problem by buying good shoes, but whenever I visit a decent shoe store I get gnarled with miserliness, scowling at the goods and casting dark looks at the clerks. I just cannot imagine why six ounces of steak goes for fifteen dollars, while one pound of leather goes for one hundred and fifty. They will tell you it's only the finest leather, that the cow spent its life immersed to its snout in lanolin, that the leather was then tenderized by having one hundred ancient toothless crones gnaw on it for a year, after which time it was joined to the sole with the finest of jute, handpicked by a man who will reject eight miles of twine before choosing a centimeter. And, they always add, it's made in Brazil.

Oh, yes, *Brazil.* Home of the highly paid manual laborer. Why not sell the shoe for $151.00, and double his salary?

There are, I grant, some expensive shoes that feel so good you wonder if they are evil and have been waiting for you and you alone so they can possess your soul. (If the Devil was to manifest himself through inanimate objects, he would be wise to do so through comfortable shoes.) But only gigolos and their subspecies, inordinately successful young mortgage brokers, buy such shoes. The rest of us sigh and buy a pair of wing tips, which look like your feet were peppered with a small meteor storm, or tasseled loafers, which contain a jaunty little bow no man would wear anywhere but, inexplicably, on his feet.

These items are sold to you by a questionable fellow who either is putting himself through college or has taken the job for the express purpose of handling the arches of strangers. I can think of no other alternatives. Why anyone would choose to spend their life kneeling before the redolent hooves of strangers is a mystery to me; the job has as much appeal as free-lance jockstrap fitter. Old-time shoe salesmen were small mild round creatures, soft and mild, and were regarded like the eunuchs who tended the harem. When in fact they probably arrive at work with their brains a roiling cauldron of lust and anticipation, much like an ordinary guy would show up for a job as a breast adjuster in the bra department. The newer line of clerks, I have noticed, simply ask your preference and hand you the item, much like a fast-food counterperson, except that they ask if you want socks with that instead of fries.

Whatever their personality, all shoe salesmen operate according to a tidy script. Line number one: "How does it feel?" You, the customer, have adopted a noncommittal facial posture, and are looking at a corner in the ceiling, as if the level of comfort is something that can be rationally deduced. Second line of dialogue: "Walk around in it, see how it feels." What, walk around? In shoes? What a novel suggestion! Thank God the inflated price of this item reflects the cost of keeping your professional expertise on staff. Third line of dialogue: "They'll stretch out." Translation: after they have worn your heel to the bone, they will lose interest in inflicting pain.

My wife tells me it is much the same for women, except the clerks are far less friendly and have the private smirk of someone who has skimmed off the best and paid employee discount. Very Soviet. But I cannot imagine it is worse for women. Not when I pass the shoe departments that take up whole floors of department stores. Women moan about the lack of good shoes, as they do the lack of good men, yet in both cases, seem more than content to settle. Perhaps one compensates for the other: I have seen women prepare for a date they are not greatly thrilled about by spending their lunch hour buying six pairs of shoes, the post-lunch adoration of which nearly brings the woman and her coworkers to orgasm. Why go out at all?

It is easier for women to buy shoes, and I don't want to hear any nonsense to the contrary. I know full well that women get their shoes not by asking for something in their size but by announcing to the clerk the type of mood they are in.

Customer: "I feel demure, worldly, and businesslike, but with a tint of sluttishness."

Clerk: "I have just the pair."

Women also understand the erotic power of shoes better than men. Men are convinced that there is, in every fitting room, a schematic of a heel with the height graded according to the sexual message being sent off.

.2 inches: Barbara Pym novels make my heart skip.

.75 inches: My calves are this good from running, thank you.

1.5 inches: I'm going home with my husband, and that's how I want it.

2.3 inches: Exactly .2 centimeters taller than the bimbo whom my husband ran away with.

4.2 inches: Hello, boys! None of you can have this.

5.8 inches: Howdy, fellas; everyone can have this.

Feminists insist that high heels exist solely to contort the female body into unnatural positions, and the reply is, well, yes, if you're lucky.

They are footwear as weaponry, a device designed solely to make one's legs look more attractive. Men have no equivalent, except for boots, which some men think makes their past look more attractive.

Men are forever cursed when it comes to shoes. It's in our makeup, and there's no escaping it, no matter what we do. Why, right now I'm wearing my wife's high heels, and let me tell you: My ankles are killing me.

Death to the Taster's Choice Couple

ᔑᔑ

YOU UNDERSTAND, DON'T YOU? TELL ME YOU DO. TELL ME that you've found yourself watching a TV commercial, realized that you've seen this particular ad about 37,203 times, and suddenly felt such an intense hatred for the ad that you wanted to spring from your chair, stride across the room, and slam your boot in the tube. Of course, you don't. If there is anything worse than wondering how stupid they think you are, it's asking the same question while your foot is embedded in an inert television set.

But surely you want to. Tell me that I am not alone in this. I was watching something stupid, like *Married . . . With Carbuncles* or similar fare, when a commercial for Burger King came on. The ad, which heralded a new line of Teenage New Kids Mutant Turtle Ninjas on the Block (Uh-Huh!), ended with the line "Sometimes You Gotta Break the Rules." I felt a vast tsunami of irritation crest in my brain—what the devil do they mean by that, anyway? Which rules do the brave folks at Burger King flout with such cheek? Will I walk into a Burger King tomorrow and be flung against the ceiling because sometimes you've got to break the rule that gravity results from planetary mass? Will an overworked fry cook fling knives into my throat because sometimes you've got to break the rules of civilized conduct that restrain us all? Can I break the rule, unwritten but understood, that keeps us from standing up and saying, "HEY! COLON CANCER AND HEART DISEASE AWAIT!"

The commercial wants us to think that the folks who run Burger King are hip, freewheeling, unconventional madmen who will stop at nothing to deliver the sine qua non of burgers, while the rest of the industry stands aside, mouths agape. This is nonsense. As far as I can tell, the fast-food industry has only three rules: pepper your chain with bitter, autocratic managers; force your senior citizen employees to wear uniforms that make them look like pathetic echoes of the teenaged employees; introduce interesting menu items that are available "for a limited time only" and then snatch them away for no apparent reason.

I see no reason to believe that any of these rules have been declared breakable.

This is not to pick on Burger King's food. I eat fast food and plenty of it, much of it from BK. The point of this screed is to point out the idiocy of advertising—how perfectly fine clients can get saddled with preposterous campaigns. Some examples come to mind.

AT&T

Judging by their latest campaign, America's peace of mind is being destroyed by an unnamed, unscrupulous long-distance company that is calling people up, promising fabulous rates, and then hanging up when asked to put their offer in writing. We see scenes of demographically correct people walking around their domiciles, each filmed in the fashionable style that looks like a well-respected but hopelessly alcoholic cameraman has been given one last chance but cannot stop stumbling over the cables. From the tenor of these ads, you'd think the Dixie Cup & Kite String Phone Company was making threatening phone calls to everyone in America, slinking away when asked to step into the light of day. The message: When these incubi slither up to you, invoke the holy trinity of AT&T,

and Goodness will prevail. Now, a word about your stopped-up bowels.

So far, it's pretty much what you expect from an industry that rakes in the gelt by flaying our confident veneers, exposing our insecurities, and drizzling lemon juice on them. This much I can understand; to sell a product, you have to make people miserable. What puts the cheese grater to my nerves is the attitude of the people in these commercials. They are personally offended that the evil usurper will not put things in writing. One man is so discomfited by the experience that he has apparently stopped on the street and is pouring out his story to us as though he expects absolution. Another man is shown pacing his apartment as he grapples with the evil one; he enjoys the intellectual combat but cannot restrain his manly disdain. An executive gives a humorless, what-fools-these-mortals-be chuckle as he tells the tale: they said I'd save money. (Spoken like a man who can write it off.) The more I see this commercial, the more I wonder, If these people were approached by a long-distance company whose satellite network consisted of ten tall guys on ladders with semaphore flags, and this firm did put it in writing, would everything be okay?

It got worse. When the tide of firms unwilling to put it in writing stopped lapping at the shores of this green and pleasant land, a new threat emerged: misdirected calls. Again, this is not something that has personally plagued my life, but it befalls the citizens of the commercials with hideous regularity. One man in particular seems trapped in hell: every night I watch him attempt to call Phoenix and he gets Fiji; a burly man picks up the phone and says, "WANANANANOAH," whereupon the man looks at the phone with disgust. Night after night: "Hello, Phoenix?" "WANANANANOAH."

The implication is that other phone companies operate according to the principle of phonetics, which is why Phoenix gets you Fiji. Presumably when you call your friend Maurice, you get Mauritania.

The horror does not stop there: the man cannot get Instant Credit for his call. Were he dealing with AT&T, gouts of coins would probably gush from the phone and knock him flat, and he would pick himself up with a wry grin. No, he is dealing with Dixie Cup & Kite String, and DC&KS operators are under orders to respond to all billing inquiries with high-handed reminders that he has abandoned AT&T for a low-rent assemblage of grifters who will probably disappear tomorrow, taking their billion-dollar satellite network with them and setting up shop under a new name. The man slams down the phone in disgust and walks away with the universal expression of CAN YOU BELIEVE WHAT A YUPPIE ARCHETYPE LIKE ME HAS TO GO THROUGH, casting nasty looks back at the phone.

In short, the entire series of commercials seems aimed at those who lack all sense of perspective and who are either ruing their apostasy or singing the plainsong of the faithful. All I know is that I have never had a problem with my long-distance; never. So when AT&T called me up to ask if I'd like their services, I simply said, "WANANANANOAH."

They didn't know what the hell I was talking about, either.

Taster's Choice

The epitome of the coffee commercial used to be those Mrs. Olson spots for Folger's. You remember: husband drinks coffee, makes a face as though he has been served broth of quicklime; wife is grief-stricken, staggers around looking for the fainting couch. Then that grinning Teutonic she-wolf of the percolator, Mrs. Olson, steps in to administer a brisk lesson in coffee selection.

"It's mountain-grown," she says in that chilling voice, fit for one of those epicene Nazi commanders in bad forties movies. "The richest kind." Next thing you know, hubby is banging back the bean by the potful, and domestic tranquility reigns.

Coffee is a dull sell, though. The makers try to tiptoe around its purpose—namely, lift-off juice. Spark plug in a cup. Most commercials thus employ the Difficult Waker, someone who has to be dynamited from REM sleep lest they fall down in the shower and hurt themselves. So we see surly, gummy-eyed mummies changing into bright perky workers, merely by smelling the coffee. Even decaf ads have people waking instantly once the cup is placed in their hands, as though there is something inherently galvanizing about hot brown water.

There are other images in coffee ads, such as the ones for flavored coffee powders; here, women are urged to make a cup and stare reflectively into space. But until recently, sex was not a big theme in coffee commercials. Until Taster's Choice came out with a series of commercials, all presumably tailored to lead its characters into the sack.

Spot #1 concerned a British Woman who was giving an elegant dinner party—pearls and prawns and petit fours. She had attended to every detail but somehow forgot to purchase coffee. (Sure. *Sure.*) The woman runs next door, where Ordinary Bloke, early-thirties handsome variety, is more than happy to oblige her with freeze-dried flakes. Woman returns to party, where someone asks if she's met her neighbor, and she replies very Britishly that she's "popped 'round for coffee," making it sound like she regularly exchanged sexual favors for a cup or two.

The whole enterprise reeks of contrivance and snobbery, and what's worse, there's more: it's an on-going series. In Spot #2, British Woman pops 'round unannounced to Ordinary Bloke's place, arms full of groceries, and says, "You saved my life the other night." At which point the Bloke would be well-advised to knock her bags to the floor and search through the groceries for some coffee, just to make sure she won't bother him again. Because *he already has a woman over for dinner,* and she is already at full perk, so to speak. Instead, they engage in sodden banter and part.

Spot #3: Bloke runs into British Woman at a dinner party. They make allusive references to freeze-dried coffee; Bloke asks her out. Perhaps at a restaurant they can find out they both like ketchup and bring to two the number of banal commonalities that link their lives. In Spot #4 they are at her door, the date concluded. There is some tension—perhaps Bloke pitched a whizzy-fit in the kitchen when he caught the sorry Frog bastards brewing coffee instead of dumping hot water over little winking shards of coffee molecules. She invites him in anyway—for coffee. With unfailing monomania, he insists it must be freeze-dried. Spot #5 takes place an hour later and finds British Woman ready for bed—either solo or with accompaniment, it's hard to tell; being British, she displays all the brio and passion of a cold pancake. He begs for one more cup—perhaps the one that will send him over the edge, turn him into a coffee-crazed serial killer. Who knows? She's let this guy into her house knowing no more than that he likes coffee. Maybe he's okay; maybe he's a narcoleptic serial killer who hates to nod off in the middle of work.

She hands him the jar of coffee . . . his hands close around it . . . end of commercial. At press time, this was all the world knew.

I have never wanted more for two people I disliked to go to bed and get it over with. Just so these commercials can leave the air forever. I dread the next one; I imagine it will take place entirely in the dark, and that British Woman will confess to being a virgin, after which we will hear the button on the lid pop up to indicate the factory seal has been broken. I hope his filter leaks.

Burnett Realty

These I doubt you've heard; they were radio ads confined to a Midwest market. But they are illustrative. Each ad consisted of a singer moaning ecstatically about realtors, interludes of drums madly thwacked, and a female choir singing "Burnett . . . Burnett fire!" The ad concludes: "Burnett Fire. Burnett *Passion.* Burnett Realty." It's as if the entire firm consists of oversexed arsonists.

No slight intended on the folk who work for Burnett. I think they're ill-served by the ads. The ads probably scare away the old folks, who fear that if they call Burnett, they will get Little Richard with a tank of napalm strapped to his back. The ads, of course, impress those of us who could not care less about commission cost and are concerned primarily with getting a passionate realtor. But most people, I think, find the ad irritating and change the station when it comes on. Doesn't matter if the music is catchy, Prince-like—they're hawking *bungalows,* for heaven's sake.

Here's what happens. A group of otherwise sane executives, dressed in suits, meets with the advertising people, who are all in black and thus hip. The ad people, who have put together a fabulous campaign that's sure to win awards and, incidentally, might actually help the client, explain what they want to do. The suits, all aging baby boomers, are so afraid of appearing unhip that they nod vigorously at the suggested campaign, approve it, and privately carp like people in an AT&T ad when it fails.

The suits really yearn for the days when boomer tunes were hip and every ad had some tired boomer anthem ("And now, Edwin Starr for Compound W: 'WARTS! *Huh!* Good *Gawd,* y'all! What are they good for? Absolutely nuthin'.' ") But those days will not come again. So they do what business people seem unable to resist nowadays: yield to the instincts of their advertising agency. It's the rule: Thou shalt not question the wisdom of an advertising firm with many industry awards in their lobby.

Maybe so. But, you quavering executives, sometimes you gotta break the rules. What, you don't know what that means? Exactly. *Exactly.*

Columbophobia

I'D BE CONTENT TO CALL COLUMBUS THE SCUM OF THE EARTH, but he spent so much time at sea. Call him the scum of earth and sea, then. No, wait; he probably leaped up when he found America. Scum of earth, sea, and air, then. Doesn't matter. I will still celebrate his day in the time-honored way: sleeping 'til noon and watching game shows.

Columbus Day does not loom large as a holiday. It has no heartwarming songs. Greeting-card stores shun it as a distraction from pushing pumpkin-themed merchandise. Families do not sit around a large table and eat a big dead bird in honor of it. Even TV advertising, which cannot resist making George Washington wink from a large cartoon dollar and say, "I cannot tell a lie: these are hot deals!" ignores it. (Which is unusual: Columbus sighting discounted car parts through a spyglass and crying, "Bargains ho!" would seem to be a natural.) No one ever realizes with a vague nostalgic pang that Columbus Day is "really for the kids." Saying "Merry Columbus Day" to people you pass is like saying "happy elevator ride."

You get the idea. This year, however, we have to think differently about Columbus Day. Spain, for example, is throwing a party in Barcelona, complete with three ships that will sail all the way to New York, where they will be blasted out of the water by the USS *Wisconsin*. (Just to remind Europe that Things Have Changed.)

The celebrations here, however, will be somewhat strained. To see why, we need to examine how the views on old Chris have moderated.

The old view of Columbus as seen through my second-grade textbooks: Unsmiling, wig-wearing gym-teacher type who was determined to find a new spice route to Cathay. (Translated by teacher as "pepper from China.") Ran into a speed bump called the Americas. Planted a flag and said, in English, "I claim this land for Spain." Went home and gave the address to the Pilgrims. A week later, the colonies declared their independence. Helpful song: "In Fourteen Hundred and Ninety-two, Columbus sailed the ocean blue."

The new wisdom on Columbus: Hitler with an astrolabe. Warty white guy who swaggered into Eden, hitched up his pants, cried, "Start killin' the natives, boys, we got shopping malls to build." Invented the concept of slavery, which no one had ever thought of before that moment and then left, pausing briefly to found the Republican Party and cough in the face of the natives to make sure they all expired of unusual diseases.

Helpful song—well, there isn't one. The standard anti-Columbus position contains so many points of view it's hard to sum it up in a handy rhyming couplet. But let's try.

"In 1492" is out, as it implies that history is the property of the Western calendar. "Columbus sailed" is nominally accurate, but insults other cultures with a seafaring tradition. "The ocean blue" both betrays a chauvinistic attitude toward the tint of that particular harbor and suggests as well that the color-blind cannot appreciate the event. Hueism, pure and simple. Plus, this simple ditty says nothing of the pain and suffering that resulted from Columbus's journey. Remember, a value not stated is a divergent value reinforced. So then:

"In a year recognized by disparate cultures as one of the revolutions of the earth about the sun, Columbus, engaging in an Iberian derivation of the navigational technology that existed in varying degrees of sophistication around the world, sailed across a body of water, which was interesting inasmuch as it allowed him to further his Eurocentric agenda of racist imperialism."

That is what it comes down to: Columbophobes are determined that everyone beat themselves in the head with the bones of history until we admit that this entire America thing has been a horror story from the git-go, that the day Columbus landed should be a day of mourning.

The truth, as ever, is between the two shrieking opposites. Pro-Columbus advocates ignore the fact that this continent was conquered by men of hideous, stupid, arrogant brutality. People who love that previous sentence forget that people of equal arrogance and brutality inhabited the land before the white guys showed up. The history of mankind is dung and diamonds, enlightenment winking up at the sun from a heap of superstition and suspicion.

Let's all agree that Columbus was, like most humans, no saint. (Not even the saints were exactly saints, in all probability.) But we're not here to fix his sins; we're here to build the sort of society his blinkered little brain could never have imagined.

Or was he really that shortsighted? Consider that enigmatic entry in his diary: "Have seen land. Great rejoicing. Have validated my theories as well as provided excellent pretext for federal holiday."

Maybe he knew what he was doing, after all.

Righteous Bacon

WHILE THERE IS NO FIRSTHAND EVIDENCE THE UNITED STATES had God on its side in the Gulf War, it seems fairly obvious that we had meat on our side. Iraqi troops dined on rice and boiled leaves; we had Slim Jims and burgers, and hence prevailed. But the Agriculture Department hasn't learned that lesson, and is now preparing to abolish the cherished Four Food Groups—the Allied Forces of Nutrition that carved the dinner table into equal spheres of influence, gave meat equal time with limp, green spinachy things that squeak against your teeth. The Four Groups are hereby to be replaced by the "Eating Right Pyramid." The base consists of grains and cereals, with fruits and vegetables making up the next level, a few thin bricks' worth of meat, cheese, and milk near the top, with fats and oils—yum!—surmounting the structure.

The reason is simply, Americans eat too much fat and oil. This makes it sound like we live on a diet of fried professional wrestlers, but it's true. You could open up a chain of restaurants called FATS 'N' OILS ("Try our lard combo platter!") and you'd make a million. After all, nutritionists unhappily admit, it's fat that makes things taste good.

And fat is everywhere in food—lurking, undetected. That would be fine if your body just left it alone; but no, tiny cells in your stomach form a bucket brigade to pass fat to your circulation system, where other highly specialized cells trowel it on your arterial walls. Eventually your ticker decides to act like an Indy 500 race car thrown into reverse gear. The coroner is forced to write, "Cause of death: bacon." (The fact that it usually takes forty years of meat-eating to have your arteries completely bricked up suggests that the cells are not only highly specialized, but also unionized.)

So yes, fat is bad. I know I've cut it from my diet: no more ordering the "free-range fat in fat sauce" at the restaurant, and when the host says, "More fat, anyone? There's plenty," I say no. I now subsist entirely on a diet of particle board—for the fiber—and tofu, which is the culinary equivalent of Play-Doh. For greens, I smoke cigarettes. Hey, it was a plant, once.

While I recognize the need for a healthier diet, I resent having the usual scolds shoving fistfuls of sprouts down my esophagus for political reasons. Eating meat is seen by some as just one more symbol of the decadent, impure West. Why, look at the noble, unspoiled Eskimos. They eat fish and don't suffer from highly symbolic heart attacks, as do Westerners. Granted. They also have epic poems built around the idea of "The Bone in the Throat."

Besides, it's not as if Eskimos have to shoulder their way through dense herds of cattle to get to their fishing hole. Put a few million cows on the tundra and see how eager they are to have fish for the 1,203,309 time.

If other cultures eat healthier foods, it's because that's what the planet turns out in greatest quantities. Plants do not have to be chased, wrestled to the ground, and violently done away with. Plants stand there and take it, and come back next year: plants never get the point. There is no particular ethical virtue to relying on plants, and no stigma should be affixed to those who prefer something that moved around, had eyes, and argued incoherently before you slayed it.

Not to suggest meat eaters are somehow more valiant, brave, forthright, etc. I think there's something uncivilized about meat eating. It begins with a nasty barbarism, for example. Cows are not led to perfumed couches and ushered on to the Great Pasture with hay-scented sleeping gas. If most recipes that called for meat began with the instructions "Apply nail-gun to cranium of beast; render and dress," there would be a lot more Lentil Lasagna Surprise showing up on the nation's tables.

Most of us manage to get past that fact. I eat meat because I grew up with it and like it. Why do I like it? Successful PR, for one. The cherished Four Food Groups, it turns out, was a concept devised by the dairy and meat industries in the late forties and early fifties, a wonderful device for making sure we all spent breakfast hurling rendered intestinal casings stuffed with bovine organ by-products down our gullets BECAUSE THAT'S WHAT YOU DID IN THE MORNING. It makes one relieved that the escargot and vinegar lobbies weren't strong in those days.

It's amazing that it took nutritionists this long to abolish that uninformed manifesto. The late forties, after all, was the era in which cigarette ads proclaimed that "Nine out of ten doctors prefer smoking unfiltered Luckies in a coal mine full of loose asbestos!" and other dubious notions. But no one has challenged the Four Food Groups until now. You'd think someone in the sixties would have lobbied for an additional group, so in addition to cereals, dairy products, meats, and fruits and vegetables, you'd also have hallucinogens and downers. Apparently everyone was enjoying their meals too much to pay the Four Food Groups any attention.

But now we have the pyramid. Just like the pyramid on the back of your dollar bill, with fats and oils located in the segment with the eye on top, watching to see if you've gained any weight. Some critics—and you should have no trouble believing this—say that the choice of a pyramid was wrong, because it puts french fries and ice cream on the top. (As if people whose diet consisted entirely of rice and sticks would promptly belly flop into a tub of butterfat upon seeing the new diet guidelines.) The PR firm that designed the pyramid says that they tested an inverted pyramid on consumers, but women rejected it because they felt that it looked like it would fall over.

Of course, women always think that their eating habits are

going to fall over on them. Men, on the other hand, probably liked the pyramid. Think of the old ones in Egypt, assembled with slave labor. Guys look at the Eating Right Pyramid and think, *Hey, slaves conquered in war will bring bales of Lucky Charms to my door. All right.*

So that's what the war was for!

Bring the Little Ones Unto Me, So I Can Kill Them

∽∽

IF YOU HAVE COCKROACHES, YOU'LL BE PLEASED TO HEAR there's a way to get rid of them forever.

1. Pile your belongings in the street; burn them.
2. Move; leave no forwarding address.
3. To ensure you don't bring cockroach eggs to your new place, skydive nude to your next apartment.
4. Repeat until you think nothing of turning on the kitchen light without a baseball bat.

Anyone who's ever had cockroaches knows the despair that comes from harboring these evil beasties. They are indestructible: the other day I gave one a swat that should have left a small, roach-shaped dent in the sheetmetal of the stove; when I looked, the roach was still intact. Probably thinking, *HOLY HELL! MAN! WHAT WAS THAT!* but intact. Off it scuttled.

They are innumerable: according to the commercials, a few idle roaches scampering across your floor means a vast colony pulsing behind your walls, a billion-legged army running around the rafters. Knock a hole in the wall and they'll gush

204

out like water from a dike. Kill one on the counter, and you can almost hear the rest laugh: *Crunch All You Want! We'll Make More!*

They are, worst of all, two dimensional: they can fit through anything. A cockroach can run full-tilt at a closed dictionary and vanish between its pages. It can slip between a stamp and an envelope. As the rest of us proceed with the standard three-dimensional assumptions, we are constantly unprepared when the roach heads for a cereal box and disappears between the box and the picture printed on its surface. You can't win.

Actually, you can. You can call an exterminator, who comes in and drenches the joint with methylethyldethylschtrethyltrioxidate, which is cockroach for "dessert." Then you stagger around light-headed for a month, covered in hives, and your vision is so fuzzy you don't actually see the roaches.

If you don't like the chemical approach, you can try boric acid, which roaches hate. It gums up their breathing tubes and smothers them. A lingering death: you like that idea. You want to put a stethoscope to the walls and hear them wheezing. I am currently giving the house the boric treatment, and it seems to be working: the roaches are slower, like smokers who've climbed a few flights of stairs; I half expect to see them dragging tiny tanks of oxygen.

But it still leaves me with something worse than cockroaches.

Ants.

Most people don't regard ants as worse than roaches, but they are: they are the Nazis to the roaches' loot-and-pillage Huns. Ants have it all figured out. Ants have a plan.

For a while I had two ants lost in my study. I regarded them as harmless pets, staggering around the room with no idea what they were doing, lost in a shag hell. Occasionally I'd see them meeting up with each other and having ant confabulations with their antennae.

Ant 1: "Where the hell are we?"

Ant 2: "I'm sure I have no idea."

I paid them little mind, which was my mistake. Ants may have no idea where they are going, but they have a highly developed mechanism for getting other ants to follow. (See "political campaigns" for further details.) By laying down an invisible chemical trail, ants are able to bring all their friends into your house, and eventually someone finds the food. It's like letting drunks loose in a shopping mall: sooner or later, someone is going to stumble on the McDonald's.

In our case, the food was located three floors below the ants' point of entry. One of the two ants must have made it down there one day. I wish I'd been there when he beheld the garbage can; his antennae must have stuck straight out and twirled around in delight. He headed back up the stairs via the baseboard, squirting the ant equivalent of EAT AT JOE'S NEXT EXIT as he went.

Before I knew it I had ants, ants, ants: little earnest ants, and big brawny guys you could saddle up and ride, all coursing up and down the baseboard of the stairwell. The ones on the way out had some speck of food—coffee, sugar, tobacco. Not just black ants, then, black-market ants. Well, this had to stop. I tried wiping the baseboard with a sponge, to get rid of their trail: no good. I used an ammonia-based window cleaner next, but apparently ants regard a trail of window cleaner like hungry humans would look at a five-lane-wide road of pizza sauce. Still they came.

So I killed them. I sat on the top of the landing with a box of Kleenex and picked them up as they came. When the Kleenex had enough ants I would drop it in the toilet. And then the ants would ant-paddle around, some of them spinning in circles, others making sturdy progress toward the high ground of the Kleenex wad. Occasionally I would see two ants meet in the water and bat antennae together.

Ant #1: "What the hell is this?"

Ant #2: "You tell me."

Then I'd flush and watch them all gurgle down. And go and fill up another Kleenex.

I should mention that my wife had been gone on a business trip for three days; I was also starting to talk to myself and laugh out loud for no reason.

My diligent anticide paid off; word got around and the ants went elsewhere. But another colony heard of the ripe pickings available in our garbage pail and invaded from the apartment below us. Small ants, these. Tiny. A box of commas come to life. You can get the entire invading army in one session of vigorous stomping, providing you tell your neighbor that you are practicing Slavic folk dances so they don't wonder why the apartment above seems to be inhabited by spastic Cossacks shouting, "ANTS DIE NOW! ANTS DIE NOW!"

But they'll be back. Humans inhabit such a tasty world. I can caulk up the doors and windows, lay down a foot-high drift of boric acid around everything, and still the insects will come. At least they're not big; if ants and cockroaches were the size of small dogs, I would end up sitting in the kitchen all night with a shotgun and a whip, drinking whiskey and muttering the litany of madness.

As it is, I just have this rolled newspaper. Front page: campaign news. It'll do. Sure, I can't kill them all.

But maybe I can bore them to death.

Talk, Talk, Talk

᪣᪣

FINALLY, A RADIO STATION THAT'S DROPPED ALL PRETENSE. WDDQ of Aden, Georgia, has scrapped its country music for and gone to nonstop commercials. No music. NO talk. NO boring news or useless weather. Just incessant bleats for money. But not any old commercials: no, WDDQ blares naught but ads for businesses controlled by the station's owner—restaurants, motels, gas stations, and an outlet mall. All these glories beamed at the helpless heads of the locals all day, all night.

It must have been a cruel moment when the station cut for a commercial . . . and never came back to the music. You wonder if they did it gracefully, playing commercials with *boom-chicka* background music, segueing to commercials whose double entendres are sordid enough to qualify as country music. "Here's Henny Penny Kitchens, located near you, with that all-time favorite, 'Grab my breasts and pry my thighs! The drive-thru's open! Try my pies!'"

This is not unexpected. AM radio, long eclipsed by the superior sound of FM, has struggled for years to carve smaller and smaller niches. There are all-sports talk stations, which pump out nothing but stat-addled fan blather; there are all-weather stations, which probably serve as nostalgia channels for those serving prison terms in solitary confinement. There are formats targeting children, businessmen, homemakers. We are mere years away from spinning the dial and hearing some beefy-voiced fellow announce that you're tuned to "WTVC—talk radio for the pet animals of red-haired transsexual penny-stock investors, all the time!"

The result has been predictable: local listeners have relocated to archaic, old-fashioned stations that occasionally play music in between the ads and swap meets. But it makes you wonder if all-commercial radio really is the most effective way to blow off your audience. Surely there are other formats that would alienate people with greater alacrity—formats that could make people switch stations within seconds of tuning in.

Some suggestions:

- All-Dial-Tone radio. At the sound of the tone . . . nothing in particular will happen.
- All-Uncomfortable-Sensation radio. A narrator will read from a list of uncomfortable things. "Good morning, it's nine o'clock. Leading the list this morning: Hot cotton on your back teeth. Getting a papercut as you lick an envelope. Stepping on a crunchy beetle. And now, the weather: A trickle of sweat down the cleft of your buttocks."
- All-Paranoid radio. Unintelligible conspiracy theories read by a speed freak.
- All-Fundamentalist-Preacher radio. See above.
- All Poke-in-the-Eye-With-a-Sharp-Stick radio. For fifty-nine minutes and fifty-five seconds, nothing but the sound of a penknife working on a branch. If that doesn't drive them off, the top-of-the-hour announcement will:

Announcer 1: "At the sound of the tone, it will be three o'clock. Now, where'd I put that—oh, here it is."
Announcer 2: "AHH! AHH! AHH!"
Announcer 1: "And now, the temperature."
Announcer 2: "NO PLEASE GOD NO NOT THE TEMPERATURE!"

Perhaps this is a bad idea; some people would actually wait around for fifty-nine minutes to hear that.

- All-Siren/Blown-Tire radio. The station will alternate the sounds of a siren with the sound of a tire blowing. No matter which you happen to hear, you'll immediately turn your radio off and pull over.
- All-Baby-Monitor radio. Constant broadcasts from the homes of concerned, slightly overprotective parents.

Perhaps even these formats might encourage the perverse to linger and listen; radio stations breed strange loyalties. Cancel the All-Baby-Monitor format, and you're sure to get people who call up and complain, say they wanted to see how it all turned out. ("Did he git over that colic and go on to live a productive life? Well, did he?") But at least they'll be honest about their intentions: to make people turn off the radio and perhaps talk to the person in the passenger seat. Maybe that's the point behind all-commercial radio: to encourage conversation.

Suggested topic: what might be on a little further down the dial.

Turn That Racket Down

∿∿∿∿∿∿∿∿∿∿∿∿∿∿∿∿∿∿∿∿∿∿∿∿∿∿∿∿∿∿∿∿∿

THE RENEWAL NOTICE FOR MY SUBSCRIPTION TO A FAMED music magazine came in the mail the other day, and I realized it was a referendum on my youth. Renew, and I revalidated my self-image, born fifteen years before, as a hip, vital guy who could not only name the players in bands I hated but name the bands they used to be in, which I also hated. Let it lapse, I suspected, and I would immediately become a deaf and cranky Old Person whistling "Jimmy Crack Corn" to take his mind off his gout.

I renewed. The pert and pouty models in the magazine's last fashion supplement had clouded my judgment; if I ever met them I'd have to have something to talk about, and if it meant being conversant with the latest offering from Bloody Froth or 30-Weight Sputum, then so be it.

But this cannot go on forever. At some point I am going to have to take a deep breath and admit that I have lost touch. For some time I've noticed that popular music is not only foreign but hugely irritating, like the headache from a night spent celebrating a stranger's birthday. Apparently, I was temporarily distracted—by the job, the house—and when I looked up popular music was sprinting ahead, wearing a satin tour jacket for some band I'd never heard of. Perhaps it happened the day the water heater broke, and I was knee-deep in a rusty ocean. Maybe that was what was knocking at the front door: my youth.

HOW I KNOW I HAVE FALLEN BEHIND The building in which I work has an immense record store; the popular CDs are downstairs, tapes are upstairs; beyond lies jazz, and in a room past jazz, classical. Two years ago I would have lingered downstairs, checked to see what was playing, and bought it like a dutiful robot programmed to consume all things hip and vital. Now I drift in like someone who's returned for a class reunion and decided to take a look at the old school. I find myself wincing at the thudding din pounding from the speakers, my bowels uncoiling from the beat; I head upstairs as soon as I can. I pass through the tapes section, where they are playing something that sounds like trash cans being fed into a woodchipper, and slide into the jazz room. Cool saxophones here, voices with a seen-it-all resignation of one whose libido has crow's feet. There is melody here. It almost seems subversive. Then I proceed through the door to the classical section, hidden away like a blind pig. Orchestras toil in this room. Tuxedoed virtuosi labor at catgut and brass. Counterpoint swirls. Intellect and passion combine and argue. The apex of civilization. BUT NO PERT 'N' POUTY MODELS! I end up buying a symphony by Bruckner, a devout Catholic and lifelong virgin, and slink back out into the sound of spasming gonads, feeling like I am wearing tweed underwear. I feel so old it is a wonder that my appendages do not slough off. *Mister—this your arm?* Thanks, sonny. Let me tell you about the Sex Pistols. Why, I remember when— *That's okay, mister. Really.*

So what happened? Did I get old rapidly—or did popular music get worse?

How do *you* think I'll answer that one?

But I'm right. Popular music has gotten worse. Newly coined adults have for decades been beholden to curse their antecessors' musical taste as being noise, and for decades they have been wrong. I am lucky to live in an age in which, by God, popular music now is actually noise, as in:

RAP, THE OUT-OF-TOUCH ADULT'S DREAM Fifteen years ago, these were the cranky questions posed by newly out-of-touch adults:

Why don't they play drums like they did?
Why can't they play guitar like they did?
Why doesn't anyone sing the way they used to?

New questions posed by freshly minted thirty-year-olds today:

Why can't they play drums?
Why don't they play guitar?
Why isn't anyone singing?

Pop music has, in short, gone downhill fast, and the wreck at the bottom is called rap. I am not generally fond of it, with a few exceptions: I spent the week leading up to my wedding listening exclusively to "We Got Our Own Thang," by Heavy D; I attribute the constant repetition of the phrase "Don't be down with anybody, let them all be down with you" apt preparation for keeping the reception line going. I have a dozen or so rap singles for play in my car but feel self-conscious when I play them, for two reasons.

1. The sight, glimpsed once and never forgotten, of a white kid in daddy's Porsche around Minneapolis, listening to "Fight the Power" and nodding his head in complete agreement. *Excuse me, son: the Power pays your insurance.*

2. I fear I look as though I am trying to accumulate Black Points. Let me explain. I know some people who seem to regard each rap record purchased as a set of stamps they can lick and place on their karma card, proof that their soul has clean fingernails. That they are in touch with The Street. There is something pathetic about white folk who buy a record about shooting black people and believe it automatically entitles them to membership in the Black-Experience Club. If hard-core rap was sold exclusively in the neighborhoods the lyrics describe, you'd be amazed how many people would decide to explore jazz.

If I don't like most rap music, it's not just because it's noisy and unlettered, and requires perhaps less musical aptitude than is required to play "Heart and Soul" on a church basement piano. It's not because the message is often harsh and uncompromising. It is simply because I have come to a point in my life where I have winnowed down the list of people who are allowed to yell at me.

Permitted:

- Spouse
- Boss
- Parents, and, depending on the context, In-laws

Not Permitted:

- Politicians
- Street Drunks
- Musicians

I'm more than inclined to give people a listen, if they express themselves in a civil manner. When their angry face is looming from my TV set and bellowing like a gored ox, I don't care if they're reciting recipes (PUT THE BATTER IN A BIG GREASED PAN! PUT IT IN THE STOVE AS FAST AS YOU CAN!/BAKE FOR AN HOUR 'TIL YOU SEE THE SUCKA RISE! SERVES TEN HOMEBOYS UNLESS ONE OF THEM DIES!), I just want to turn the channel. It's not something I want to carve time out to endure.

And please—*please*—do not suggest that my attitude toward rap means I am insulating myself from the harsh realities of life, closing my eyes to the solutions espoused by rap. One does not become an expert on the collapse of the Texas economy by listening to weepy country-western tunes. You can get a clue about Hitler if you listen to Wagner, but few clues to whether to mount an invasion in Normandy or Calais are found in the Ring Cycle.

THE REST OF THE SORRY HEAP OF LOSERS So, besides rap, what is there? Much dreck. Here are the current rock and roll genres:

Death Metal

Bands with one-word names like Anthrax, Slayer, Megadeth, Tetanus, Psoriasis, Seborreah, Pyorrhea, Colitis. Band members dress in black, play very fast, and sing about how everything is hopeless and how war is wrong. Audience: Teenaged boys who live in a prosperous, draft-free society and believe that the record of human perfidity is a valid excuse for sleeping through math class.

When I listened to this stuff: Never. Life is too short to spend every moment being reminded of the fact.

Stupid Drunk Evil Boogie Metal

No real pattern in the names, aside from a vague internal rhyme: Twisted Sister, Quiet Riot. Group names frequently have umlauts over letters in their names to indicate allegiance with Satan; thus, Higgly Piggly becomes the ominous Hïgglÿ Pïgglÿ. Band members have names reminiscent of English royalty, like David St. Pepto, or names redolent of evil, like Bismollah Sixx. Songs are generally grungy messy thrashings about sex and suicide, thus giving their audience at least one thing they can successfully execute. (Devotees frequently raise their hands with the index and pinkie fingers extended, thinking it refers to the horns of the devil, when it is actually a sign expressing solidarity with the Brotherhood of Careless Band-Saw Operators.)

Classic Rock

Music for people who, by some odd turn of events, are still in the same job they were in twenty years ago.

Lite Rock

An oxymoron. This is the fluffy, bouncy stuff that makes sorority girls feel nasty and/or sad and, ten years later, makes them pause while diapering a child and briefly feel a stabbing pang for youth, lost forever. Naturally the format is very popular. Men are not immune: a sure sign of age is hearing on a lite rock station a tune you once considered a "good driving tune." (One station in my listening area advertises its product as "not too hard, not too soft," thereby appealing to the Baby Bear Boomers in their audience.)

Indie Rock

Also known as indie-thrash, under-indie, indie-post-punk-thrash, depending on whether the rock writer is, like so many, paid by the hyphen. The main difference between this and other highly spirited incompetent garage bands of the past few decades is that these bands wear only plaid shirts, do not wash their hair with discernible regularity, and come from Seattle, thus constituting a New Voice.

There are a dozen other splinters, each with its own philosophy, worldview, and haircut. On any given weekend I can happily twitch and twirl along with any of them, but I will come to life only when someone puts on an Elvis Costello record from 1978. At that point I recall that I am now of the age of people who hated Elvis Costello when he first came out. Yet here I am, thirty-three, and I love it.

Lord. What narrow-minded people they were.

The Sound of One
Hand Lathering

∿∿∿

INSTRUCTIONS FOR READING THIS ESSAY ON SHAMPOOS:

Empty brain.
Read piece; forget.
Repeat.

Most of you, of course, will stop at the second step, and
that's good. The eternal shampoo-instructional loop is not
meant to be taken to its logical extreme, or you would shampoo until the bottle blurted bubbles, the hot water ran dry,
and you staggered from the shower scalded and puckered,
arms aching, scalp raw. No, you laugh every morning at the
shampoo bottle: repeat? *REPEAT?* You think I'm stupid?

But you are stupid. We are all stupid. We are pawns, dupes,
bleating sheep who believe our wool is unique and deserves
special care. Shampoo is just gooey soap with perfume and
an ad campaign, and we are idiots to buy it.

I realized this the other day when I was out of shampoo
and was forced to wash my hair with Lava soap. Lava contains actual shards of rock and is favored by people who clean
horse stables and cap oil wells. My hair turned out just fine—

217

in fact, my scalp sang all day long with that pleasant, freshly healed feeling.

You could wash your hair with bargain-brand dishwashing detergent, and no one would notice. But we've bought into the notion that our hair has special needs. It's Oily. It's Dry. It's Permed. It's Stressed. It's Sad. It's Ambiguous. It's Tough on Foreign Policy but Liberal on Social Issues. There's shampoo for long hair. Short hair. Shampoo for skinheads who don't want their bright, fresh tattoos obscured by oily buildup.

We all buy into this nonsense. When presented with the options, we buy the shampoo that fits our conception of our hair. If you have oily hair, you cast envious glances at the Normal Hair bottle, and hate the people who buy it. If you have dry hair, you console yourself with the knowledge that at least you don't have to buy the Oily Hair shampoo. If you have normal hair, you pity everyone, and it's an enjoyable feeling. You suspect it's all nonsense, but you don't want to risk the nightmare of inappropriate shampoo.

But none of this shampoo is appropriate. In a perfect world, we would have choices like these:

- *For Psychotic Hair.* This is for hair that defies all attempts to do what you tell it to do and flies off in a dozen directions the minute you step away from the mirror. Contains ten percent Thorazine.
- *For Normal Hair.* Contains five percent hallucinogenic drugs. You're too damn normal. It's time you passed a fire hydrant, and it winked at you.
- *For Hair Whose New Color Is NOTHING Like the Color on the Box! Nothing At All!* Contains a solution that will strip your head bald in seconds. It's also poisonous, in case you're really upset.
- *For Anchorman's Hair.* To combat the effects on hair that has been hosed down with epoxy every day for the last twenty years, this gentle relaxing solution of turpentine and bourbon loosens up the tightest hairstyle.
- *For Hair You Wish You Had.* Contains the sweat of models and the essence of the espresso left behind when high-priced stylists were called away from their ciga-

rette break because their three o'clock had arrived. Special conditioning agents lower your IQ while you bathe.

This would be closer to reality, but it would still be a lie. We really don't need special shampoo at all. Consider one damning fact: Body hair gets boring old bar soap every day. Yet no one has ever described their underarm tufts as "limp and unmanageable."

And it gets worse. We laugh at "Repeat" and then unquestioningly accept the next line, "Apply Conditioner." No one has been able to explain precisely what conditioner is. As far as I can tell, this is the procedure:

Shampoo: removes oils.

Conditioner: puts them right back in.

"Repeat" I can understand; it was a simple attempt to double the sales of shampoo. And it worked. But "Apply Conditioner"—what audacity! You can imagine the shampoo makers putting that line on the bottle with the expression of a bomb-squad technician snipping the last lead to the fuse. Will this be the one that blows the whole charade in our face, makes them go back to washing their hair on Sundays with the flakes from the bottom of the laundry soap box?

Of course it didn't. We bought conditioners like good little zombies, feeling we would somehow break up a set if we didn't buy both identical bottles, and the store would be left with an uneven amount of shampoo and conditioner, and they'd KNOW WHO TO BLAME.

And so they came up with the next step, a pure blatant act of contempt for us, the sheep: a substance that's both shampoo and conditioner, like Pert Plus shampoo.

We all know this is theoretically impossible.

It actually enters the realm of philosophy. I know this is typically Western and empirical of me, but I was brought up to believe that certain things follow in sequence. You live, you die. You sow, you reap. You clean, THEN you condition. It's very Lutheran.

If that wash-rinse-repeat cycle smacks of Hindu reincarnationism, then there's something damn near Zen about Pert—serene, enigmatic, a mystery that deepens with contemplation.

Yin and yang, clean and condition: each idea contains its opposite. Pert may be a plot to erode our intellectual foundations, make us more accepting of internally contradictory beliefs. Perhaps it will start to carry parables on the back to be read in the shower.

A young man approaches the old master, asks to be taught the secrets of healthy, more manageable hair. The master says nothing but points to a bucket of mud. The young man is confused and leaves, but returns the next day and repeats the same request. And again the master points to the bucket of mud. This continues for ten years. Finally, in exasperation, the young man pours the mud over his head.

The ancient master smiles. "As you can see, one must understand dirty before one can understand clean."

Moral: The truth can sting. Or, as the shampoo bottle puts it: avoid contact with eyes.

Gobblercide

ᘙᘙ

ENJOY THAT TURKEY, YOU MURDERER. RIP ITS INCINERATED flesh with gusto, you heartless sod. White meat? Dark meat? Blood-soaked bones marinated in fear and terror, anyone? Have a nice Thanksgiving.

The above sentiment has been brought to you courtesy PETA, an animal-rights organization based in the Washington area. While those are not its exact words, those are the sentiments. "THANKSGIVING," their posters read, "IS MURDER ON TURKEYS."

The nation's capital, it should be noted, is not paralyzed by throngs of people marching on the turkey's behalf. It is difficult to mobilize public concern for dead birds when the human murder rate is high enough to make recent census statistics wholly inaccurate. Nevertheless, the animal-rights lobby is set to press hard in coming years, with the intention of making everyone feel dismally guilty about eating the bird.

Why? Animal rights activists contend, correctly, that turkeys are raised in inhumane conditions. They are crowded together in small pens and forced to live noisy lives before getting shoveled into the abattoir. Admittedly, there are more pleasant existences. But we are discussing turkeys, not gurgling infants or even smart smiling dolphins. Turkeys. A creature whose IQ actually increases when you cook it.

Well, here is the total life-experience in the normal turkey habitat, i.e., the predator-infested wild:

Hungry. Not hungry. Sleep. Awake. (Repeat until ripped apart by morally neutral wolf.)

Here is the life of a turkey raised for your table:

Hungry. Not hungry. Vaguely irritated about someone always being in your face. Sleep. Awake. (Repeat until ripped apart by a union member.)

Here is what the animal-rights activists seem to believe a turkey's life is like:

Born into the world with the same hopes and dreams as you or I. Sleep—perchance to dream. Appalled at the filth of its surroundings, absolutely *appalled.* Death at the hands of ignorant beings. Father, forgive them, for they know not what they do.

Beyond the problem of poor conditions, turkey advocates believe that we shouldn't eat birds because, well, they have feelings too. If an animal can feel pain, the argument goes, we have no right to kill it for food. Not when there are all those yummy insensate grains and unconscious gourds we could be eating.

My philosophy of food is based not on whether a creature feels pain, but on whether I can catch it and kill it without being killed myself. (Modern supermarkets have simplified this task immensely.) I do not regard eating meat as immoral and will never grant hamburger the same ethical value as, say, my sister, and just as I don't burst into a vegetarian's home and shove flank steak down their horrified gullets, so should the animal-rights activists desist from trying to make me feel guilty about the frenzy of gobblercide that currently grips the nation.

The hectoring PETA posters complete an effort begun years ago by various scolds and ax-grinders to make Thanksgiving a joyless occasion of dread and self-loathing. With the elevation of the turkey to martyr status, there is now absolutely nothing in Thanksgiving to celebrate.

Let's go down the basics.

• It is cruel to flaunt our bounty. The whole idea of Thanksgiving—taking time out to hoover up the products of

Mother Earth down our greedy gullets—just points out our selfishness. The United States, for example, contains just one seventeenth of the world's population, yet throws away enough candied yams to give everyone in the Saharan subcontinent a twelve-minute sugar rush. This is unfair to all those people who do not yet have the opportunity to waste as much food as we do.

• It is a Eurocentric holiday insensitive to Indigenous American people and thus glorifies European values. After all, Europeans came here to escape the lack of religious freedom in Europe, and . . . well, it doesn't matter that they didn't like Europe and its values, they were *from* there, which is bad enough. Anyway, they came here without invitation and invited the locals to a meal instead of killing them, proving themselves to be . . . wait a minute. Okay, then, Europeans came here and, according to legend, learned fertilization techniques from the natives and out of gratitude asked them to share in the . . . oh, never mind.

• It is cruel to be thankful while others are not thankful. This is the corollary to the point above: while we dominate the world in terms of gravy consumption, the gravy is not spread to an even depth across our own land. We cannot have Thanksgiving until everybody has exactly 4.5 grams of white meat. As the Bolsheviks put it, until every man has one drumstick, no man deserves two.

The point, you see, is not to change anything, but to succeed in making others feel guilty. So have a nice time, you murderous, world-raping glutton. And pass me a wing.

Spokescreatures

∿∿

I watched too much TV as a child. There was a ten-year period in which I sat transfixed before the screen, letting the cathode rays imprint their inanities into my skull like a chef rubbing spices into raw chicken. You could mark my growth not by height-lines penciled on the wall but by carving key dates into the TV set. Sept. 27, 1969: Sight of the three girls from Petticoat Junction disappearing into the Hooterville watertower leads to fevered dreams. Dec. 19, 1970: First frankly carnal appraisal of middle Brady sister. May 13, 1971: Allowed to watch all of Carson for the first time. Nov. 4, 1971: First comprehension of smutty double entendre made on The Match Game, also realization that something was not quite right with Charles Nelson Reilly. And so on.

All of those shows I now regard with horror. I have never been one of those who spend the precious coin of mortal existence watching The Donna Reed Show for its supposed ironic value, particularly if The Mary Tyler Moore Show is playing on another channel. But as much as I forswear TV today, I cannot deny its influence. The other day I was at the supermarket and noticed that whenever possible, I had purchased a brand of food that had been hawked by an animated spokescreature. Madison Avenue had sunk its claws in and sunk them deep. That explains what follows. I never gave this to my editors; I didn't want to worry them.

The Jolly Green Giant

When I was growing up in North Dakota, the knowledge that the Green Giant company was based in the adjacent state of Minnesota was somewhat discomfiting; I didn't like the idea that this lurid golem probably could walk to my house in a day. But he never did walk around. He just tilted his head back slightly and issued that laugh—merry but *too* merry, bone-chilling, if you thought about it coming from a sixty-foot biped standing over your house. When we got color TV, I could see how his skin glistened, a sick oily green soaking in the sunlight, a nauseating fecundity shining from his manic eyes, and I began to fear the Giant.

I knew we were supposed to feel as though the Giant was a great benevolent spirit, happily stuffing peas into plastic bags for the good of all, but I never bought it. First of all, he never did any of the work. Just stood there while the presumably terrified townspeople did his will. It would not have surprised me to see a terrorist act during a commercial—a little house explodes under the Giant's foot, a suicide squad rappels up the Giant's thigh and blows off a testicle, etc. Even if he didn't control the town and bend it to his will, I did not buy him as a benign creature. Someday, I thought, that Giant's going to turn on us. Not a word but that damnable *hohoho,* which may be in his tongue the phrase "I shall consume your young with butter sauce." Try singing the jingle with that notion in your head. "From the valley of the Jolly— KILL YOU ALL!—Green Giant."

Years later the advertisers came up with a small ambulatory weed-child, Sprout, who was sort of the Green Giant's only begotten son, made cellulose, sent to intercede on our behalf with the Giant. Sprout scampers about in a presumably amusing fashion, getting into scrapes of all sorts. He is not interesting or lovable and can be regarded as pure Giant propaganda.

This would be of little consequence had not the real Giant disappeared from the ads entirely, replaced by an animated version of himself. I can only conclude that something truly dreadful has happened in that village—or revolution is underway, and transmissions from the Valley have been successfully stopped.

Charlie Tuna

It took years to understand the true perversity of Charlie Tuna. As a child, I was initially confused by Charlie's suicidal desires; given that he was a tuna, and Star-Kist was in the business of catching, asphyxiating, and mincing tunas, it just didn't make sense that Charlie was constantly petitioning for their attention. Moreover, his failure to grasp the standards by which he sought to be judged—*taste good* vs. *good taste*—seemed to indicate an intellectual failure inconsistent with his obvious abilities. Indeed, as a tuna capable not only of standing on what appeared to be vestigial legs but of reasoning his way through various schemes, it would seem that he would not only grasp that tasting good was the overriding criterion but use his abilities on behalf of other less fortunate tuna, to save them from their fate.

Charlie, I came to realize, is one of many quislings in the animal kingdom. It is not unusual to find grinning pigs beaming from BBQ ads or winking turkeys with Pilgrim hats extolling the purity of a particular brand of drumstick. The older I got, the more I understood of the world, the more I realized that these creatures had cut a deal. In this context, Charlie Tuna makes sense. In his constant rejection—*sorry, Charlie!*—he encouraged other tuna to feel good about their capture and slaughter. They could neither stand nor walk, yet they were good enough. How they must have jeered and hooted at him as the nets drew them upward.

But there is a deeper deception here. Charlie wears a beret, has black-framed glasses, and speaks with a broad New York accent. He is the model of the 1950s leftist intellectual. On one hand, this is a way of explaining his suicidal impulses; Charlie could be reefer-crazed, nihilistic, or driven mad by the "artistic temperament" often attributed to amotivational coffeehouse habitués. But for Charlie the Modern to want to belong to Star-Kist is for him to say, "Take me into your administration, Ike." The suggestion is that the neurotic self-hating modern, so characteristic of the postwar intelligentsia, harbors deep desires to belong to the mainstream. This assures us that as much as Charlie Tuna professes to detest us and the values we have, he is so covetous of them he would die if his death meant our acceptance.

The Doughboy

Few have a visceral reaction to Charlie Tuna, but nearly everyone has an opinion about the Pillsbury Doughboy.

You love him or you do not. You find his impish ways charming or cloying. I personally like him but understand why some people find the notion of a fat and toothless creature shilling for sugar-laden dough products off-putting. The Doughboy, however, inhabits a darker territory than Charlie Tuna. Charlie was bent on suicide; the Doughboy sells the very substance of which he is made. He wants you to take dough and subject it to witheringly high temperatures—indeed, he takes great delight in seeing great tubes of fleshy matter contort in agony in the oven. Why?

Again, you could trace it to the death wish. The Doughboy is much like Speedy Alka-Seltzer, who danced around glasses of water knowing that one drop would cause his body to suppurate. Speedy was like a hemophiliac demonstrating Ginsu knives; you had to admire the sheer bravado and reckless courage.

But the Doughboy never seems to be in any danger. The Doughboy will never go into that oven. He will constantly come up with new variations of dough to distract us and make us believe he is invaluable. He is the equivalent of seed corn, never to be consumed. (Besides, he may have internal organs, which would make for a gruesome pastry. It is possible that the finger that palpates his abdomen in every commercial is actually prodding for some sort of skeletal or muscular array.) If times were lean, of course, the Doughboy would indeed be put in the oven—hunted down through the house, his happy squeaks changing to shrieks of terror, as the famished poked knives under the sofa, looking for him.

In early commercials, the Doughboy sprang from the roll of dough, like Adam culled from the dust. This is no longer shown, probably at the Doughboy's request—best to distance himself from the yummy dough, pretend he is a disinterested middleman. But it does raise the question of where the Doughboy comes from. If he still comes from the roll, can one strike ten rolls and have ten Doughboys on the counter, chattering and capering, getting into the flour, falling into the disposal, etc.? And if the Doughboy assures safety by distancing himself from his doughy origins, would not the presence of ten Doughboys make him less unique and realign him into the edible category? It is tempting to find out, to see if ten Doughboys will fight to the death until one emerges. Scientists are encouraged to note the next time a strong earthquake strikes a grocery store, and hundreds of jostled tubes produce platoons of Doughboys. It would be interesting to see if, indeed, pitched battles form—whether the Doughboy has innate society-building skills that would allow for the formation of different sides, or whether there would be a stomach-poking, limb-rubbing, anarchistic free-for-all.

Breakfast Cereal Spokescreatures

THE TRIX RABBIT Silly rabbit, he was ever told; Trix are for kids.

Why?

THE COCOA PUFFS CUCKOO Was this cereal the predecessor of crack? Here you have a scrawny, wild-eyed bird who not only cannot control his desire for a tiny brownish sphere of indeterminate composition but every commercial break was shrieking for more; when he ingested it, he promptly bounced screaming off the walls. When you see this commercial nowadays, you want to speed the poor creature into a treatment program. Sure, it would be hard at first, and no one likes to think of the Cuckoo Bird shivering on a bare mattress, feathers soaked with sweat, beak chattering while grotesque visions of a balanced breakfast swim tauntingly before his eyes. But he'd be better for it.

THE LUCKY CHARMS LEPRECHAUN Let me get this straight. Here's a creature who, like the Trix Rabbit, is driven by the need to possess multicolored vitamin-fortified grain products. When he succeeds in grabbing a box, he flees, with children in hot pursuit. Cornered, he calls upon supernatural powers and summons up a mode of escape. ("Oh! I'm trapped! I'll make a hydrogen-filled, rigid-framed dirigible to get away!") It is obvious Lucky can make objects appear at will; why then need he steal the cereal? Can't he snap a finger and have crates of the stuff fall from the sky? What's more, why not have steel cables snake from the ground and lash around the legs of the pursuers, holding them in place and making the need for complex escape mechanisms irrelevant?

TOUCAN SAM A creature from which all could learn. Breezy, vaguely British, confident, unmindful of his huge, garish nose—indeed, proud of it: *I follow my nose! It always knows!* A can-do bird.

You can imagine Sam's advice to his colleagues.

To the Trix Rabbit: "Have some spine, man! Stand up! Demand your Trix!" To the Cuckoo Bird: "Good God, my fine fellow, control yourself! One spoonful at a time! That's the spirit!" To the Doughboy: "Frankly, my good chap, you giggle in a *most* unmanly fashion. Let's suck in that stomach! Shoulders back! That's the ticket!" To Charlie Tuna: "Off your knees, my friend. You're a fish, and a fine one! Demand, not ask! When that hook comes down, take it!" To the Green Giant: "Ho ho, indeed! We'll see how jolly you are when your eyes are pecked out!"

Perhaps that's why we don't see the Giant on TV anymore.

Toucan Sam got to him, pecked out his jellies on behalf of the other creatures he had terrorized for so long. Blind and mad, the Giant now plots his revenge.

Ho ho ho.

Ho ho ho.

Ho. Ho. Ho.

A Wing and a Prayer

~~~~~~

YOU, TOO, CAN BE AN AIR TRAFFIC CONTROLLER! JUST TAKE this simple test.

Two jumbo jets are screaming to earth, and you note that you have assigned them both the same runway. Your response:

1. "Close enough for government work."
2. Call up the pilots and play scissors-stone-paper to determine landing order.

A plane is taxiing around the airport in dense fog. You note on your video monitor that you have directed it to the runway where the aforementioned two jumbo jets are landing. What do you do?

1. Turn off the screen and put your fingers in your ears and make a loud humming sound until all the commotion is over.
2. Casually ask a coworker if planes have reverse gear.

When you are in communication with the pilots, you

1. Give clear, concise, accurate information.

231

   2. Use a high-pitched voice so they can't identify you on
      the cockpit voice recorder.

Which of the following does not constitute proper landing
instructions?

   1. "Hey, planes! Ollie-ollie-in-free."
   2. A series of instructions based on the concept of "getting
      warmer" and "getting colder."

When you are driving home at night and mistakenly run a
red light and plow into another car, your explanation to the
police:

   1. Wind shear.
   2. Deregulation.

I know, I know—this maligns the 99.9 percent of air traffic
controllers who put in a shift without making huge machines
play bumper cars on the runway. But this past week has seen
testimony on two recent air disasters. In the collision of two
planes in Detroit, a 737 coming in for a landing smacked into
another 737 that had also been directed to the same runway.
This is like the car rental agency assigning Luciano Pavarotti
and Orson Welles the same Yugo, and propelling them via
cannon fire into the lot. Meanwhile, in Los Angeles, they're
investigating how a 727 hit a small commuter airplane. Normally the wee ones don't stray into the path of the lumbering
grown-ups, but apparently the pilot of the smaller plane got
lost in the fog while taxiing around. Perhaps they were under-
standably nervous; you don't want to get lost driving in L.A.,
lest you end up in a bad neighborhood. A small commuter
plane, stripped of its wheels, hood up, seats ripped out, is an
all too familiar sight.
   But one believes that air traffic controllers are supposed to
keep this from happening, and you suspect that the plane
committed the sin of taxiing into an area of the screen obscured by a Post-It note reading, "MILK, BREAD, VISINE."
   An explanation frequently given contends that the nation's

air traffic system has not recovered from the mass firing of controllers that followed their strike, held eleven years ago. In retrospect, that was a bad move; go back and watch footage of the striking controllers walking the picket line, and you'll note that not one of them ever bumped into each other. Clearly these people knew their business. In fact, the argument can be made that the strike was ineffective because of their training: each striking worker stayed exactly eleven miles apart from any other as they picketed, giving the impression their numbers were few. (And, of course, there was their refusal to drop flaps and assume a lower altitude of reimbursement.)

But we've had eleven years to train a new batch. Surely they're pros by now and are not staring at their screens with their tongue stuck out the corner of their mouth, brows furrowed, looking like the class dummy asked to perform long division. You have to believe that the phrase "Hey, boss! Is this supposed to happen?" does not echo frequently through the control tower, nor that someone spends an hour trying desperately to direct a plane that is actually a piece of lettuce sneezed onto the screen by the guy on the previous shift. Surely they know what they are doing.

The problem is that they are being asked to do the impossible, which is never to screw up. As a member of the National Transportation Safety Board put it recently, "We are relying too heavily on perfect human performance combined with luck to assure the safe movement of aircraft in and around today's busy airports." There you have it. If we could rely on luck and perfect human performance, no one would ever have a disappointing first date.

The solution is simple: first, throw money at the problem. Hire more air traffic controllers. More controllers means that someone won't misplace a plane like a thimble in the sofa cushions because he's pulling a long shift and confusedly believes the words GAME OVER will signal the end of his day. Second, do away with the weird names they give planes, like DW2934 and LW39203, and give them names like Bob and Rachel, just to remind them that they are not guiding license plates through the skies, but huge barges loaded to the gunwales with chattering, hopeful humanity. Third, install traffic lights on the runways. This is actually being done in Houston. Let us hope there is no caution light, or cockpit recorders may reveal the navigator said, "Hey, it's yellow—punch it."

Fourth, hire Iranian air traffic controllers. During the early moments of the 1991 Gulf War, the entire Iraqi air force decamped and ran for the border like cats dipped in gasoline; Iranian air controllers had to deal with over a hundred strange planes cruising in at high speed and begging for landing coordinates. They obviously know their business.

Then again, when they do have crashes in Iran, the cause is usually not "pilot error" but "will of Allah." Which would be fine with most of us. Putting your fate in the hands of an unseen omnipotent being—that's what Americans do every time they fly.

Except our version has an ulcer and is overdue for a coffee break.

Confessions of a Public-Radio Leech

~~~~~~

THE TRUEST SIGN OF SPRING IN WASHINGTON IS NOT THE AP-
pearance, for four and a half minutes, of the cherry blossoms.
It is the pledge week, the biannual strong-arm session for
public radio listeners. The announcers would have you believe
that burly men with spanners and blow torches are in the
wings, ready to dismantle the station if you don't fork over.
I'd send them money if I thought it would shut them up. One
year I did contribute to public radio, and damned if they
didn't rise up six months later and put the lumber to my
conscience again. Now I have the same feeling I get when I
pass the beggar with the HUNGRY, NEED BUS TICKET
HOME TO TENNESSEE sign for the fifteenth time. *Buddy,
get a job. Or a new sign.*

The local public television station has come up with what
it believes is a fine metaphor for publicly funded media: in a
fund-raising commercial, a woman is shown checking out at
a grocery store and is told by the cashier that she needn't
pay now, she can go home, cook up the food, and maybe pay
them someday if she likes the food. The ad suggests that this
would be a crazy way to run a business.

Well, no argument here. Even crazier would be for the grocery
store to deliver its top quality foodstuffs to my doorstep every
morning, then stand outside my house twice a year, cap in hand,
with a hangdog look. *But you ate the food!* And tasty it was.

Since I am a public-radio leech, I'd better give my reasons.

235

1. I am not costing them money by not paying. Radio is not like a newspaper box; if I pop a quarter in the box and stagger away with an armload of *Posts,* I deprive everyone else of a paper. If I listen to public radio without paying, this doesn't mean someone who did pay turns on their radio and gets static. The day police can pull me aside and cite me for defrauding NPR, I'll pay.

2. National Public Radio, while a fine news organization, has a tendency to announce its political agenda through a bullhorn. The day Allied forces rolled into Kuwait and Iraqi soldiers stood up in their trenches and surrendered with such alacrity they appeared to be doing the Wave, NPR's Morning Edition ran an interview with a pacifist. Someone suitably grim and religious, who droned on about sanctions. As I strode to work, listening to this sonorous moral luxuriousness on my headphones, my blood pressure spiked so high I began to emit a fine red mist. I swore off NPR for days after that.

I know that journalists are supposed to get The Other Side for objectivity's sake; I pretend to do it all the time. It's just that if NPR was present when God separated light from dark, they would have interviewed a spokesman for The Light/Dark Coalition Working Group. And followed it with mournful, tasteful jazz music.

3. The pledge sessions themselves. The stations around Washington operate on the challenge system, wherein a corporation or rich person, like a stern parent, gives money but makes conditions: unless a certain number of people call and pledge money, the station will lose the grant. Which seems vindictive and punitive, rather like the famous *National Lampoon* cover: Buy this magazine or we shoot the dog.

Hour after hour, there is the sound of old Rover thudding to the floor. Time and again, I have heard the host morosely announce that the challenge has not been met. The stink of defeat hangs over the show; it becomes unpleasant to listen to. After a while, you don't feel guilty for not contributing— you began to resent the capricious jillionaire who set such unreal conditions in the first place. Although if some harried gotrocks called up and pledged a hundred thousand if they'd just KNOCK IT OFF FOR AN HOUR, you wonder how the station would respond. Probably by having an auction to sell silence to the highest bidder.

When not coming down on you like ten tall buildings, they bribe you: compact discs, book bags, umbrellas, plaster casts of Cokie Roberts's jaw, whatever. You get these indispensable items if you pledge large amounts of money, of course. If you chip in five or ten dollars, you get . . . satisfaction. The deep kind that comes from knowing you've paid for the goodies showered on high-dollar patrons the next time pledge season waddles around.

Worst of all is what pledge does to the hosts. They wheedle; they get cranky, hectoring the deadbeats and spooning gooey familiarity over the names of those saints who do call and pledge. Deprived of a world event to deplore or a good record to introduce, they seem lost and uncomfortable, as if they are scolding the child of a second cousin. Or they become emotional: They really need us. They can't stress this enough. They're depending on us. They sound exactly like me the last time a girlfriend walked out on me, except that I didn't go on about it day and night for ten days. And I didn't give her a book bag when she came back.

Public radio ought to be a regulated utility. Meters could be installed on all radios; you could have someone read it twice a year, figure out how many minutes you'd heard, and charge you accordingly. This would lead to innovative technological services, such as firms offering to Wagner-proof your radio: for a small fee, your radio can be equipped to detect the interesting instrumental passages and shut itself off during the long declamatory passages.

Having said all this, I now feel so damn guilty I will give them some money. But whatever they end up sending me, I hope it isn't an umbrella. I saw a woman walking down the street today with an umbrella stamped with the logo of a local public radio station. The fabric had come untethered, and one of the spokes stood out like the bony finger of the Ghost of Future Pledge Sessions. That umbrella probably lasted six months. Exactly.

Listen closely come pledge time, and you can hear tote-bag handles coming off all over town.

President Me

vvvvvvvvvvvvvvvvvvvvvvvvvvvvvvvvvvvvvvvvvvvvvvvvvvvvv

PEOPLE LEAN AGAINST THE BARS, POINT IN AT THE CREATURES moving in the cage, snap pictures, mimic the curious antics of the species on display. It would be a normal exhibit at the zoo, except that I'm describing the White House. Pass it any day of the week, and you'll see a crowd lined up to get a glimpse of *Presidentus Americanus.* Since he never comes out, let alone swings from the trees and snatches away the peanuts people have tossed, most people are disappointed. All that gambols on the lawn are the *Stiff-Haired Newscasteri,* a variety of parasite able to feed off the body of its host without actually getting near it.

Every time I see that crowd, I am reminded anew of how awful it would be to be president. I'd last about a week in that house before I showed up on the doorstep in my robe, clutching a shotgun and demanding everybody get off my property. Imagine if you woke up, looked outside your window, and saw fifteen tour buses pull up, full of people who are about to walk through your house—which, of course, is a mess. I would be madly scrubbing the toilet bowl before an aide pulled me away and reminded me that I was the leader of the free world.

The perks of the presidency, of course, are nice: room and board, free haircuts, and a fawning staff, part of which is legally obligated to die on your behalf. It's tempting, in a way. But I would make a bad president. Here are some reasons why:

• Would be unable to pursue vice-related activity. I think running down to the corner store for a six-pack is pretty much out of the question when you're president, as is strolling out to the White House fence and offering to buy a cigarette for a nickel. And let's say I wanted to rent an adult video. No more slinking unnoticed to the sleazy part of the video store, oh, no. People would watch amused as the six secret agents who surrounded me moved slowly through the aisles to the ADULT rack and stood there, looking in opposite directions.

• Couldn't help triggering nuclear war. There's just something about knowing you could do it that would make it sooooo irresistible. Since we all know there's a button in the Oval Office that launches the missiles, I just know that on a slow rainy afternoon when there's nothing better to do, I would sit there and press it gently, seeing how far down it went before it went *"CLICK!"* Then, of course, I would spend the rest of the afternoon under my desk, waiting for the sirens and hoping no one found out and blamed me.

• Tendency to abuse position to realize personal fantasies. Like showing up on the set of the next Batman movie and asking if I could drive the car. And try on the mask.

Hell, I'm the President; hand me that costume and let's make a movie.

• No more lotteries or contests. I don't buy lottery tickets; if you look at the fine print, they always say, "chance of winning anything other than the contempt of the clerk who sold you the ticket is 1:1,000,000,000,000,000." But I don't like the idea of being unable to buy a lottery ticket, which would be the case were I president. The lottery industry lives in fear of the President of the United States buying a ticket and winning; try telling folks it's not fixed after that happens. Besides, nothing would be less dignified than holding a press conference down at the lottery redemption center to get the big check. Although for once when the winner said, "No, I don't have plans to quit my job," you wouldn't think he was an idiot.

No more contests, either, for the same reason. I'd miss those thick brown letters full of stickers and personalized letters. Although I would like to send off a few subscriptions addressed to PRESIDENT OF THE UNITED STATES, just to get computer-generated contest letters that refer to me as MR. STATES.

"DEAR MR. STATES," they'd say. "HOW WOULD IT FEEL TO SEE A BRAND-NEW CAR IN THE STATES DRIVEWAY AT 1600 PENNSYLVANIA AVENUE? COULD THE STATES USE A MILLION DOLLARS?"

And you know, they could, what with all the federal cutbacks. Maybe I should run for president, enter some contests. The newscasters on the White House lawn could get great footage of me toddling down the driveway to mail the entries. When the STATES win big—and they will; as President, I'll see to that—well, let's let them say I have no domestic policy.

Those Pesky Nukes

IT'S SUCH A RELIEF TO KNOW THAT SOMEONE ELSE IS GOING TO have a nuclear war instead of us. The Korean peninsula, circa 1999: smooth smoking glass. Ditto the Pakistani-Indian border. Future astronauts are going to be leaning out of their ships and combing their hair in the reflections where those countries once were.

North Korea, it seems, is close to getting the bomb. Experts are divided; some say they will have it by Thursday morning; others, scoffing at the likelihood of the North Koreans achieving that level of technical sophistication so quickly, say it will be at least Thursday afternoon.

"A bomb is an incredibly complex machine," said one expert. "I think it's safe to say that there will be plenty of North Korean nuclear technicians late for supper next Thursday. It may even be Friday before they finish gluing it to a Scud. So while we should be concerned, we should definitely drag our heels in doing something about it."

The West has already protested through the usual channels, waving satellite photos of their nuclear facilities in the faces of relevant diplomats, but North Korea insists that its nuclear facilities are producing only electricity. An interesting claim to make about buildings that have no power lines attached to them. Perhaps the North Koreans will say the building is a giant battery, and the Eveready Bunny will show up in high-altitude reconnaissance photos, waving a drumstick. Make that five thousand Eveready Bunnies, shouting slogans in unison.

This past week nukes were in the news back home as well. The nuclear weapon-manufacturing industry, it seems, has hit a bad patch. They concentrated on a single fad-driven item— hideous weapons of mass destruction—and failed to diversify. If they'd made nukes, flavored coffees, and novelty keychains that made clever sounds—things we really need, in other words—they'd be fine.

But no, it was nukes or nothing. Not for them the lessons of the Pet Rock. Not for them the warning example of CB radio. That's the thing about building the means by which to bring about the end of the world: you think the good times will go on forever.

Now they are trying to stay alive by offering to take the nukes apart. There's not much else they can do, as nukes have limited uses. Imagine reading this ad:

IT'S GROUND ZERO FOR HOUSEHOLD PESTS

Nukem, the only pest-controller with extra-strength U-238. Simply set the launch codes and place where you have a problem. Originally developed to kill massed hordes of fanatical Communists, Nukem kills even the most stubborn vermin.

Someday, ants may have perestroika. Until then, there's Nukem.

(Not responsible for genetic mutations. If ants grow to height of seven feet and eat the family dog, consult a professional.)

No, I don't think so. Nor will you see ads for any of these products:

Minuteman Stump Removal Service
MIRV's Strategic Demolition & Wrecking

MX Overnight Delivery (Simultaneous Delivery of Independently Targeted Packages Our Specialty)

All you can do with the damn things is take them apart and close up shop. Right?

Wrong. Russian businessmen have announced they have a totally new use for nuclear weapons: waste-management. Chetek, a private firm in Moscow with ties to the Soviet ministry that makes nuclear arms, has announced that they will take your trash, bury it deep in the ground, and nuke it. I immediately drew several conclusions.

- It couldn't be any noisier than the two guys who pick up my trash.
- When Khrushchev said, "We will bury you," he was really pleading for customers at the new Soviet landfill; mistranslation set back international relations for decades.
- Anything that makes Pampers radioactive cannot be a good idea.

The price is right. For as low as $150 per pound, the Soviets will blow up anything you want, and even better, they'll come to your neighborhood to do it. There's your New World Order: from standing toe to toe with one hand on the nuclear sword to asking the Sovs to fly in a nuke and handing them a check on arrival.

It is probably not a good idea. I think letting the geniuses of Chernobyl rig up a nuke on the edge of town pretty much defines the "not in my backyard" syndrome. On the other hand, it does show that nukes are not the one-note Johnnies we thought they were. After forty years of shaking them at one another, the U.S. and the U.S.S.R. have decided that all they're good for is blowing up biological waste.

Problem is, some countries define "biological waste" as the people on the other side of the border.

Pundit for a Day

〰〰〰〰〰〰〰〰〰〰〰〰〰〰〰〰〰〰〰〰〰〰〰〰〰〰〰〰〰〰〰〰〰

BIRDS FEED THEIR YOUNG BY EATING A MEAL, FLYING HOME, and regurgitating it into the outstretched beaks of their chicks. It's a similar situation with reporters—except that they are bored with the meal, hate the chicks, are aware that half the chicks loathe them, and they regurgitate over a cellular phone.

Well, perhaps that's too harsh. You can't judge the press corps by one day on the road. But you can certainly try. Here, then, a day on the media-elite express—a trainload of scribblers and pundits and, incidentally, the leader of the free world, desperately scrabbling for reelection. Can I help? Can I hinder? Let's see.

The trip begins in a hotel lobby in suburban Atlanta at eight thirty in the morning. Since I have joined this caravan between stops, I have to find someone to credential me—i.e., give me the tags that identify me as a legitimate member of the press. I love tags. All reporters love their tags. They let you go places other people can't. They bind you to the tribe, separate you from the masses. Make way! *I've a badge.*

I spot a man in a blue suit; he has the telltale curly wire coming out of his head and disappearing into his collar; this means he is one of the special super-secret government robots that protect and, in all likelihood, control the President through mental telepathy. I tell him my name, and he doles out my badge with a smile. It has a picture of a train wheel on it; it reads, "THE TRIP OF THE PRESIDENT OF THE UNITED STATES." I fit it on the chain that holds my House-and-Senate tags, thinking

A) My folks would be so proud.

B) How do they know I'm not a mass murderer? The Secret Service, I mean. (My folks know me pretty well.) All I did to get this badge was call up and tell them I worked for Newhouse News Service. *And they bought it.* Maybe next time I should try a wholly fictional service—say, Gotham City Press or the Pluto Tribune or Trotsky-Engels Disinformation Bureau.

I keep these thoughts to a minimum; those curly wires no doubt pick up brain waves. I take my place in the line to board the bus. First, a dog comes by and sniffs our bags for undetermined substances. (One reporter looks anxiously at his bag with the expression of a man convinced the dog can detect hard-core pornography.) The dog is excited, which leads me to wonder if he has discovered plastique or gunpowder. I then realize that any dog presented with a quarter ton of used socks and underwear would be thrilled. I watch the dog plunge his snout into my bag, and of course he moves along. My luggage is pronounced nonlethal. I have the same thoughts I have whenever I am waved genially into the press balcony at the House of Representatives—*sure, I didn't set off the metal detectors, but how do you know I don't have plastic explosives in my shoe heels? Come on! Look lively!* Next we get patted down by stoic Secret Service men, and then a guy in a uniform passes a metal wand up our inseams. Perhaps to check for metal; perhaps to check for the lack of testicles. ("Okay, you're a journalist who's been thoroughly co-opted by the promise of access; you can go.") Then we're put on the bus. It's nine A.M. You can hear the hangovers if you listen closely.

We board the train at 9:20 and trash it by 9:22. Well, not completely. It's a luxury train—old cars from the thirties and forties perfectly restored, spacious and clean, with historical plaques posted fore and aft in every car. But screw history: we have to work. Within moments we have found the outlets, plugged in extension cords, whipped out the transformers for our computers, and made the train a rolling UL nightmare. Then we turn on our machines. And wait.

The intercom crackles to life, and the President begins to speak. Heads snap up: for a moment, I believe that the President will tell us that the Chief of Staff will be along to collect our tickets. But no, it's a live feed of a press conference taking place on the other side of town. Since we're the Expanded Pool—i.e., the second-class citizens, behind the White House Pool—we're not allowed to cover that event. We have to cover it from here. From a train. Going nowhere. Heads bend and labor at the laptops, soaking in news.

The President describes the prime minister of Canada as being "very pro-Canada."

"Well, there's a switch," someone mutters.

An hour later the President arrives on board—or so I assume, because the train shudders and pulls out. None of us have seen the man, but we believe he is Back There at the end, like the Wizard, like God, like the Principal. I wander back through several cars until I am stopped by Secret Service men: my badge is the wrong color. It will not get me any farther.

"What color would I need?" I ask.

They give me looks of pity.

I consider taking a running leap at the door, so I can blow it open with my explosive heels, then recall that I don't actually have any such thing. Back to my seat. In the press car the conductor has come along to explain how to avoid snapping our ankles when we get off the train. Apparently it is dangerous terrain beyond.

"Whatchoo had before, with the gravel on the bed? That's gonna seem like a foah-lane highway. You gonna be walkin' one leg up and other leg down here. Crooked-like."

No one is listening. With an hour to go until the next stop, the Expanded Pool is whiling away the time with its favorite pastime: conspicuous cellular phone usage. At least half the reporters carry phones, and in a curious reversal of the laws of plumage, the smaller the phone, the more impressive. One reporter with a phone the size of a matchbook paces the aisle, talking to his editor. It is important that you be seen to be connected, tethered by invisible lines. The indispensable can never be out of touch.

Gorgeous Georgia countryside unrolls beyond, the sun racing the trees. No one pays it any mind. Everyone is bound by the habits of the office cubicle: head down, shoulders hunched, phone cradled, fingers tapping the laptops. My seatmate, a brusque and high-handed sod from a large East Coast paper of record, is hard at work already; from his skull radiate little jagged beams of contempt for everyone who does not work for his paper.

He has a cellular and is making calls. I have no such thing. I do, however, have a better computer than he does. And I have prepared for this moment. Before I left, I wrote a small program containing maps of our journey and loaded the program with several bogus features: when I hit a certain key, the computer will say, in a robotic voice, "Please insert Georgia coordinates now" or "Satellite uplink established." I call up the program and start making it talk.

The man from the paper of record steals a glance at my computer. "Did your company buy that one for you?" he asks.

They did not.

"Yes," I reply.

"Destination Norcross," the computer says. "Accessing long-distance codes."

My computer is bigger than his too. I almost want to let out my belt.

There are four stops today, the first being Norcross, Georgia. The train slides into a Capra set: a quaint Main Street, apple-cheeked citizens, languid blue skies, flags snapping from eagle-topped poles. A brass band waddles into patriotic song, and a great cheer erupts as if this is an inspection by the National Dentist. Scream *AHHHH!* Let's see those molars!

The train disgorges the horde, which stumbles through the

loose gravel of the track bed to the observation platform. I wonder if we are going to collide with the crowd, be forced to hack a path by swinging mikes or sticking pens in people's rears. No; we stride through a roped-off corridor of our very own, barreling along like steer through the chute, stone-faced and all business, bearing the great load of duty and perhaps a TV camera.

Behind the yellow rope, the great and famous mingle. There's Newt Gingrich! There's Marlin Fitzwater, whose face looks as though God stopped before he finished the details. Marlin is taking Instamatic pictures of the crowd, which is taking pictures of him.

The President, meanwhile, is giving a vigorous denunciation of his rival; it is a rather broad speech, a cannon load of lamprey eels shot into the ocean in the hope that they will land on a shark. He tosses in a few local references, the equivalent of a rock star on tour calling out the name of a local radio station; he then produces the political version of a mass, simultaneous orgasm by coming down unequivocally in favor of the Atlanta Braves to win the Series. (The other team was Canadian, thereby providing a presidential candidate's dream: a politically neutered World Series pick.) He does the tomahawk chop, a gesture associated with Atlanta—and the crowd again shrieks its glee.

By now I have strolled down to the tracks and am alarmingly close to the President. This is probably as close as I'll get in my life. The man looks unbelievably normal, just someone's dad in a Windbreaker. A nice guy. Still chopping, the President of the United States turns to his wife, and I hear him say:

"Chopmania."

There are no other reporters present, so I am certain no one else heard him say this. I am in possession of an exclusive presidential quote. I hold it tight to my breast the rest of the day.

The Norcross stop was the blueprint, repeated three more times over the rest of the day with little variation. You could stick a new dateline on the story and send it out three more times, changing the color of the school band uniforms and the time of the day.

Actually, that's what quite a few have to do. There's a strange contradiction at play here. Dozens of reporters will have to file stories at the next stop. But how can they simultaneously file a story and report on the next stop, so they'll have something to file the stop after that?

Simple. *It is not necessary to observe an entire event in order to report on it.* There's a printing press on board, and the President's staff—polite, well-dressed folk with that high Republican grooming—presents you with a transcript of the event after it's over. In the case of Norcross, the train hadn't been moving a minute before printer-damp copies were handed out. And they were the real thing too: some of the President's trademark stop-start fit-pitching oratory is included, along with real audience response.

Yes. (Applause.)

Booooooo.

Four More Years!

On to the next stop. Laptops open, heads bend, phones click open. The man next to me calls a Washington pundit from his seat on the train, reads him the Norcross speech, and asks for a comment.

Both the pundit and the reporter agree that the speech was a failed effort and all too typical of this campaign. The spin is so sudden and stern I retire to the restroom to comb my hair back into place.

Next stop, Gainesville, where the first filing frenzy will take place. Gainesville appears to be the rusty-drum-disposal capital of the South; one junkyard actually has discarded Dumpsters sitting in larger Dumpsters. Makes sense, really. The air is sullen with grain dust and the smell of the dog-food plant up the street. Why here?

Because there be Republicans here, matey.

"MURCANS!" shouts a cameraman as he stumbles off the train. "LET'S GO SEE THE MURCANS!"

Bedlam awaits. Reporters surge through their roped-off pathway, shove their way to the phones, and fall on them like locusts. Half the reporters don't need phones—they need the cord in the back, the thin plastic vein through which they can pump their nourishment. The phones are discarded beneath the table, where they lie in a pile like the husks of tough and unappetizing nuts.

Perhaps twenty reporters are bent over the table, shouting over the din of the speech, whipping their computers through the download. One man in a blue suit sits on the dusty ground, fastidiously batting away the cigarette ashes someone is flicking at him.

Having nothing to file, I wander around the crowd. There seems to be an inordinate number of heart-stoppingly gorgeous young high school girls. Maybe it's the water, the grain dust in the air, or perhaps the fortuitous intersection of good genes and massive intermarriage. Whatever, it works. Half the nation's future models will come from this town.

Of course! That's why the President stopped here: it's the strategic model reserve.

I return to the speech and note a man standing on a train adjacent to the Presidential train. I mean, standing on a train: he's on top, vigorously translating the speech into sign language. When the President gets to the bit about being endorsed by policemen's unions, I note that the sign-language guy mimics the pumping of a shotgun. Whether this is the sign for *police* or *union,* I can't say.

No one I talked to on the train afterward noticed the girls. (They all recalled the dog-food smell, though.) The big difference between this speech and the last was that Bush called Ross Perot by name instead of just calling him "my feisty friend," as he did at the last stop.

We'll have to wait for the transcripts to confirm it.

The next stop isn't for two hours, so there's time to attack the buffet line in the dining car. Free lunch at sixty-five mph. We line up thirty deep for our choice of dry lunch meat, dry bread, dry croissants, cheese, and dry salads. Dry is the word for the car too: not a drop of booze in the house.

People have begun looking forward to the daily dole of grog. Alcohol is regarded as inevitable. Not to say that the train is a load of parched souses waiting to flop into a drink, but this life must have its compensations.

An English correspondent has voiced fears that Gaffney, our evening destination, is a dry town.

"Who knows if there's a drink to be had there?" he cries. "That's the problem with America—you cross a county line and you're in a dry county, land of the heathens. And there's never any warning."

There is more to do than write and look forward to liquor, though. You can hang out with the Secret Service men and watch for snipers.

One agent—late twenties, regulation haircut, regulation shades, regulation I-could-kill-you-but-it-would-mean-forms-to-fill-out expression—is standing at a window between train cars, frowning at the kudzu-choked forest beyond. "It's tough," he says. "Someone could be in there and you'd never know it."

But there are no snipers. Just Americans. It seems that the entire state has assembled to watch the train pass—in small towns, on roads, in fields, they're there, waving from the bluffs above, waving from their cars. We pass elementary schools that have let everyone out to watch their president go by. Small factories where everyone has put down the tools and waited for the train. Curious, the farther you get from big towns, the fewer teeth people seem to have. You can tell you're getting near a major population center when mouths are reasonably full once more. When the waving folks sport empty gums, you're halfway.

You slide through a small town and see children running down a hill in the cool autumn light to wave at the train, and it's an instant gut-check. Does it make your heart pang with love of country? You're new. Do you shout, DON'T TRIP AND FALL UNDER THE WHEELS? You've been at this too long.

The Secret Service agent looks at them impassively and gives them a thumbs-up that makes them squeal.

"You can do it too," he says. "You've got a white shirt and a dark tie. They'll think you're with the President." He stares out at the kudzu. "You handle the waving, I'll do the looking."

I start waving and smiling and pointing. I recall a story about the President, how he loved to "light people up" by making eye contact, pointing, and watching their faces spark with delight. By God, he has a point: it's fun. I grab as many faces as I can as the train slides past, grinning and giving curt, efficient gestures of goodwill. There is fraud at the heart of this—I'm not anything like what they think I am.

But they are who I think they are. They'd probably be disappointed to think I am merely a citizen, like them, and no doubt livid to find I was with the media—sort of like someone who discovers the beautiful woman who's been flattering him all evening is really a man.

Oh, who cares. It is a lovely day, and I'll never see this many people predisposed to like me again. Their love is broad and general, and I'm happy to handle the wobbly beast for a few seconds. Put us all at the same table in a café, and I know full well I'd get bored with them because they didn't know what *The Washington Post* had said, and they'd come to suspect me for being the sort who leaves small towns and goes to big places and makes fun of them.

But the train is moving just slowly enough for us to lock eyes and get along. I love them all. I have this deep, painful desire to live a life so calm that the passing of a train is cause for assembly. But then I find myself wondering what the crowds will be like up the road, and I know I'd rather be here, lying and waving, than down there watching the show pull out of sight.

That's the nice thing about access. You can be sentimental, professional, cynical, and curious in the same moment. It is easy to confuse the rush of emotions with genuine humanity.

Cornelia's next. It's getting old now. I've been on the campaign trail a total of seven hours, and the excitement has faded. As I walk along the train bed, I note a strange gelatinous substance scattered along the tracks. It does not explode when I step on it, which is good. I decide it is Bubba Larvae.

Eventually large men with big smiles and a two-days' growth
of beard wiggle out and take their place in the community.

The filing center is in an old train depot, and there's the
standard argy-bargy with the phones while the event rages
outside. An old man, who no doubt used the depot when
trains came through Cornelia decades ago, stands with his
nose to the glass, watching the frenzy inside. He takes a picture and moves along.

By the press stand, several irate citizens are complaining
that they can't see, now that the media have arrived.

"Ah've been waitin' here all dayuh," says one man, bitterly.
"And now ah can't see a thing."

And then you realize why some folk hate the media. It
makes so little sense to them: the people with the best view,
who get to be close to the fun, are the same people who
don't seem to care about any of this. They don't look excited.
They don't smile and they don't clap.

And they leave things out. Folks know there won't be time
on TV for all the details, but once it would be nice to see
the networks show they appreciate all the effort that Cornelia,
South Carolina, has put into this event. How nicely the band
played. How cute the cheerleaders were; how the entire Web-
elos Scout Troop had worked for a week on that sign. It'd
be nice to hear the networks mention these things and do it
without making it sound like they regard the inhabitants of
Cornelia as critters from another planet.

Instead, if they do see their home on the big news tonight—
and they probably won't—they'll see someone saying the
President is in trouble and fighting for his political life. Give the
media a pretty picture, and they stick it in a big black frame.

"There's a bumper sticker," Bush is saying from the back
of the train. "Maybe you've seen it—says, 'ANNOY THE
MEDIA—REELECT BUSH!' "

"Yeah," says a national-TV White House correspondent to
another reporter. "Problem is, that's the only reason." He's
close enough for the people on the other side of the rope to
hear the comment.

So what if they do?

*　　*　　*

Anything annoys the media if you repeat it enough. There's a phrase in President Bush's speech—"Don't listen to those nutty pollsters." The first time anyone heard it they smiled—it was such an archaic coinage, something one aging Vegas hipster would say to another. By the second use it sounded like the title of a Jerry Lewis movie, or perhaps a mid-sixties Disney movie starring Dean Jones. By the third usage it had stuck in everyone's brain, had been passed around as the choice locution of the day, and had become the catchphrase that was simultaneously in everyone's mind. Walk around the train and say it, and people said it right back to you, like a blessing passed between members of a religious order: may the Nutty Pollsters be with you. *And with you.*

It's night now, the train rumbling through dark country. Which makes the approach to the day's final stop all the more dramatic: beaming teens line the tracks waving sparklers, cheering. A sulfurous reek fills the car, which makes heads snap up from their laptops. (You can hear the necks crack.) And then it's back into the maelstrom. This event is much different from the last, in that it's dark outside. And it's bigger: fifteen thousand people howling as one, throats open in joy. Searchlights roam the roof of the sky; a band thrashes "Hail to the Chief" to pieces, and a billion white balloons flock into the sky, rice cast on deep water.

A marble-mouthed ancient gets up and reminds us all that JOAHGE BUHSH WUN TH' PUHSHUN GUFF WOAH! A lone Democrat passes out Clinton fliers to the reporters. (He later returns to bum cigarettes.) The President appears to deliver the Same Speech, and this time he hits every line like a man at a county fair Test-Your-Strength booth. Every line soars high and hits the bell. The crowd would have shouted "AMEN" every other few words, but they're white; instead, they clap and howl *WOOOOO* and wave signs and pour vast undiluted admiration toward the guy in the beam of the lights.

It ends with a barrage of fireworks, big boomers you feel in the gut. We stagger away, sated with rhetoric and spectacle. The reporters are ushered to the buses that will take us to the hotels and sit for half an hour while the ceaseless tide of people surge past around us. A couple of Italian journalists stare in wonder at the A-1 Gun Shop and its sign: CLOSED FOR PRESIDENT'S VISIT.

And then it all just goes to hell. We arrive at our accommodations to find the hotel has closed its kitchen. It has one confused man on duty to process the surly multitude.

And it doesn't have a bar.

Reporters get their keys and stalk off to their rooms, grim death in their eyes. One of the Brits is howling in indignation, cursing America; someone tells him that if he practiced American self-reliance, he'd bring a flask and shut up already. And so the day gently ends.

One day. And, quite probably, a good one, as these things go. Now, imagine this over and over and over, for days, for weeks, for months. The same happy yelling masses, the same speeches, with cramped buses and indistinguishable motel rooms at the end of it all. Imagine having nothing to do all day but suck it in and spit it out.

It is quite possibly the only job that can make you sick of America. Republican, Democrat, Independent, who cares? Let's get it over with.

Vote, already. Let the reporters go home.

Manly Tweeters

∿∿

WHEN THE PIECE OF STEREO EQUIPMENT A MAN BOUGHT FIVE years ago blows up or melts down, he generally has one dominant emotion.

Gratitude.

Now he gets to buy something new. In fact, he's vaguely angry at the machinery for not breaking down sooner. His once-fancy box of lights and dials used to look like a missile-guidance center; compared to what's out there now, it looks like a Brownie camera. He's missed two, maybe three pointless technological leaps. But thank God his investment is now a worthless pile of wires, and it's time to get a new system.

Or is it? First, take this test.

My receiver is broken because:

A) I dropped it.
B) I spilled a beer down the ventilation grill.
C) I spilled a beer while dropping it.
D) I had a beer while looking through the stereo catalog and decided it was broken, so I dropped it to make sure.

What exactly do you mean by *broken?*

A) It just doesn't pick up AM stations like it did before I moved into this lead-lined basement apartment near the tinfoil factory.
B) It's located too far from an outlet.
C) The batteries on the remote are dead.
D) There's a weird hum coming from the speakers. Granted, I play only Tibetan chants on the thing, but still.

Can it be repaired?

A) I don't understand the question.
B) I suppose you'd give a hamster a bone-marrow transplant.
C) Yes, it can be repaired. *But I can always open another beer.*
D) What, and forgo my duty to the Japanese trade surplus?

If you answered any of these questions, you are not a man. A man would simply look astonished, then impatient, then bored, waiting for all this silly self-reflection to pass so he can go out and get some new stuff.

Those of you currently ruminating over the notion of new stuff are in for a bit of a disappointment. While there's plenty of cool gear out there, most of it will be replaced within the week by something whose appearance is slightly different and hence better. You are guaranteed of no more than seven days supremacy over everyone else. Time was, stereo styles moved with the sluggish pace usually found in auto manufacturers' boardrooms; a man had at least a decade before his equipment went out of style. In fact, let's tour the recent past, and show just how things have been moving.

The Sixties

The last gasp of simple, basic record players. The tone arms were as heavy as barbells, the needles were plain-spoken things that looked like railroad spikes, and the speakers— attached to the turntable by hinges—were covered in a weird metallic fabric in patterns usually found in the suits of Paul

Drake, the investigator who worked for Perry Mason. It was also the great age of the 45 RPM record player—cheap boxes whose rugged construction ensured that when your father threw the damn thing across the room because you'd played "See Me, Feel Me" for the seven hundredth time that day, the tone of the sound would vary not a whit.

The Seventies

Here is the birth of audiophilia, which is defined as "the desire not only to have sex with your woofer but to have everyone be impressed by the way your tweeter described the event." The simple record player, like cold taffy struck with a hammer, was split into several component units; each unit had huge heavy knobs, which made the act of turning the treble up from nine to ten feel like a skilled and finely calibrated operation. Something called "loudness" was introduced, a device that made it easier for neighbors living below you to get the gist of your musical selections.

It was also the age of quadrophonic sound, which required you to buy four speakers in order to hear every delicate nuance of a Black Sabbath record.

The Eighties

The advent of the compact disc. Some believe that the CD succeeded so quickly because of its superior sound, but that had nothing to do with it. CDs were instantly beloved because of those motorized trays that whirred out when you pushed a button. Men saw that tray pop out, and they groaned and closed their eyes and reached for their wallet. The sound could have been akin to a wax cylinder, and we'd have paid billions. To be absolutely crude about it, the CD tray was a record player that put out.

The Nineties

Here's where the problems began. The nineties have yet to introduce a technology that makes men salivate. Digital-audio tape players were too expensive, and they didn't do anything new: digital tape drawers opened like normal tape drawers. (If the players had come with a robot arm that chose a tape from your rack based on a verbal command, they'd be standard equipment now.) Besides, they looked like little VCR tapes. Given that the average American home contains 293 unlabeled VCR tapes whose contents are an utter mystery, men rightly realized that they would end up with hundreds of mysterious cassettes that not only cost a great deal but, like normal cassettes, left the house in the middle of the night and migrated underneath the driver's seat of their car.

This is not to say they don't have a new pointless advance waiting for us in the shop.

I went to the stereo store the other day, looking for a receiver. I found a cheap and chunky model that offered digital effects—you could make a recording sound like it was being performed in a big hall or blared over the speakers in a dance club. This setting was called Disco and instantly made you think you should be well-dressed, drunk, and shouting at someone who probably won't give you her phone number, anyway. That's the new technology: through the scrupulous application of digital technology, the most painstakingly recorded music now sounds as bad as the band that played at your high school prom.

Oh, but there's more. This unit adds surround sound to your VCR sound—a recent concept that places you square in the middle of the action. With surround sound a joke, for example, can go not just over your head but behind your head as well. If you're watching *Top Gun,* a jet doesn't just go left to right like it does on those old, boring stereo VCRs; it goes through your clavicle and exits above your third vertebra. Of course, if you're not watching *Top Gun,* it's because that's the movie every damn salesman put on the VCR to sell you the glories of surround sound, and you're rather anxious to see if it works with other films.

Of course it does! Here is how surround sound works with other classic films:

The Enemy Below

A classic submarine movie. All the dialog on the German sub is carefully placed below your floor. You can either put someone in the basement who shouts up what's being said or phone your neighbor and ask them to leave the phone off the hook, so you can listen.

Pillow Talk

All of Rock Hudson's dialogue seems to be coming from the closet in the hallway.

Paint Your Wagon

Clint Eastwood's first musical. Here, surround sound is capable of pitching his voice into a country on the State Department's list of terrorist nations.

JFK

Wait until you get to the part about the Magic Bullet.

How does it do it? Take a look at the back of the receiver, and you can see it's different. No more Manichaean divisions like left channel and right channel; now it's a looser world, more accepting of the world's diversity. Now you have front inputs, rear inputs, center inputs. Wow! Cool! A whole new world! Gotta have it, *gotta*—

Hold on. That's *three* speakers.

They did learn something from quadrophonic sound, after all:

Wait twenty years and subtract one speaker.

Hellish Hints

~~~~~~

WHO IS HELOISE, AND WHERE DOES SHE GET THESE HINTS, ANY-
way? And who asked her? Get away from me with your
hints! Leave me alone!

I am not rational on the subject, you must understand.
All "household hints" columns mystify and annoy me. Their
notions of thrift look more like pathological stinginess; their
suggestions for recycling drab everyday items into drab everyday decorations conjure nightmares of tacky Cub Scout craft
projects. Reading these columns is like being trapped downstairs on a rainy day with some nickel-pinching lunatic.

Heloise is not alone; there are dozens of hint-droppers in
papers across the land, helping the harried homemaker by
imparting the mysteries of hearth and scullery. And she has
help: half the column consists of hints from readers who have
discovered that the plastic bag that covers the newspaper
makes an excellent mackinaw for the dachshund and must
share the discovery with America.

If you are not handy in the world of get-by and make-do,
here is what the average column looks like. (Note: Some of
these may actually work.)

Dear Betty: Next time you sever a limb, try cauterizing the
wound with a Teflon waffle maker! Heats up fast and cleans
up in seconds. Sincerely, Helen.

Betty says: Right you are, Helen. Also, dental floss makes

261

a great suturing thread, and you can use the needles you have for stitching up the turkey.

Hint: Don't throw away that piano! The wires can be used to make the coil for that hydroelectric dam you've been meaning to put in. A coffee can makes for a great spool too.

Dear Betty: Want to make a tasty and nutritious meal out of those leftover banana peels? Put them in a coffee can and bury them to a depth of seven feet. Leave them there for two years. When you dig them up and open the can, the odor will actually cause birds to fall from the sky. Cook the birds at four hundred degrees for half an hour. Sincerely, Ethel.

Betty says: And try a tasty banana stuffing! Remember, small birds are harder to stitch than a turkey; try using dental floss.

Hint: Big coffee cans make an excellent storage place for smaller coffee cans!

Hint: Your pet needs dental care too. Liquid Paper makes an excellent tooth-brightener. And to remove those hard-to-get-at stains on Fido's back molars, why not feed him a mixture of baking soda and vinegar, clamp his jaws firmly together, and then ignore his frenzied expression as the chemical reaction does its job? *Hint:* Release his jaws slowly or built-up gases will cause him to fly helplessly around the room.

Dear Betty: When I am dining out, I save the paper sleeves that cover drinking straws. When I get home, I iron them flat, apply an intricate design with an ink-dipped pin and a jeweler's loupe, and give them successive coats of lacquer over a course of several days. Presto, a stiff, decorated piece of paper! It can be a bookmark or just something to carry around and show to people. Yours, Edwina.

Betty says: Bravo! Don't forget to save the straw, either. Coated with clay and kiln-fired, they make a great carrying case for Q-Tips. Decorate with nail polish.

Dear Betty: I've found that I can cut my water bill in half by running the water only half as long. Sincerely, Hermione.

Betty says: Absolutely! And you can save even more if you load empty coffee cans with cloud-seeding chemicals and project them into the sky with a rocket, and then enjoy a fresh outdoor shower when it rains. Why not make a rocket by laminating a wrapping paper tube with nail polish, then stuffing it full of bicarbonate and vinegar, and shaking it until it leaves your hands with a thunderous roar?

Hint: Did you know that if you lash together five hundred coffee cans with dental floss, you can harness the wind and be pulled to any destination you choose?

Hint: Don't throw away those little bits of soap! There could be a depression tomorrow! Instead, boil them down on the stove, turning them into a viscous broth that will set off your smoke detectors! Do this twice a month so you know your detectors are working.

Dear Betty: I've found that light bulbs can be substituted for onions in most all recipes and are an excellent source of fiber. Sincerely, Calpurnia.

Betty says: How true! But grind them fine. You don't have to have a fancy glass-grinder—simply tie unused coffee cans with dental floss to an old housecoat and roll around on the light bulbs until they are a crunchy powder.

Hint: Dropping a bowling ball on your foot is an excellent way to sustain a compound fracture of many hard-to-heal bones!

Hint: Don't throw away that dead ballpoint pen—bury it in the yard and include it in your prayers!

Hint: Bubble-gum is perfect for getting wax out of table-cloths. And wax is perfect for getting bubble-gum off the floor. A mixture of wax and bubble-gum, when stretched to a thickness of .001 millimeters, is a perfect substitute for dental floss. And don't forget, if you wrap dental floss tightly around a coffee can and put it in the oven, and shout, "THE POWER OF BETTY COMPELS ME," your husband will have more beers than usual and watch you out of the corner of his eye.

Hint: They all laugh because you're cheap! Why don't you just show them who's crazy?

Hint: Why not make some armor-piercing bullets with the Teflon from an old pan? Why not refuse to give up until you speak to Betty?

Betty says: Mwahahahahaha! Your soul is mine!

Tomorrow: Removing brimstone from linen.

Instant Dogma

~~~~~~

As a post-boomer—someone who was not around for Woodstock and frankly glad of the fact—I noted with pleasure the use of John Lennon's song "Instant Karma" for a shoe commercial.

I applaud, for that matter, any Bronx cheer in the holy temple of the sixties. We people in our early thirties grew up tired of immediate elders lauding anything put out by the messy, stuporous crew of the sixties as the ultimate expression of Western civilization. We did not embrace their music the way they did, for one simple reason: we weren't there. Whereas all around us was music of our times, punk: loud, snarling, nihilistic racket that made the twangy yowlings of the sixties sound like a Lutheran hymn. What our predecessors called freedom had curdled into indulgence and self-righteous cynicism by the time we got around to sprouting pubic hair. We inherited that sardonic attitude and let a decade of oil shocks, Watergate, Gerald Ford, and other unending mediocrities turn us into smirking, barking, alienated maniacs.

Those were the days!

Every generation has its angry moments, the period of high-minded fury before you get down to the real work of selling out and bowing before your corporate overseers. This time in your life is marked by rambunctious songs. My father had "Northwest Passage" by Woody Herman; I had "Anarchy in the UK" by the Sex Pistols. (Granted, I'd never been to Britain, but my father had never been to the Northwest.) Rock music, however, was ennobled in the sixties as the Voice of the Most Important Generation Ever, and hence the ditties of that age were regarded as more than just entertainment, a soundtrack for the obligatory period of reflexive socialism and unshaved copulation. No, these songs were Statements. They contained Philosophy.

Thus the collective drawing of breath by the boomers when "Instant Karma" was impressed to sell shoes. The boomers had endured the use of "I Want to Hold Your Hand" to sell Taurus autos in the mid-eighties, mostly because the car and the ads appealed to both their long-sundered youth and the materialism they had embraced. But using Lennon—the great martyred genius himself—well, *this* had gone too far.

Never mind the absurdity of selling fitness by using the music of a man who spent the B-side of his life lolling dazed behind the dark walls of The Dakota building. Never mind that the idea of "instant karma"—the immediate payback for one's accomplishments—is antithetical to the long, hard grind of athletic training. What's delightful about the boomers' reaction is their slow horror at discovering how well their high-minded art serves mammon. In fact, I never liked the song *until* I saw it used as a commercial.

This is not going to be a problem for my generation bracket. The music of our heyday cannot possibly sell anything, except perhaps caffeine pills and suicide machines. Examples:

"I am an ANARCHIST! I am the ANTICHRRRRIST!"—the *Sex Pistols,* "Anarchy in the UK."

What on earth can you do with this? "I am an ANNUAL CLEARANCE! I am COMPETITIVELY PRRRRICED!" No.

"Let's have a war! So you can go DIE!"—Fear.

Perhaps: "Let's have a SALE! SO you can go SAVE!"

Impossible. Even if you could find the appropriate product or lyric, the sound would make anyone dive for the remote control. Our music, after all, was purposely unlistenable, the equivalent of someone blowing a bazooka full of stinging insects into your ears. Great for days of dateless fury, fine for frat-boy bash-ups. But eventually you realize that the problem with nihilism is that there's nothing behind it, and that while it is fun to be an anarchist, the dental benefits are nonexistent.

My generation, however, did not suffer a loss of ideals upon entering the real world, as we had very few ideals in the first place. The music reflects this—punk became a cartoon of itself within a year, and New Wave, which was essentially well-educated nihilism with catchy melodies, devolved into the bubbling mud of dance music that plagues us to this day.

Which, the injured boomer might cry, proves that their music was better! They had Ideals! They had Love in their Hearts and Right on their Side!

That's one way of putting it. You could also say that they spun out a bathetic idiom of clichés and unexamined platitudes whose credence arose from its supposed relevance, rather than any intrinsic merit. Take the song "Eve of Destruction"—a plodding rant that rivaled "99 Bottles of Beer on the Wall" for invention and melodic wit, ending in a sing-along chorus about collective extinction. This could only come from a generation as ahistorical and self-righteous as the boomers—something to sing with a sad, smug smile. The grown-ups won't listen to us, so the planet is doomed.

My generation listens to that song in rapt horror, realizing that it was, in those days, a prerequisite to getting laid to agree that extinction was nigh. We did not worry about it. Between inflation rates that mirrored our age, scary ranting maniacs in the Middle East, the usual warty crew of bastards in the Kremlin, and the standard gang of idiots in Washington, we *knew* we were going to end up as loose carbon atoms blown high into the atmosphere. (At least we'd get to travel.) I recall that a great topic of discussion was not how to prevent our extinction but the best way to enjoy it. Heading up to the roof with a bottle of wine was a common favorite. Not even one last moment of sensual pleasure; that was never discussed. With a thousand phallic cylinders headed your way, a gentleman would feel inadequate to the task. No, it was the roof. Red wine. The big flash. The final thought of comforting clarity: no more hippies.

The generation that followed us has, to my dismay, turned out not to be clear-eyed seekers of hope and truth but sullen whelps who went past NUCLEAR DESTRUCTION and proceeded directly to DEATH BY OZONE DEPLETION. They are besotted with the sixties as some great shining age of truth, wear tie-dyed patterns that look like what you'd get if you stuffed a cow full of Day-Glo paint and shoved it off a rooftop. The sixties is a musical to them, and their life is a revival.

But the people against whom they rail are the boomers themselves, now the grown-ups. Now they are in charge of the ad agencies that pull their levers; now they are the ones who are supposed to make a difference. And all they can do is hold the rearview mirror in front of their faces and pretend they're looking ahead. No doubt the boomer looks at the Lennon commercial and consoles himself with the fiction that this is an homage to them, proof their tastes are timeless.

It's proof their tastes are marketable. And when they pass from the earth, so will the market they represent, and hence the tastes used to reach it. The need for shoes is more enduring than the means to promote them.

In short, my elder brethren, repeat the following whenever the commercial comes on the air:

A) He was a rather bad poet.
B) He wrote a couple good tunes.
C) He's dead.
D) Can we get on with our lives now?

Contrude Not with the Ketchup of Mine

∿∿

As the saying in Washington goes: If it moves, reelect it; if it doesn't, regulate it. The most recent example of the latter: The Great Ketchup Reclassification Controversy.

The USDA has decided to review the standards by which ketchup is graded. Nothing drastic. Current "dual grade nomenclature" would be replaced by single letter-grade designations, meaning that "U.S. Grade A or U.S. Fancy" would be dropped for the more prosaic "U.S. Grade A." These classifications will be based on color and consistency. Sound controversial?

It isn't. No one would be forced by the Evil All-Powerful Government to make ketchup with the consistency of newly poured cement. Labeling ketchup with the government grade is voluntary, anyway, so companies could thumb their nose at the new standards and go on making whatever they liked.

This wouldn't be an issue if the USDA, good public servant that it is, hadn't invited letters from the public on the matter. It's standard form. They'd do the same if they decided to establish a medium beet circumference. Ketchup, however, is the lord of condiments. Everyone has an opinion about ketchup, and generally a strong, irrational one. Somehow, either through jokey, inaccurate news stories or people's own muddleheaded refusal to respond rationally to an issue, America got the idea that the government was about to either

A) make ketchup thicker.
B) make ketchup thinner.
C) A and B simultaneously, and at huge taxpayer expense.

Nothing of the sort was to happen, but the people rose as one and demanded their thoughts on ketchup be heard. Hundreds of letters had reached the USDA by the June twenty-sixth deadline. Here are some excerpts, all of which are guaranteed true. I have removed the names for legal reasons, and because I'd probably misspell them, anyway.

• Missing the Point Entirely, Pt. 1
V.F. of Brewster, MA, was aghast. "I am completely against spending any money to determine the preference of people to thick or thin catsup! Feed the hungry children— they couldn't care less if it's thick or thin. Let's be sensible."

• A Plea to Avoid Unnecessary Physical Trauma
After a plea not to make ketchup thicker, P.S. of Long Beach, NY, ends with this plaintive postscript: "After pounding on the bottle for hours, it leaves my hands red."
On a similar note, Mrs. R.G. of Kirkland, WA, issues perhaps a veiled threat: "I don't need to hit the bottle any harder than I do."

• Missing the Point Entirely, Pt. 2
From "Long Time Consumer" in La Plata, MO: "I for one do not want Heinz or Hunt's changed any way because it's perfect. I'd thank politicians to leave the catsup making to Heinz."

• A Child's Garden of Happy Ketchup Opinions
From M.C., of Lebanon, OR: "The idea is stupid. All of us think it is stupid. I think people should buy what they

like." (Drawings of McDonald's fries and a bottle of ketchup fill the bottom of the letter.)

• The Boomer's Lament, or the Larger Implications of Ketchup

From T.K. of Floral Park, NY: "I was born in the early sixties, and original products of my day no longer exist. Everything in today's market is new and improved. New formulas have been added. Bright new labels have replaced original labels as to lure customers in a subliminal state to purchase the item ... I am fed up. This goes way beyond the ketchup issue."

• Get Your Cotton-Picking Gummint Mitts Off MY Ketchup!

From Mrs. M.N., also of Lebanon, OR (what is happening there, that this issue has so gripped the townsfolk?), this blistering broadside: "Why on earth would you want to pass laws about catsup? Heinz is perfect just the way it is and all the others are not good so why bother wasting time and money passing laws to make them thicker? Everyone I've mentioned it to thinks it's silly and none of my family would touch anything but Heinz. P.S. Any restaurant that wants me to eat there better serve Heinz, too."

• Still Has a Che Guevara Poster on the Wall

"Viva viscosity!" shouts M.S., North Babylon, NY. "Down with narrow neck bottles!"

• American Ingenuity Isn't Dead, Just Increasingly Sarcastic

From M.H., of Tulsa, OK: "Why don't you do something about the black stuff that appears around the opening of the bottle? Shoot, if folks want thick ketchup, let them use that stuff."

• Please, Not to Be Tampering With Ketchup of America

This letter, meticulously printed and signed, Your Critic, appears to be the work of someone for whom English is a recently acquired skill. (As opposed to other letter writers, whose mangling of English was something at which they had long excelled.) It reads, in part: "Yes, I know that the market of competition will always be but if Ketchup is good enough to savor of the taste buds, then why contrude with it? If Ketchup is to be ketchup, let it stay ketchup and we will live happily ever after. But is not the whole idea of produce a product with a flavor that will stir-up the taste buds with mild thinking? I am wish you all a great success in the market of sales. I will be waiting for a response as time is vulnerable."

• No, They Just Want to Contrude with Your Mind
E.R. of Silver Beach, New Jersey, fit her disapproval on a postcard, but had room to add this parting indictment: "Is these little things done so you can make high wages?"

• Save the Earth, Knock It Off Already
"Don't you people have anything better to do than sit around and harass the ketchup business?" asks M.H., of Nevada City, CA. Switching gears in a postscript, she notes that "if you make it to the point where there has to be thicker ketchup it will mean more tomatoes, and with the water shortage . . ." Here she trails off, presumably to let the dire ecological consequences of thicker ketchup present themselves silently in the reader's mind.

There are dozens more. Several key lines of thought appear.

• Older folk don't want thicker ketchup, because it's hard enough to get out of the damnfool bottle now.
• Unrecyclable plastic ketchup bottles are the spawn of the Devil, albeit a convenient one.
• Water that collects on the top of the ketchup—what the USDA calls "free liquid"—is regarded as a nauseating fluid that denotes cheap, substandard ketchup.
• Everyone wants wide-mouthed ketchup bottles. Everyone.
 —Tampering with the ketchup formula is un-American.

(Several writers allude somberly to the Lessons of New Coke.)

- Finally, the one point that shows how divided this nation remains after two hundred years: No one can even agree on whether it's ketchup or catsup.

Thicker, thinner; catsup, ketchup: wars have been fought over less.

Credit Where Credit's Not Due

EITHER THE BANKS ARE DOING BETTER THAN WE'RE BEING told, or they've decided to open a vein and die as quickly as possible. I can think of no other reason why they have sent me eight credit card applications in the last two months. Me: the deadbeat.

For most of my adult life, I had the typical credit policy of an English major: loan me money, and a little later I will give you a well-written explanation as to why I can't pay it back. The result was the credit rating of a Bangladeshi bond.

I ascribe much of this to a curious way of looking at bills. For a few years I seemed to regard opening a bill as the equivalent of paying it. Simply ripping open the envelope flipped the little PAID switch in my brain. As no such relays were triggered in the computer that generated the bill, I inevitably received a thin missive, devoid of scent strips or ads for luggage or an enticement to visit one of those hotels that, to judge from the pictures in the brochure, seem to have nothing more to offer than the opportunity to throw my laughing wife in the air while I stand in a shallow swimming pool. This life was no longer mentioned. The letter was solicitous, concerned, with the overly polite manner common to the first visit from an enforcer. The letter usually said that perhaps it had slipped my attention, but I hadn't paid my bill; if I had done so, why, disregard this notice.

Which I did. I knew the bill had not slipped my attention, nor had I paid it, but as long as the company was still in doubt about the matter, I saw no need to rush things. When they knew I was serious about remaining in arrears, why, then we'd talk.

And talk we inevitably did. The company would call and use my name with that questioning inflection that's a dead giveaway of the dunning agency, and I would promptly pant as though out of breath and explain that I had just run three miles chasing the mail truck to hand in my payment. There is nothing they can do when presented with a story like that, no matter how patently fictitious it is; all they can do is pretend to be relived and go away. You could tell them that the dog ate the bill, and you were running castor oil through a garden hose into the beast to get it to cough the damn thing up, and they would pretend to make a note in your file and volunteer to send a fresh one.

This, of course, is indefensible behavior. It stemmed not from a desire to cheat evil capitalists, or even rampant prodigality, but out of sheer laziness. Even when moved to write out a check and put it in an envelope, for example, the entire initiative was frequently defeated by the need to fix a stamp to the envelope. I never have stamps. Stamps could fall from the sky like manna every Monday and Thursday afternoon, and I would still forget to stick my tongue out and catch a few. Whenever I have the presence of mind to buy more than I need, they go into my wallet, where they adhere permanently to a photograph; this is why people think my mother was Harriet Tubman, and my wife appears to be cradling a huge bald eagle in her arms.

But those days are gone. Now I get my bills paid within a decent interval. It was the mortgage payment that taught me good skills, I believe; the implication was that a late payment meant they would not only assess a charge but demolish my residence. (Hey, with my credit, they were the only terms I could get.) Somehow my credit rating repaired itself over the years, like new skin healing over a rash. But I always thought the scar would be ever indelible and was surprised when the financial establishments of the world decided I was not just deserving of a credit card, but a fistful of the damn things.

They began arriving in the mailbox shortly after I left my tenured-for-life union job and set up with an organization where staff turnover was so high the company car was a tumbrel. While my pay had increased, this was mere rouge over the same old complexion: the cost of living in my new city was twice that of my previous life, and I was actually making less money than before. This didn't matter to the computers that spit out these come-ons: my income had hit the level where it was time to start draping the leaden garlands of debt around my neck.

"Because of your excellent credit," the letters began, "we would like to offer you this unique offer." I felt a bit like a plain-faced wallflower at a dance who hears someone shout, "Hey, gorgeous," and cannot believe the comment is addressed to her. Excellent credit? Was this a joke, a nasty jape? Perhaps all the cruel popular kids in high school who tormented the homely had gone on to careers in credit-card disbursement. They'd send me a card stamped with a code indicating it was a hoax, and I'd use it in a restaurant only to end up red-faced, burning with shame, when the waiters laughed and pointed and waved my card around.

I ignored the letters. Wouldn't give them the satisfaction. Then a certain phrase began appearing on the envelope: pre-approved. Preapproval has never struck me as a wise idea, what with Original Sin and all that. How could they approve me when we'd never met? And if they could do that, *Where the hell were these people when I was single?*

Eventually I winnowed the offers down to two cards:

First Bank of Pork Fat, Arkansas, Gold MasterCard. This is a typical rotating charge card that allows you to load up immense amounts of debt and pay it off a nickel at a time, while an interest rate of 234.9 percent is compounded every five minutes (not counting a lunch break). The credit limit is determined by actuary tables—I cannot, for example, charge more than ten thousand dollars, for I will not live long enough to pay it off if I submit only the minimum payment. The little hologram has a picture of Sisyphus pushing a rock up a hill.

American Express. This is the famous green one with the soldier on it, the one that makes you pay in full every month or the soldier comes over and takes off your head. I have always wanted this card for its supposed cachet; getting one was a sign that you had entered a select and prestigious club, and besides, all my friends had one. All I had to do was pay a seventy-five-dollar fee. Why? Don't ask! Now start charging! And pay up!

This card offers many services, detailed in a brochure so thick and glossy that it partly explains where my seventy-five dollars is going. Few of these services seem to apply to my life, or the life of anyone I know. For example:

- If I lose anything aboard the Concorde, they will pay for it, up to ten thousand dollars in Krugerrands that may have fallen into the seat cushions.
- If I buy the Concorde with the card and crash the plane, they will reimburse the purchase price.
- If I purchase over one hundred thousand dollars in traveler's checks, a professional forger will sign the things for me.

Worthless. Here are the services I *need* from a credit card:

- If I rent a car with the card and get in a fatal accident, they will replace my life.
- Meals and drinks that I later throw up will not be charged to the bill.
- Waving the card a certain way will make cigarettes materialize out of thin air.
- Edge of card sharp enough to draw blood, making waiters who want you to leave hesitant to grab it so quickly.
- Hootchy-koochy holograms for those idle, bored moments.

And, the most important service of all:

- Option of deferring payment until I get some stamps.

I have the cards now and use them like a dutiful slave of the prevailing financial order. I realize why I felt so naked without them before, why I had always coveted them: they give you a sense of safety, of belonging, much like the vassal felt comfortable within the shadow of the master's castle. They are my identity papers, showing which large, faceless institutions own me. I haven't always believed that the banks and their faceless owners controlled the world, but I know better now. It was very subtle, the way they tipped their hand: sending those cards after I got the raise. How did they know—unless they know . . . *everything.*

And since they know everything about me, I'm sure they know that I'll be a little late with the payment this month. I am certain they will understand.

Cap'n Santa

〜〜〜

WHEN THE NEWS BROKE THAT THE GREGARIOUS BILLIONAIRE
had vanished at sea, rumors were as plentiful as gulls at a
garbage heap. There were allegations of financial misdoings,
of murder by foreign agents, of suicide. When his portly
frame was fished from the brine and laid to rest, his heirs
may have hoped the rumors were put in the grave as well.
No such luck.

Santa Claus, it now appears, was not the man we thought
he was.

A beloved figure who had come to symbolize Christmas,
Claus was at the time of his death worth an estimated $3.8
billion. But like so many other figures of the eighties, Claus—
whose real name was Clauserawski—had built an empire on
paper. As the charges of financial wrongdoing multiply by the
day, it is instructive to trace the history of this extraordinary
man.

He first appeared on the financial scene in 1974, when he
purchased a manufacturer of wooden toys. Shrewdly capitaliz-
ing on the new market for "natural" playthings, Claus made
millions with his line of simple blocks. It was hard not to
make money in that market, but Claus was regarded as a
marketing genius—partly because of his relentless gift for
self-promotion.

"He was the sort of man who absolutely filled a room," said a broker who arranged the financing for the deal. "Everyone remembers him for that ho-ho-ho and jolly manner, but he was a shark when it came to numbers. There was no ho-ho-ho in negotiations, I'll tell you that."

Where Claus came by his cash was never discerned. He had a peculiar habit of paying for multimillion-dollar deals with change, often delivered in thousands of red kettles. Added to his peculiar quirks—arriving for business meetings by the roof instead of the lobby, leaving meetings by laying his finger on his nose and ascending in empty elevator shafts—gave Claus a magical reputation in the financial community. Lending Claus money became a sign of prestige.

"Oh, bankers would stay up all night waiting for him," said one man who dealt with Claus. "They'd set out the 'cookies,' as we called them. First, of course, it was cookies and milk, but as the years passed any deal that involved minimal risk to Claus and maximum risk to the investor was referred to as 'cookies.' Then they'd fall asleep and wake to find all the contracts signed."

It was these "cookies" that proved to be Claus's undoing. By the end of the seventies Claus had amassed a network of entertainment companies, privately held and well-performing. But Claus sought to diversify his holdings, and using his businesses as collateral, he issued vast quantities of junk bonds to finance a blizzard of takeovers that stunned Wall Street.

In *Visions of Sugarplums,* Clement Moore's incisive investigation into the scandals of ClausCo, the author described the mercurial billionaire.

"One would almost laugh in spite of one's self at the sight: this absurd man in an absurd suit of red and white, belly a-quiver as he strode chuckling through the darkened office. He looked more like a clown beloved by the childish and imbecilic than a captain of industry, but to the lawyers and ministers of finance who slumbered around him, he was a prince, a king. He said not a word but went straight to work, signing contract after contract, as though he was pulling the money out of some bag that would never run empty."

For a while it appeared that the bag was, indeed, bottomless. Shares of ClausCo stock were snapped up as soon as offered. Meanwhile, Claus began appearing on the society page as frequently as the business page. He left his wife for a svelte model who appeared in the catalogs for his lingerie company, Santa's Choice. He partied among the elite in Palm Beach, where tabloid photographers caught him nude on a boat surrounded by leather-clad elves. (CALL HIM SINTA! screamed the headlines.) The public seemed to love his antics; free-spending, generous, and impossibly rich, he was a symbol of all things dear in the eighties.

But insiders knew that the true picture was not all rosy cheeked. Claus's toy companies had long abandoned the traditional wooden horses and rag dolls that built his fortune and had concentrated on luxury items for the upscale tot. This market collapsed following the crash of eighty-seven, but Claus refused to see the coming period of austerity, issuing more and more stock.

As investigators are now discovering, the Claus empire was built largely on shaky assets shuffled between divisions. Claus appears to have raided over $1.6 billion from his employees' pension fund, leaving nearly 250,000 workers—whom Claus dismissively referred to as "elves"—without any future. At the time of his suspicious death, ClausCo was scrambling madly to pay suppliers for the toys that would give children a merry Christmas, and regulators were probing allegations that the catastrophic fire that had swept his reindeer's stable was intentionally set for the insurance money.

More allegations are expected as the sad tale unravels. Last week Claus's sons, Willis and Trevor Claus, resigned as heads of ClausCo and authorities seized records at the palatial retreat in northern Canada. With the company in arrears, it is expected that there will be no Christmas this year, although President Bush has insisted that the nation will see signs of Christmas by spring.

This may be Claus's legacy. Perhaps the seeds were there for all to see, years ago. As Moore notes in the end of his book, "Few who worked with him will forget the taunting couplet he would cry as he left the building. 'On Maxwell, on Campeau, on Drexel and Burnham! On Milken and Boesky and Pains in the Sternum! Let's make our pile now, and let's slink out o' sight! Merry Christmas to us, and to you, long dark night!' "

The Life and Times of Wile E. Coyote

‏ഗ്

From *The Journal of Animated Mechanics and Physics*, Sept. 1984:

UPON THE DEATH OF WILE E. COYOTE, GENIUS, SEVERAL crates of files were made available to researchers. It is impossible to underestimate the importance of these documents in tracing the life of this mysterious, and oft-reviled, individual. Forgotten in his later years, embittered by the failure of his many inventions to bring him the success he believed he deserved, W. E. Coyote never doubted that history would validate him. Discerning the truth of those beliefs requires that we start with the record. And the record is impressive.

THE EARLY YEARS It appears that inventing chose W. E. Coyote, not vice versa. As we read in *A Single Puff of Dust*, his autobiography (unpublished), Coyote was not the standard American entrepreneur, with a lonely childhood of tinkering behind him. He was an adult, reacting to necessity with adult practicality.

"It was a matter of hunger, really. Pure and simple. Dog eat dog. Coyote eat bird. Due to intense interspecies competition, the available food supply had, by 1949, dwindled to a particular avian genus *hotroddus incredibilus*. It was not a particularly intelligent prey, for evolution was content to give it the means to evade its predator by sheer speed. In most environments, there would be compensations that would favor the predator—terrain, for example, that was better suited to my loping gait than the furious scurryings of the bird, or areas in which I could, with the assistance of fellow coyotes, trap the prey and devour it.

"Unfortunately, the ecosystem in which I lived had been the testing grounds for the American freeway system; between 1945 and 1948 the U.S. Army Corps built a vast system of empty and unused roads that threaded through the area, giving the bird a free and untrammeled means of escape." (See also *Road to Nowhere: The Forgotten Freeways of Arizona,* C. Jones, 1984.)

Coyote's manuscripts show how he first attempted to best his prey with sheer speed but soon discovered this was impossible. It was then he decided to use mechanical means to assure a steady supply of food.

Contrary to popular belief, the bird was immensely plentiful; documentaries of the period may have suggested there was but one roadrunner in Arizona, when in fact U.S. Game and Wildlife records of the time indicate that there were as many as fourteen thousand present in the state, all possessed of the same idiot cheer and brazen speed. (The impression of one bird, able to avoid Coyote's various devices by luck and guile, was one that appears to be the creation of the documentaries, and was a source of particular bitterness for him later in life.) Coyote then set about constructing a variety of traps. Such as:

GRAVITY-DRIVEN. Gravity, alternately the boon and bane of W. E. Coyote's life, was not widely employed by his fellow carnivores. Coyote described how he came to discover gravity, independent of Newton.

"The first time the bird demonstrated its tremendous capacity for speed, I had a reaction of shock so strong it manifested itself in several bizarre symptoms: my jaw fell to the ground, my tongue rolled out like a red carpet and draped

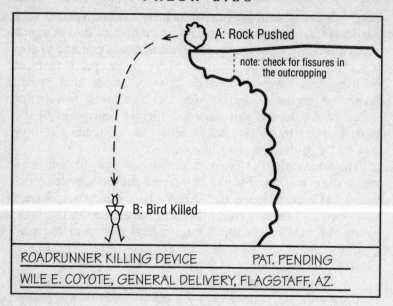

itself slack against the pavement, and my eyeballs popped from my skull and bounced around on the ground, requiring me to paw through the dust to find them. The more this happened, the more I began to wonder if there was not some elemental force at work."

This suspicion led to the first of the ingenious blueprints that have come to constitute Coyote's legacy.

If the crudity of the concept is amusing, it is instructive to note that the device comes from a quadruped previously thought incapable of grasping rudimentary physics. Coyote himself reserved an indulgent sense of amusement toward this first invention, as he notes in *Single Puff*.

"Like other great theorists, I had assumed a static universe in which the variables—density/structural integrity of the rock outcropping, presumed inaction of the bird—would behave as I pleased. This was not the case."

One hears the wry, sarcastic voice of an older Coyote in that passage. For evidence about what really happened upon the first testing of his invention, we need to go elsewhere in the Coyote archives, to an interview with Charles Jones, on hand to film what he had been told would be a major advance in interspecies competition.

"We had two cameras set up—one to shoot Coyote on the rock cliff, the other to get the bird being killed. There were a lot of jokes between the crew about the project; no one really believed this would work as advertised, but it wasn't the sort of thing you could ignore—fail or succeed, it would be great for the last segment of the newsreel. We waited for about five hours; I remember it was hot, incredibly hot, and a few of the guys were taking breaks in the shade; Mr. Coyote kept yelling down for us to keep on our toes, for that damned bird—that's how he said it, 'damned'—could be along any minute. Around seven o'clock we were getting ready to pack it in, when Coyote yells that he sees a plume of dust in the distance, and the bird is on the way. So it's places, everyone.

"The bird just screams through. I mean, screams. Didn't even see it pass, just this blur of blue and red feathers. I look up and see Coyote is still shoving away at the rock, trying to get it to drop over. Hasn't even noticed the bird's about fifty miles down the road by now. Then the cliff gives way. Oh, the look on his face. Priceless. The whole cliff face falls apart, and Coyote goes crashing down onto the road. The rock never moves all the way down. We all rush over to see if he's okay—and, of course, he was; that was his real gift—and we're trying not to laugh. He gets up with this great show of dignity and stalks away and disappears over the hill, not saying a word. And of course the rock, which fell down with the cliff, starts to roll down the hill after him. We hear this little 'ow!' from the distance. About a week later I got this very nice letter asking if he could buy the film back."

Jones, of course, would go on to film the majority of Coyote's inventions and provided the means by which Wile E.'s fame was spread. But while Jones was developing his film, Wile E. was hard at work at his improvement.

Again, Coyote has made a conceptual leap, from the notion of gravity as a universal force to not only the concept of the fulcrum but the theory of equal and opposite reactions. In his zest to see his theories realized, however, Coyote neglected to calculate the precise amount of force required to loft the rock,

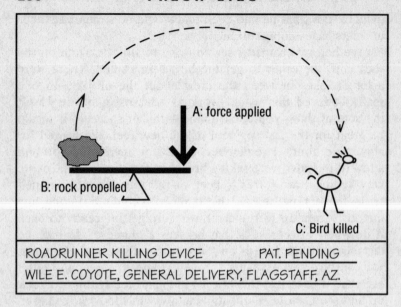

A: force applied

B: rock propelled

C: Bird killed

ROADRUNNER KILLING DEVICE   PAT. PENDING

WILE E. COYOTE, GENERAL DELIVERY, FLAGSTAFF, AZ.

as well as the placement of the fulcrum. When the device was first used, Coyote himself applied the force by jumping on the board; the rock flew straight up into the air and smashed down on his head, temporarily compacting the lanky inventor to a height of two feet, three inches. Again, Jones was present.

"His body was pleated like an accordion, his arms were dragging behind him, and he made this horrible wheezing sound when he staggered off the board. I think we were all too horrified to laugh. It was pretty obvious he was in total shock; he started walking back to his cave, muttering and making that awful sound. Then he keeled over and started to convulse."

The impression given by the documentaries is of a creature with extraordinary recuperative powers, and while this has enhanced Coyote's mystique, it was merely good editing. Jones notes that it often took two years to film a documentary consisting of four or five inventions, as each new device required longer and longer hospital stays. (Coyote in his later years laughed off his vaunted stamina, saying in an interview that it kept the investors coming.)

By this second invention, the pattern for the next thirty years was clear: a brilliant idea, a flawed execution, a certain amount of physical trauma, all captured on camera. One more element remained, and it fell into place while Coyote was recuperating.

THE ACME YEARS Enough has been written about the mysterious ACME corporation to warrant only cursory remarks here. Suffice it to say that before its takeover by leveraged buyout and dismantling in the late eighties, before revelations about its role in the international arms trade industry sullied its name, ACME was one of the nation's most beloved industrial concerns, supplier of ingenious machinery to king and citizen alike. Founded in 1912 as McKimson & Sons Notions, the company's first catalog offered a total of fifteen devices; by the time a convalescing Wile E. Coyote found its catalog in a hospital smoking lounge, it was a hundred pages thick.

"I knew at once I had found a source of inspiration unequaled. As I paged excitedly through the book, my mind made lightning-fast connections between the products, grasped at once how these disparate items could fit together in wholly new combinations. Each device by itself was amusing, benign—the skis, the small refrigerator, the electric fan. But put them together, and you had a machine that spat ice cubes into the fan, which produced a torrent of snow on which the skis might move. Thus I might ski down upon the bird as he passed. These were the raw materials of devices as yet unrealized; it would take the spark of divine genius to pull them together. And I had that spark."

Hopeful, prideful words; ominous as well. Coyote had the spark but all too often applied it to ACME explosives. In 1950, using royalties from Jones's documentaries, he purchased a vast quantity of ACME gag dynamite, believing it to be genuine. A forerunner of the various proximity-fuses and "smart" weaponry ACME would later develop for the military, Gag Dynamite employed something called an "optically-triggered fuse." Simply put, the dynamite would not explode if the user looked away, eyes closed, hands over ears. When the user, confused by the refusal of the dynamite to explode, looked at the fuse, it burned down with astonishing rapidity and detonated. Due to a catalog misprint, the gag properties of this explosive were unclear, and unfortunately Coyote never realized why the explosives only blew up when he picked up what seemed to be a dud and peered at it. He would discover his mistake years later and sue, leading to the landmark gag-liability laws that made Coyote a rich man, paupered ACME, and made them ripe for their subsequent takeover by Robert Campeau.

(ACME recalled the product in 1967, when the military wished to divert all production to the Southeast Asia war.)

"It was funny at first," Jones recalls. "He just didn't get it. Once he rigged up a barrel full of dynamite, suspended it over a plate of bird seed. Lights the fuses. Along comes the bird, eats the food; Wile drops the barrel. Doesn't move. Of course, the pulley had rusted; he'd been playing with some ACME rain-seeding equipment the previous day and nearly rusted out everything he had. Naturally he goes to the road and stares after the bird with that look he had that made you love him, that combination of bafflement and plotting, like he's already figuring out how to do it better next time. Naturally the barrel falls right down on his head. He manages to pound his way out, but he's still wearing the top of the barrel, which has dynamite attached to the inside of the lid. He runs off to hide from what he thinks will be the blast, and we do this long dolly shot to keep up with him—you laid tracks all over when you were shooting Wile E., let me tell you. I shout for the boys to zoom, because I know what's going to happen. Sure enough, he peeks out and looks at the dynamite. Kaboom.

"It looks funny on film, but, you know, he lost three fingers in that one; he had prosthetics on both hands ever after, and if you look close you can tell they're rubber."

Coyote's inventions grew more baroque as the years passed, and while none proved adept at killing the bird, that goal increasingly seemed besides the point.

"Kill the bird, yes; always, kill the bird. But in an ideal sense. By 1953 I had sufficient income from various patent revenues to purchase foodstuffs, so the capture and death of the bird was no longer a matter of personal survival. By then it had become something more—an emblem, perhaps, of a struggle that can occur when one species has the advantage of speed, and the other has a substantial line of credit from a major catalog house."

Jones sums up the mid-fifties Coyote this way:

"We'd arrive to film his latest invention, and there would be this incredible apparatus spread all over the desert. Like the system of pipes that was supposed to carry a bowling ball about thirty miles and drop it on the bird's head—he later sold that one to the post office, I remember. Anyway, we'd all be sitting around waiting to film, blocking the shots with Coyote, and one of those damn birds would run past, stop, and start pulling bugs out of the ground. Invariably one of the crew would take out a gun and blow the critter's head off, you know, just for sport; the things were everywhere, and you got so tired of them and that goddamn *Beep! Beep!*. Wile E. never paid us any mind. He'd be snacking from the catered buffet, look up, and then go back to his diagrams. Eventually everyone in the crew had some roadrunner feathers in their cap.

"It got to be that whenever you proposed a complex way of doing something, you'd be 'doing a Wile E.' And of course when you wanted someone to knock off the bullshit and get to the point, you'd tell them to 'just shoot the bird.' "

THE LATER YEARS The termination of ACME's consumer products division in the sixties coincided with the end of Coyote's period as an inventor and his rise as a popular icon, chiefly among the youth. Coyote was never comfortable with his new devotees, suspecting that they regarded him less as an inventor than as an antihero who symbolized a technocratic faith in machinery and ingenuity. Included in the archives are notes of a disastrous speaking tour of college campuses he took in April of 1967. Aged and nearly infirm from a lifetime of accidents, Coyote was also suffering from the early stages of degenerative 'toon-morphology (DTM), whereby his body would suddenly assume the shape of previous injuries.

"It began horribly, horribly," Coyote wrote later about the

tour. "The indignity commenced with a showing of some of the first documentaries. The laughter of the audience was immediate and hearty; most telling, they laughed at my first appearance, thus telling me that they had been primed by previous viewings to see me as a comic figure. Having never seen any of Mr. Jones's films with a theater audience before, I could only speculate that, unbeknownst to me, audiences had been holding me in ridicule for years. It was under these conditions—silent fury and humiliation—that I took the podium for the first public-speaking engagement of my life."

The shock triggered an attack of DTM, and according to a review of the lecture, "The Guru of the Desert," Coyote reverted to an accordion shape on his way up the steps to the stage. The audience, thinking this to be a gesture of solidarity, immediately burst into cheers and applause; this so unhinged Coyote that his body assumed a very rare and deadly form of DTM, turning into a thin puddle of coyote-shaped liquid that flowed slowly down the steps. Paramedics revived him, and he was able to go on with his lecture.

"I was perhaps a minute into my speech when I knew that I was not what the audience expected. They had come to hear their own tidy values reinforced, to hear that I, like them, rejected the deterministic and rational view of life, that my unceasing attempts to dominate the bird was a comment on the futility of conflict. Instead, I gave them my theories and philosophies full-strength, and they turned on me."

" 'You mean,' cried one teary-eyed brat, 'that you were actually trying to kill the bird?'

" 'Yes,' I thundered, 'of course I was.'

" 'But killing is wrong!' she mewled. 'How can you look at the record of death and destruction caused by imperialism and tell us violence is an appropriate reaction to conflict?'

" 'Bugger imperialism!' I shouted. 'I was a coyote, and a goddamned hungry one at that! Here you sit all well-fed and content, and you have no idea what it is to have your supper out-race you! Have your cafeteria workers hurl their slops past your fat little faces at a speed of 126 mph every night and then come and tell me about the inappropriateness of violence!' "

It was perhaps Coyote's most painful moment, made no easier by the appearance of three large lumps on his head—again, a manifestation of DTM. The sight of someone with fresh and painful signs of concussion defending violence was sufficient to restore some of his lost credibility, however; several in the audience saw this as a brilliant expression of man's duality, made all the more pointed by the fact that it came from a creature who was, essentially, a dog.

Coyote never completed his lecture tour. He was a heavy drinker in his later years, and the stress of public controversy and his illness caused him to drink himself to incoherence before his appearances. He was a cantankerous and argumentative drunk, and when he appeared on a panel with Elmer Fudd—by then the revered elder statesman of his generation—he got into a bloody fight with Fudd over the issue of guns, which Coyote abhorred. Given that Fudd was known for his conservative viewpoints and support of the gun lobby, Coyote's belligerence was applauded.

"I remember little, which is probably just as well. But I had long hated Fudd—his complaisant face, his reactionary views, his long history of reflexive support for the gun lobby. When he had the gall to dismiss my work as the product of 'an unnecessawily compwex mind' and posit that 'guns don't kill wabbits, peopow kill wabbits,' I reached some sort of breaking point. I remember the feel of his hot, fat little neck in my claws, with his voice coming out in pants: 'O deaw. O gwacious me.' There was a glorious moment in which I remembered that I was a coyote, not a human being, and thus had full rights to behave like a morally innocent carnivore. To hell with the inventions; what had they got me but ridicule and sorrow? I sunk my teeth into Fudd's throat."

Luckily for Fudd, of course, the teeth were but denture plates, and Coyote was too weak to do any harm. But the rest of the tour was called off following the incident, and Coyote withdrew to Arizona, from which he would venture no more.

About his suicide attempt, the archives say little. It is known that Coyote shot himself with an ACME gun, but succeeded only in blackening his face and making small, circular holes in his ears. While his despair may have deepened, his capacity for invention did not: in his last years he produced a variety of devices of astonishing complexity (see plate 28). None were built. He died, broke and alone, on Friday, June 26, 1982.

Two days before his death, there is this sorrowful note in his diary:

"Sleepless night. Fudd may be correct. Life's work for naught? Despair at every turn."

The archive's greatest revelation, however, is the next day's diary entry. Coyote defenders had long asserted that he actually caught the bird before he died, and this may be the proof. The lack of corroborating evidence from Jones or independent observers has long made biographers skeptical. Arthur Davis, in the widely praised but bitterly divisive book *The Fudd Conundrum,* posits that Coyote was actually an unwilling part of an ACME management scheme to depress the stock price by constantly demonstrating the implausibility of its goods in the documentaries. Thus, Davis argues, it was unlikely that anything ACME sold to Coyote would ever have worked. But Coyote defenders turn Davis's argument against him and state that if Coyote did catch something, it would be in the interests of ACME to keep the matter hidden.

The truth may never be known. But it is instructive to note that Coyote took delivery of a shipment of unnamed ACME goods on June 24, the day before his death and noted laconically one day later:

"Meat somewhat tougher than expected. Prefer fois gras."

Pasted in the diary are two feathers—one red, one blue.